Many Adventures Followed

by Roger Young

Many Adventures Followed

ISBN 0 646 45661 X

1st edition published by Xulon Press, Longwood, FL 32750, USA.
July 2005. ISBN 1 59781 460 1

2nd edition published by Roger Young, c/o P O Box 246, Wendouree, VIC 3355, Australia. February 2006. ISBN 0-646-45661-X

3rd printing (Australia) July 2007.

Printed in Australia
by FRP Printing Pty Ltd., 9 Traminer Crt, Wendouree, VIC 3355.

TM Books, P O Box 246, Wendouree, VIC., 3355, Australia
Email: tmbooks@ncable.net.au

To

our grandchildren

and to

everyone who has an interest in supporting the work of
Christian missions in general and the work of
Mission Aviation Fellowship in particular

Roger and Rose Young February 2006

ACKNOWLEDGEMENT

Special thanks to Ros Atkinson for her patience and many helpful suggestions while editing my manuscript, and to Neil Walters of FRP Printing for his help in designing the front and back covers.

FRONT COVER is a composite of two photos:

1. MAF Cessna 185 in flight over mountains near Wewak, in New Guinea.
2. The Highland Highway between the Daulo Pass and the Asaro Valley. (in 1967).

CONTENTS

Notes:

Throughout this text "miles" means "nautical miles" as this is the unit still used in air navigation. Road distances have been quoted in kilometres.

Altitudes and mountain heights are given in feet, as this is the unit still used for aircraft in this part of the world.

FOREWORD

It is always refreshing to read a book written by a person who has experienced life with its ups and downs and who tells it like it is! It is even more refreshing to come to the conclusion and find the author giving praise to the Lord who called him into a lifetime of effective ministry and sustained him through the highs and lows which are a part of life.

This is such a book. It is a catalogue of the experiences of an ordinary man working in partnership with an extraordinary God in a lifetime of serving others as a practical missionary in mission aviation.

Roger Young's experiences provide fascinating insights into the daily life of a mission pilot and aircraft engineer who, together with his wife and children, followed the call of God on their life and used their gifts in serving the Lord and His people in the remote areas of our world.

I trust that you will enjoy reading this book as much as I did, and that, at the end of it, you too will give thanks to the Lord for all He has done. My thoughts as I finished reading returned to the words of the song written by Andre Crouch:

I thank God for the mountains, and I thank Him for the valleys,
I thank Him for the storms He's brought me through,
For if I'd never had a problem I wouldn't know that He could solve them,
I wouldn't know what faith in God can do.

Through it all, through it all
I've learned to trust in Jesus, I've learned to trust in God,
Through it all, through it all,
I've learned to depend upon His word.

Read – and be refreshed!

Rev. Dr. Bruce Searle
Dean, Department of Mission Aviation
Bible College of Victoria
Melbourne, Australia
February 2006

THE QUESTION

"Mister Young. Are you awake?" The voice seemed to come from afar, and I chose to ignore it. Have you ever been there – in that dreamy world of semi-consciousness as you recover from a general anaesthetic?

"Mister Young. Are you awake?" Bother that woman. No! I am not awake. This is a pleasant and peaceful place, and I don't want to leave just yet. Perhaps soon ...

"Roger. Wake up!" This was a different voice. But the command was specific and personal. It could not be ignored. I opened my eyes and found that I was looking straight into the face of a trusted friend.

"Bibi. What a pleasant surprise! What are you doing here?" A rather silly question really, since Bibi was a nurse and this was the hospital where she worked. But she did not interpret it as a silly question.

"I was just going off duty when I saw them bringing you into this room, and I knew that if you were back in hospital again then it could be serious. So I came to find out why you are here."

As my eyes began to adjust to the scene around me I realised that Bibi was not the only nurse in that room. Another nurse stood beside the bed, and I knew from the look on her face that she was not really happy at what she obviously considered to be interference with *her* patient. Bibi was now backing away. Then, as she turned to leave, "I'll come and visit you tomorrow."

"Thanks Bibi. You do that. I'll look forward to seeing you then."

True to her word Bibi did visit again the next day, but being staff she had the advantage of not being restricted to visiting hours, so we had plenty of time for informal chatting.

Now I need to tell you that I had entered that hospital as a patient quite convinced that I would walk out again after I had recovered from some fairly radical surgery. But not everybody was so convinced. And it was only after I had been discharged that I was told how some of the staff responsible for my care were not so confident that I would survive.

My wife, Rose, was nine months pregnant at the time but many of the hospital staff, with their knowledge of my recent medical history, questioned whether I would live long enough to see that child born. So, although she was not actually working in the same ward where I was a patient, Bibi had access to that information. Nevertheless she respected the need for confidentiality. So when she talked about her fear of things like death and dying I was unaware of the significance of her thoughts and simply responded by talking about my faith in a God who could be trusted.

One morning as she sat and chatted she raised a question, which to me was an interesting one. She said, "Roger, I have been studying a lot about psychology lately, and it raises the question in my mind: Does God really answer prayer? Or is it just the power of the mind – some form of psychokinetics, or the power of positive thinking where the power of the mind effectively brings about the healing of the body?"

I thought about that question for a few seconds before I answered.

"Yes, I can understand, particularly in your field of medical work there would be many cases where a remarkable healing could possibly be explained as you have suggested. But I could think of many situations where God has answered prayer, even in my own life, where that explanation would not be valid."

My friend Bibi had asked a very reasonable question. But the more I thought about it, then the more convinced I became that I should attempt to record some of those experiences in writing. What I have recorded here began as my response to Bibi's question. I have added quite a few extra details since writing my first notes, but this has been done in an effort to sort-of "put flesh on the bones" as it were, rather than just present you with a bare skeleton. Hopefully you will then realise that this is a true story about a very unimpressive and ordinary human being. It is God who has been good, and it is God alone who is worthy of any praise.

Chapter One

EVEN THE CLOUDS HAVE ROCKS IN THEIR HEADS

It was mid afternoon and the usual rainstorms were beginning to spread rapidly down the mountains and into the valleys of the Papua New Guinea highlands.

Flying a turbo-supercharged Cessna 206 aircraft I had just departed from Nipa bound for Mt. Hagen, 29 minutes away. On board was a man and his wife, missionaries, and a friend of theirs who was anxious to get to a doctor today, if possible.

To fly a straight line between Nipa and Mt. Hagen would take one over the top of Mt. Giluwe, nearly 15,000 feet high so most pilots fly either north of Mt. Giluwe and through the Tomba Pass, which requires a minimum altitude of 9,000 feet, or south of Mt. Giluwe which, if one knows the valley systems well enough, can be flown at about 7,000 feet.

"Madang, this is Mike Foxtrot Quebec. Departed Nipa at two zero, estimating Hagen at four-niner. Initially via the north, and 500 feet above ground. Do you have any aircraft that could give me weather reports to the north and south of Giluwe?" I held on to the microphone awaiting a reply from Madang Flight Service.

"Mike Foxtrot Quebec, this is Madang. Roger your departure. Standby."

Another aircraft immediately broke in to give details of the weather south of Giluwe. The report was not good, indicating a cloud base about 8,000 feet with showers rapidly turning to heavy rain. Obviously deteriorating! However, a further aircraft which had just departed from Mt. Hagen bound for Nipa via the north of Giluwe reported, "No problems weatherwise. The Pass is wide open and the slopes of Mount Sugarloaf are in the clear."

Mount Sugarloaf is a 12,000 ft peak 15 miles north of Giluwe. The normal route for aircraft approaching Mt. Hagen from the west is to fly through the valley between these two mountain peaks and then enter the Wahgi valley by way of the Tomba Pass.

Encouraged by this report I pressed on with my intention to fly north of Giluwe, even though the weather did not look promising from my end. There was a heavy overcast and many rain showers in the area. Soon I was descending to remain below cloud and to follow the course of the old road from Mendi to Mt. Hagen. This road winds around the foot of Mt. Giluwe on the northern side then through the Tomba Pass.

Descending a bit more to keep beneath the cloud base I followed this road until I could follow it no further, as it climbed steeply and disappeared into the cloud ahead of me. Surprised, because of the good weather reported from the other end of this route, I began to turn back thinking I would have to try via the south. But wait a minute, there just to the left, in the direction of Mt. Sugarloaf, the ground was a bit lower and clear of cloud. "If the slopes of Sugarloaf are in the clear", I thought, "and if I can get through there, I may be in sunshine in another 3 miles."

Convinced, on the basis of the favourable weather report, that I must be nearly at the end of the bad weather I rolled the aircraft over slightly and followed the ridge down into a shallow basin two or three miles across. But there was no sunshine. All ahead of me the cloud was down on the trees. I would have to go back!

"Now where is that gap I just came through?" I thought as I turned the aircraft through 180 degrees.

"Where, where ... ?" My mind began to race. "What compass heading was I on when I entered this basin? That grassy patch below me; I didn't see that when I flew down the side of the ridge! I'm trapped!" The gap between the cloud and the trees had disappeared! "Now what do I do?"

I had been so sure that the slopes of Mt. Sugarloaf would be in the clear that I had allowed myself to be caught. "Always, ***always*** be sure there is a way out before you commit yourself to crossing a mountain ridge or entering a valley." I had been told that, and I had said the same to others often enough!

"Caught! So this is how it happens!" Cloud above. Cloud all around. Trees below. To the south, hidden in that cloud, Mt. Giluwe nearly 15,000 feet high. To the north Mt. Sugarloaf something over 12,000 feet. Most surely these clouds had rocks in their heads! And my altitude? Barely 9,000 feet, and the floor of the valley where I was now flying was not much less than that!

The valley sloped away to the west where a river ran down towards Mendi, but the trees in that direction disappeared into the blackness of a teeming tropical rainstorm. Nobody in his right mind would try flying into that!

I recalled advice I had once heard from an old pioneer of New Guinea flying. "If you ever get caught in the weather put the aircraft down, even if you have to land in a riverbed.[1] But *never* try to climb out through cloud, because if you do you'll probably fly into the side of a mountain hidden in the clouds or else you may become disoriented, lose control and crash." I looked at the grassy patch below me. It was my only possible forced landing area. I must keep that in sight whatever else I do. But this grassy clearing was perhaps a mile or two from the road, quite a distance to walk, even if we could walk out of the wrecked aircraft and make our way up to the road. And there would be little hope of finding any vehicle travelling through the area, as the road was not used very often now since a new highway had been built on the south side of Giluwe. Also the grass would be long enough to flip our aircraft on its back the moment our wheels touched the ground. What a prospect. "Is there any other alternative?"

"Oh Lord, please help me get out of this. I've made a stupid mistake and got myself in a corner. I can't get myself out, but please do something for us."

"Help me relax, Lord," I prayed as I noticed the telltale white knuckles of my left hand gripping the control wheel. "For the sake of the passengers I must not get frightened. We've got to get out. Please help me, Lord!"

As the awfulness of our situation hammered itself into my mind we continued circling within the available space. There was certainly no point in attempting a forced landing until we were nearly out of fuel or forced to do so by the weather conditions getting even worse. Perhaps we circled for only five minutes but it seemed much longer. I was due to be calling Hagen Control Tower with my position in the Tomba Pass by now so, in a voice of professional calmness, I advised Madang Flight Service that we were "Holding, due to weather, in the area just north of Giluwe. Will call again on the hour."

"Watch the weather. Any sign of a break so we can get out the way we came in?" Keep that grass patch in sight. "How are the passengers? How is the fuel? Lord, how can we get out? You'll have to do something." Thoughts chased each other around in my mind and as they went around I continued to fly an orbit as wide as the weather would allow.

Then suddenly a flash of sunlight – a fleeting glimpse of blue sky! That growing patch of sunlight on the jungle-clad lower slopes of Mt. Sugarloaf indicated a hole in the cloud layer. Fly to the hole. "How big is it? How thick is the cloud? Can I see the tops of the cloud by looking up through the hole?" Keep that grass patch in sight, I might still need it. "Is the hole in the cloud big enough to climb up through?" The smaller the hole, the tighter the turn must be. The tighter the turn, the steeper the angle of bank and the less vertical component of lift from the wings. "Can we do it? Is it safe to try?"

"Yes!" I decided to go. Mixture, pitch, and throttle controls all moved forward with one hand. "Thank God," and I meant it reverently, "for a supercharged engine." Full sea-level power right up to 19,000 feet if I needed it. Airspeed 90 knots. Too fast and we don't climb, too slow and the exhaust-driven turbocharger overheats. Rate of climb? – OK. Engine temperature? – OK. Keep the turn balanced. Keep out of the cloud. Watch that patch of blue overhead ...

"We're committed now," I realised as the grassy clearing in the trees below was now out of sight. 10,000 feet …11,000 feet. Grab the oxygen mask. Advise Madang Flight Service, "Mike Foxtrot Quebec is now climbing above ten thousand. Will advise when level." Balance the turn. Watch the airspeed. Yes, make it 85 knots for a better rate of climb. Keep that turn balanced. How are the engine temperatures? Relax ... your knuckles are showing white again! Stay within the hole and out of the cloud. 12,000 feet!

I realised I was leaning right forward in my seat. "Yes, keep that patch of blue sky in view but relax and get your head back so you can see all the instruments. Is the oxygen system working?" Still climbing up through the chimney, round and round, with the compass spinning hopelessly. 13,000 feet. At least now I was above the top of Mt. Sugarloaf and I relaxed to a normal sitting position. 14,000 feet and suddenly we had made it!

The sun shining off the top of the cloud layer was dazzling as I now looked out over an almost flat expanse of whiteness, although there were some build-ups of towering cumulus rising out of the cloud layer beneath me – somewhat like monstrous snowmen on a vast field of snow – and two of these had already developed into angry-looking cumulonimbus storm clouds. I levelled off at 15,000 feet and let the compass settle down.

Set course for Mt. Hagen – 090 degrees on the compass. Ahead a build-up of towering cumulus blocked the way, but slightly north of track I could see breaks in the cloud layer and I judged these to be over the Baiyer Valley.

"Madang, this is Mike Foxtrot Quebec. We are now cruising at 15,000 feet and estimating Mt. Hagen at time zero five. [ie: *five minutes past the next hour*.] Tracking via the Baiyer Valley."

Throughout the rest of that flight I was tremendously conscious of the Lord's presence and of His having answered my prayer, or should I say our prayers, in a rather dramatic way.

As we approached the Mt. Hagen airfield I turned to apologise to my passengers for a somewhat abnormal flight and noticed that from this distance the Tomba Pass *appeared* to be clear of cloud and hence "wide open"! But that is typical tropical mountain weather, not always what it appears to be.

After that experience I learned to base my judgements more on what I could see for myself and less on what other people said about any subject, especially the weather.

1 **WARNING**: I need to add a cautionary note here in regard to that advice about "putting the aircraft down, even if it means landing in a river bed." I have since heard of a pilot who took this advice to an extreme, and he tried to make a forced landing into tall trees. He, his wife, and three children were all killed as a result.

Chapter two

BEGINNINGS

It was meal time, and as we sat at the table I felt bold enough to ask, "Dad, do you think Graeme and I could have a clockwork model train for Christmas? We saw one in the toy shop the other day, and it only cost about two pound something."

My father put his fork down, looked at me and said, "Son, you can have anything you want, just so long as ***you*** go out and earn the money to pay for it."

We had never been a wealthy family. My parents had been married during the Great Depression years of the 1930's – in fact it was partly because of the Depression that they had married when they did. During those difficult years my father had been applying for one job after another, but was finding that a common response was, "Even if we had work for you to do we only give jobs to married men." When he mentioned this to his beloved Edith Dallimore her response was simply, "In that case we should get married as soon as possible." So they did – in an unpretentious ceremony at the nearest Presbyterian manse. My father then eventually did get the job he wanted but, with the uncertain times of depression years, he was laid off the next day. You know the old story, when things get tough in the work force the last man on is the first man off. So he knew what it meant to live in a world where you work hard to earn whatever you want in life. And now he presented me with a similar challenge. "You want it son, then you go out and earn the money."

I shot a glance at my older brother, Graeme. We thought we could meet that challenge. We had a steel-wheeled trolley (what some folk call a billycart) and we knew that one way to earn money was to collect discarded drink bottles and take them to the Bottle Man. He would pay us one shilling per dozen for beer bottles and threepence for every soft-drink bottle. Over the next few weeks Graeme and I must have walked every street in our little town looking for discarded bottles. When we had earned five shillings we went to the toy store and arranged to put the dreamed-for model train on lay-by. We eventually paid for that train and it was included with the other gifts on Christmas day.

Railway trains, and especially their big steam-powered engines, held a real fascination for me and in the small country town where I had been born we saw plenty of them. Not only was Te Kuiti on the main-trunk railway line between Auckland and Wellington, but in years gone by it had been home for a number of the men who worked to build that track. We even had a street that was commonly known as Railway Town.

One day as we walked home from school my friend and I had to stop and wait for a train to pass before we could cross the tracks. I stood and gazed in wonder as the great noisy steam-powered monster rattled past. When the noise had faded enough to be heard I turned to my friend, and with all the enthusiasm of youth said, "When I grow up I am going to be a train driver." I was not prepared for the very practical feminine logic with which this statement was received. Without even looking at me Fiona said, in a very determined voice, "Well don't expect *me* to wash your overalls!" We would have both been about five years old at the time. And I guess it is only fair to say that her comment was not an unreasonable one.

I had already learned that boys could not be trusted with certain information. If you mentioned anything to them about dreams, hopes, or ambitions in life they were very likely, at the most inappropriate time, to use that as evidence against you and make you feel very foolish. But Fiona was different. She could be trusted, and we often talked about our dreams for the future, including the kind of house we would like to own when we were grown up.

There were even times when my fascination with railway engines created a bit of a problem for my mother. Apart from an open fire-place in the sitting room, our coal-fired kitchen stove was the only form of heating we had in the house; it was our primary source of hot water, and mother used it for most of her cooking. Beside the kitchen door we had a shed full of shiny, black coal and this little boy took great delight in scooping up that coal by the shovelful and piling it into the kitchen fire. I would fondly imagine myself as a fireman stoking the boiler of a railway engine. But on one cold winter's day, having opened all the dampers to get the fire really roaring, I was just about to unload a second heap of coal into the fire when my mother entered the room. When she saw what I was doing she cried out, "Roger. What are you doing!? I've got a cake in the oven!" I guess I ruined her otherwise excellent cooking that day.

The Second World War was still in progress when I started pre-school and I have vague memories of air-raid practice drills. An alarm would sound and we would all have to flee the building and find some place to hide, out in the school grounds. But one day the bell on the Presbyterian church next door to our school started ringing and it didn't stop. It just kept going, on and on. "Whatever is wrong?" I asked. "Is there a fire, or something?" "No." I was told, "The war has ended and we are all celebrating." Of course at that point in time I had little concept of what "war" really meant and did not fully understand the reason for all the dancing and singing. I don't think it made much difference in real terms to life in our household. We had problems of our own. My mother was not in good health at all. In fact it was not long before she became so sick that the four boys in our family were all farmed out to foster care until her health improved.

In order to accommodate four boisterous boys we were all sent to stay with different folks. Graeme went to stay with friends of my parents, who lived on a farm near Drury, about 160 km to the North. My two younger brothers, David and Ian, went to stay with friends at Mahoenui and Pio Pio, to the Southwest of Te Kuiti, and I was sent to stay with the Cleary family in Te Awamutu. Muriel Scutt, now married and known as Mrs Muriel Cleary, had been my mother's nanny when my grandfather, a London lawyer by the name of Henry Dallimore, had migrated from England to New Zealand. I lived with the Cleary family for many months.

However, for some reason I have no memory of Mrs Cleary at all. In my memory it was her teenage daughter Shirley who filled the role of foster mother. But I certainly did *not* get along with Mr. Cleary. I remember Laurie Cleary (Uncle Lorry, as I called him – although I could not understand why any creature without wheels would be called "lorry") as a cantankerous Irishman. If ever I wandered about the house looking and feeling like a little boy lost, or worse still if he caught me daydreaming, he would yell at me, "Haven't you got anything to be ***doing***, boy? Don't just stand there dreaming! We've got a hospital down the road where they put people like you!" He was, of course, referring to the Tokanui Mental Hospital, and I knew it. By the time I returned to my parents' home in Te Kuiti any self-confidence had been well and truly destroyed. And when I finally did return home there was an epidemic of polio and all schools were closed. So everybody, like it or not, had to do home-schooling.

I did not enjoy doing school lessons by correspondence. But what I did enjoy was a book that my father had purchased entitled *Everyday Things for Lively Youngsters*. The book described, in very simple terms, how many of the things in the world around us worked. I remember going through that book and trying out some of the experiments described within it.

So by the time things returned to "normal" I felt like a stranger even at school in my own home town. I would like to have re-established my friendship with Fiona, but the other boys in my class made it very evident that they did not approve of boys who treated girls as friends. So, out of fear of being rejected by my peers, I avoided speaking to her. Like a frightened turtle I withdrew into a shell and found it easier to occupy my mind with experiments from my favourite book. It was not that I wasn't interested in trying to understand other people, for that is a subject which has always fascinated me. But in those days I was more like the classic wallflower, sitting at one side of the room watching others on the dance floor, fearful of scorn or criticism and lacking the necessary confidence to get up and become involved in any of the activity myself.

When I was about seven years old my father came home with a most unexpected present, the likes of which I had never seen before – the kitset for a small model aeroplane. The box contained a sheet of drawings, several strips of fine balsa wood, and a roll of tissue paper. I watched with fascination as, over a period of several days, my father tried patiently to assemble the model – a Stinson Taperwing. It was supposed to be a flying model and the propeller was powered by a rubber band. I don't know that it flew very successfully, but I was now hooked on a new hobby – aero modelling.

However, this new hobby soon proved to be a bit more expensive than could be financed by discarded drink bottles! Having seen an advertisement in the local newspaper for someone to mow lawns, I checked the address and knocked on the door of the house. When the door opened, an elderly man looked down at me.

"I have come to apply for the job you advertised – for someone to mow lawns." Mr. Jacobs smiled down at me, and with a slight shake of his head said, "I am not sure that you could even push the mower little fellow."

"Of course I can. I mow the lawns at home and your lawns look easier than ours."

"Well, okay little man. I'll give you a chance to see how you go with it."

And so it was that I started in a job which kept me in pocket-money for another eight years or more. In fact, even after I left school I would still get phone calls from Mr Jacobs asking if I would please come and mow his lawns again. During later years, when I was in high school, the occasional lawn mowing income was supplemented by two newspaper delivery rounds, and in the last two years of school with a job delivering groceries. Of course all of these jobs required that I own a bicycle. And that was a story on its own as my first bicycle was made from bits and pieces that my father had found at the local rubbish tip. Nevertheless, it was not long before I had earned enough to buy myself a decent pushbike with a three-speed gear hub in the rear wheel.

About the time I started my lawn mowing job Graeme and I also started attending *Every Boys Rally*. This was a one-evening-a-week activity sponsored by the local Brethren Assembly, and intended for boys between the ages of eight and twelve. Two of the leaders, Mr. Bob Jackson and Mr. Pip O'Shaughnessy, had been physical training instructors with the RNZAF, so we did a lot of gymnastics using a wooden horse, springboard, tumbling mats, and parallel bars. Although I had never been particularly good at team games like football and cricket, I really enjoyed the challenges and the subsequent achievements of these evenings.

The third leader involved with the Boys Rally was a man by the name of Nick Segedin. I had already met this man some time before because he was the local bloke whose job it was to fix and sharpen saws and lawnmowers. Nick Segedin's responsibility with the Rally was spiritual input and each week at the end of the evening, before we had our hot Cocoa drink and headed for home, he would present a teaching session on life-style values. In addition to these week-night meetings he also began a Bible Study group in his own home. At these Sunday afternoon classes there was always a strong emphasis on the need for every one of us to make a personal decision to accept Christ Jesus as our personal Saviour. It was after one of these Sunday afternoon classes that I returned home and wrote in my diary, "Today I was saved by asking Jesus into my heart." However, with hindsight, I have to admit that the decision at that point in time was based largely on a fear of punishment and of God's wrath. I certainly did not want to spend eternity in Hell! And this did not mean that Mrs Young's little boy Roger thereafter began to act and behave like a perfect angel. Far from it; there were days when I must have caused my parents a lot of concern as they wondered if their second son was going to turn out "alright".

It was another ten or eleven years, after the 1959 Billy Graham Crusades in New Zealand, before I began to understand that the relationship which God had offered me in Christ was based on his incredible ***love*** and compassion, not anger.

My interest in model aeroplanes took a great leap forward when I discovered a Model Aero Club in our town. This was a great help to me because I now had access to men who proved very willing to pass on their knowledge and skills. I was now able to build bigger and better flying models and move into a world where model aircraft were powered by tiny diesel engines. But, because these people flew their models on Sunday afternoon, this clashed with Mr. Segedin's classes. It was not long before the aero modelling won the competition for my attention.

One of the more successful models that I built during this time was a five-foot (1.5 metre) wingspan free-flight sailplane. Models of this size were launched using a 100 ft towline, and when the towline was released, a natty little device would set the rudder a few degrees to one side so that the model would then begin to fly in circles. The intention, of course, was that the aircraft would come back and land somewhere within reasonable walking distance. However this particular model seemed to fly particularly well and on one occasion became caught in a thermal. Instead of descending, my model simply continued to climb, and as my friends and I stood and watched it eventually climbed so high that we were no longer able to see it. We had planned a competition meeting for a few weekends after that, so other aero-modellers would be coming to our small club in Te Kuiti from all over the North Island. Having apparently lost my star performer, I went home that day with a heavy heart. But fortunately I had been warned, and consistent with normal club practice, my model was clearly marked with my name and a telephone number. Later that week I received a message from the Club President advising me that he had received an interesting telephone call. A farmer, who lived about 25 kilometres away, had found my model sailplane as he was ploughing one of his paddocks. Great news! I gladly accepted the offer from the Club President (Aubrey Haines) to drive me out to the farm and retrieve my model.

Our competition day finally arrived and, fortunately, it came with some excellent weather. We had competitions for control-line flying, chuck-gliders, free-flight sailplanes, and free-flight powered models. I watched in awe as one man demonstrated a radio-controlled model plane – the first I had ever seen.

Of course I entered for free-flight sailplanes. Entrants were allowed three flights, each of which had to be observed and timed by an approved club official. Timing began the instant the towline was released and continued until the model landed or touched the ground. The person with the highest aggregate time (total of three flights) was declared the winner. On this occasion the winner was a local boy, and emphasise ***boy*** in this case – yours truly. I would have been only about 13 years of age at the time.

This was a great encouragement to me; I had just won a competition against grown men, some of whom may have been building model aeroplanes for more years than I had yet lived.

Encouraged by my success with the sail-plane I allowed myself to be persuaded to try building a powered free-flight model. By carefully measuring the amount of fuel on board, the little 1.5cc diesel motor was only meant to run for about nine seconds. When I first flew this model the day was hot with absolutely no wind. After launching it flew beautifully, climbing steadily in a perfect circle. As we watched it continued to climb, up and up, until it eventually climbed so high that, like my sailplane had done, it disappeared from sight. I never saw that model again. It was never recovered.

The model airplane with an "adventure spirit" of its own – but it also won a competition for me, and that against men who had been building model aeroplanes for more years than I had yet lived.

With hindsight it is interesting to see how the major decisions we make in life can sometimes depend on otherwise insignificantly small events:

I was now frequently being asked what I would like to do when I finally left school. The career I wanted would have some bearing on which subjects I should choose to study at high school – which in this part of the world started at Form 3 (year 9). But, with a total enrolment of only about 250 students, the high school in our town was certainly not a large one, so there was not a lot of choice for study topics anyway.

My personal preference, of course, was to take up a career in aviation – flying light aircraft. Airline flying did not appeal to me and it seemed that the only prospects in the field that did appeal to me would be in agricultural aviation (known in New Zealand as Aerial Topdressing). I was advised against this. It was a dangerous job and there were many fatal accidents. So I had to think of something else instead. The only other career that had any sort of appeal to me was something in the field of electrical work or possibly a telephone or radio technician. But I was not really excited about any of these ideas.

My interest in radio was really a very self-centred one, mainly because there was some dispute in our house about the acceptability or otherwise of listening to the latest in popular music. It was this disagreement that had prompted me to build a little battery-powered radio receiver. By connecting the aerial to the wire-mattress of my bed-frame and wearing a set of headphones I was then able to listen to Fats Domino singing *My Blue Heaven*, or whatever else was on the latest hit-parade at the time, without disturbing anyone.

On the first day I attended high school all the new students were gathered into the assembly hall where the staff outlined something of what was ahead of us all for the next few years. We had the choice of two streams. One was designed for those students who were interested in taking up a trade of some sort, or farming, and the other was intended for those who might possibly continue on to study at university. Those who were intending to do the "M" (trades) stream were then asked to sit on one side of the hall and those in the "A" (academic) stream on the other.

It seemed a simple decision to me. If I was planning to enter some sort of a trade then of course I belonged with those doing the "M" subjects. When everyone was settled the headmaster, Mr. Tizzard, cast his eyes over the scene before him. Suddenly he pointed straight at me. "Young. What are you doing over there? I know you better than you know yourself. You belong over here in the A stream. Now move!" Apparently my sister, about four years older than me and academically brilliant, had impressed Mr. Tizzard very favourably and I was expected to follow in her footsteps. Meekly I moved across to the other side of the hall.

I certainly was no brilliant student, but many times in the years ahead I would be grateful for that authoritative direction. The mathematics and science subjects covered in the "A" stream were an essential grounding for studies still ahead of me – studies in a career that I now believe God had mapped out for me, but of which I was still quite unaware.

During the following four years as a high school student I continued to wrestle with a choice of career. I was still really keen to fly aeroplanes, but since a career as an agricultural pilot did not meet with parental approval I eventually decided to apply to the New Zealand Post Office for training as a radio technician. Once School Certificate exams were behind me I made some inquiries, found out who I was supposed to contact, and wrote the necessary letter. Days ran into weeks – well probably only three or four weeks really, but I had received no reply to my letter. The end of the year and Christmas holidays were approaching rapidly and I was anxious to begin setting plans for the year ahead.

It was during this period, while browsing through our small-town twice-weekly newspaper, that I noticed a "Situations Vacant" advertisement. The local Aerial Topdressing firm, *Northern Air Services*, needed someone to assist with aircraft maintenance work. Here was an opportunity to be involved with aeroplanes without flying them. I had not even considered such an idea until now.

I do not think anyone else applied for the job, but I did, and thus began an extremely interesting career in aviation! A few days later, in response to the letter I had written to the NZ Post Office, I received a rather confused message – verbally and second-hand – asking me to make an appointment for a job interview. I now saw no point in even trying to make that appointment.

Chapter Three

THE REAL THING

The Chief Engineer of Northern Air Services was a quietly spoken man who had a wonderful ability to inspire excellent performance from even the most mediocre of workmen, George Craig Bennett, known to friends and staff alike as "Snow" Bennett. Soon after I commenced work, Snow, along with two shareholders of the company, began talking about the very ambitious idea of manufacturing an aircraft designed specifically for aerial topdressing. Apparently on one of their visits to a movie theatre they had seen reference in a newsreel to a strange-looking agricultural aircraft, which had been designed and built in Australia. The aircraft, known as the Flying Tanker or PL7, was the brainchild of an Italian designer, Luigi Pellarini. Mr Pellarini had already designed several unorthodox aircraft including one that had effectively been a flying car – almost a typical James Bond dream machine. This small aircraft, which actually had been built and test-flown, was designed in such a way that, after landing, the pilot could simply fold the wings and then drive the machine down the highway like a motorcar. As with many of his other designs Luigi came up with another most unorthodox design and because this was the 11th aircraft that he had designed, it was known simply as the PL11. Later it became known as the "*Airtruck*".

The small staff of four was soon increased to seven men who, with a pile of technical blueprints and an even greater pile of sheet metal, set out to manufacture two prototypes of this PL11 aircraft. The machine was designed to use a Pratt & Whitney R1340 radial engine of 600 H.P. as Snow had managed to purchase a number of war-surplus Harvard aircraft which were fitted with these engines. This also gave us a supply of instruments and other sundries, such as undercarriage wheels.

Warbird fans will no doubt be horrified to know that in order to get these Harvards from Wigram, where they were stored, they had to go from Christchurch to the seaport at Lyttleton by train. They would then be shipped to the North Island. This meant having to cut the stub-wing off the fuselages, at least on one side, otherwise they would have been too wide on the railway flatcars to go through the tunnel between Christchurch and Lyttleton. We used a hand-held circular saw with a metal-cutting blade – the noise was hideous and painful to my ears. Of course those aircraft were now beyond restoration, and what we could not use had to then be consigned to the scrap metal merchants.

The fuselage of the PL11 was basically a huge round hopper capable of carrying two tons of superphosphate, with an engine mounted on the front and wing-attachment brackets on the side. The pilot sat in a little cabin perched on top of the hopper. Except for the parts we salvaged from those Harvard aircraft, or parts that were available as stock items in the aviation industry generally, everything was handmade. Wing ribs and control surface ribs were all made by forming them over carefully shaped hardwood or steel blocks.

September 1959. Pellarini took the concept of "a hopper with wings and engine attached" very literally. This was the "body" of the PL-11 Airtruck before wings and tail booms were added.

There were good reasons for Luigi's unorthodox approach to the PL11. Aircraft of more conventional design presented a number of problems: Firstly was the problem of superphosphate getting into the rear fuselage and tailplane structure. This caused big problems with corrosion, so Luigi simply dispensed with the rear fuselage and mounted two tailplanes, one on each side, attached by booms to the main wing structure. Secondly; with aircraft like the Cessna 180 and Piper Cub, the hopper was fitted in the cabin, behind the pilot. In the event of a crash landing the pilot was likely to be crushed as the cabin crumpled with the impact. In the case of aircraft like the De Havilland Tiger Moth, the hopper was mounted in the front cockpit and the pilot in the rear cockpit. Although this gave the pilot a better chance of survival in the event of a crash landing, it also meant that he tended to get a face-full of whatever chemical had been loaded into the hopper as the throttle was opened for take-off. Luigi's solution of placing the pilot in a little cabin mounted on top of the hopper was an attempt to overcome all of these problems.

October 26, 1959. The first ever attempt to assemble the entire PL11 structure. This was done to ensure that it all fitted together as expected. The picture also shows how the loader vehicle would drop the load into the *Airtruck* hopper. Next day we dismantled it all and then reassembled the airframe in a huge jig, where it was subjected to structural load testing.

During this time I also decided to learn to fly, but never with any intention of taking it up as a profession. Unless one intended to go into airline flying the only alternative at that time seemed to be aerial agricultural work. As I have already mentioned, I considered that somewhat dangerous and so did my parents, which was why they had never encouraged my youthful desire to learn to fly. Nevertheless, in spite of this discouragement, even before I had left school I did for some time attend evening lectures at the local Aero Club. The topics covered included: Principles of Flight, Meteorology, and Navigation. I had found these lectures to be extremely interesting.

Our instructor was a professional pilot by the name of Noel McCready, and one of the first jobs I had at NAS was to salvage what could be salvaged from the remains of the Cessna 180 aircraft in which Noel had been killed. Noel's aircraft had apparently stalled in a turn at low level while he was sowing superphosphate.

When you stall a car engine, it stops because the engine is running too slowly to keep going under the conditions of load which are being applied at that time. But when an aircraft stalls it does not necessarily mean that the engine has stopped. It stalls when its speed through the air is too slow to keep it airborne. At the point of the stall the aircraft suddenly pitches into a nose-down attitude and may then plunge out of control towards the ground. It is possible for a trained pilot to regain control of an aircraft that has stalled, but in Noel’s case, because he was flying so low at the time, his aircraft hit the ground before he was able to achieve this.

My first flying lessons were in an old Miles Magister aircraft. This was a low-wing monoplane of wooden construction and with open cockpits. During training operations the student sat in the front cockpit and the instructor in the cockpit behind. Since there was no canopy, only a small windscreen to shield the pilot's face from the full blast of the slipstream, it was necessary to don flying helmet and goggles and as much warm clothing as possible – preferably a leather jacket – before going for a flight. I find it hard to understand how I ever managed to avoid freezing (literally) when, on those frosty winter mornings I used to cheerfully set out for half an hour or even an hour of flying practice before starting work at 8am!

The Miles Magister was an aerobatic aircraft and, although I never learned aerobatics such as loops and rolls, it was necessary to learn spinning and be able to recover satisfactorily before being allowed off on a first solo flight. Spinning was always an exhilarating experience. With throttle closed and engine at the idle, the control column (joystick as it was often called) was eased back raising the nose of the aircraft until the airspeed dropped off to the point of the stall. Then, at this point, a heavy foot on either left or right rudder pedal would do the trick! This was the "moment of truth" for the unwary pilot who had neglected to fasten his safety harness really tight. As the nose of the aircraft suddenly dropped below the horizon such a pilot found himself, just for a brief moment, without that reassuring feeling of a seat where it ought to be. This resulted in a very distinct feeling of falling out of the airplane! The sensation is so real that the first time it happened to me I simply dropped everything and grabbed at the seat which, in turn, caused extra confusion as I had now taken my hands off the controls! But on those occasions when the harness was good and tight there was that thrilling sensation of weightlessness as the nose of the aircraft dropped below the horizon and, with the joystick held hard back, my stomach would come up to somewhere higher than it normally sits. Then everything seemed to settle down as the ground, now straight in front of me, appeared to be going steadily around in circles.

The recovery, once learned, was simple enough. First; push fully forward on the rudder pedal in the direction opposite to the rotation then, as the control column was moved carefully forward, the spinning would suddenly stop leaving the aircraft in a steep dive. A gentle backward movement of the joystick raised the nose of the aircraft and put the horizon back where it ought to be. Modern aircraft, with their little placard stating "*Aerobatic manoeuvres, including spins, are **not** permitted*" are almost a disappointment in spite of their superior comfort in comparison with the faithful old Magister. [And, just out of interest, I understand that this aircraft, ZK-AYW, is now in the Museum of Transport and Technology in Auckland, New Zealand.]

A few years later (April 1964) this flying instructor, Les Keane, was also killed in an aerial topdressing accident. Apparently, against his better judgement, Les had been persuaded to carry "just a little bit more" on his last take-off. This extra weight, together with a light gust of tailwind during the take-off roll, caused the aircraft to be so low over the end of the airstrip that the wheels caught in the top wire of a fence.

Although Aerial Topdressing was considered by some to be at the lowest end of the scale in the aviation industry when it came to safety, I need to make it clear that safe practices and procedures were *not* being ignored. On the contrary, the engineers I worked with consistently emphasised that safety was paramount. If a fault develops within an aircraft then you can't just pull over and park on the nearest cloud and fix the problem.

I remember one occasion when a stranger landed at our airstrip. Apparently he wanted Snow to have a quick look over his aircraft, an old De Havilland *Tiger Moth*, and issue a new maintenance release for it. Normally this would have involved bringing the aircraft into our hangar and we would spend the next day or so giving it a thorough inspection and fixing any defects that we found before issuing a new Maintenance Release. Civil Aviation Regulations required that this be done for all aircraft, every 100 hours of flight time. Snow went out and spoke to the owner/pilot and when he came back into the hangar he was shaking his head. I heard the plane start up and take-off. We never saw it again. But I did hear Snow talking with another of our engineers. He reckoned it would have taken weeks of work to fix all the problems he had seen in just one quick walk around the machine. Some months later I heard that the aircraft had shed one of its wings while performing an aerobatic manoeuvre. The instructor and his student were both killed in the crash.

And again, in spite of a popular misconception, most of our pilots were not of the dare-devil breed. One in particular, Johnny Johnstone, who had been an aerial topdressing pilot since 1949, was meticulous in all of his preparations when he went flying. I learned quite a lot about the theory of flight just by watching his conscientious approach to the work he did.

Another incident that left a deep scar in my emotions involved a pilot by the name of Ernie Gardener. Ernie had joined the staff of Northern Air Services while we were still in the early stages of building the PL11 Airtruck. Everyone liked Ernie. He was always bright and cheerful and he had a good sense of humour.

It was Monday 26th January 1959, Auckland Anniversary holiday. I was sitting on one of the seats at the local swimming pool, just enjoying the warmth of the sun for a while before getting back into the water, when someone – I cannot even remember who it was – came up to me and said, "You heard about Ernie?" Well I knew that he had just announced his engagement. "So, what else is news?" I asked. "Ernie is dead! Killed in a plane crash this morning." And then the messenger of bad tidings was gone, just as suddenly as he had appeared. I just sat there, stunned, gazing out at nothing in particular and feeling strangely numb.

An acquaintance I had known in High School walked past and noticed my glum expression. "Hey, Youngie'" he shouted, "Wassa matter with you? Didya girlfriend smack your hand last night?" How can people be so crass? I eventually managed to gather my things together and make my way home, saddened and grieving over the loss of a friend, and especially grieving for the bereaved fiancée.

I learned later that Ernie's loader driver saw the accident happen; saw the aircraft hit the ground. The engine was torn away leaving Ernie still strapped in his seat but with no protection in front of him as the wreckage skidded along the ground. He was still alive when Eugene got there, but he died a few seconds later. Apparently, as was the case with Noel McCready, Ernie had pulled up into a stall turn at the end of his sowing run – a very common practice as it can save a few seconds of time in the turn – but must have not left himself enough room for the recovery. And it was not as though he was a complete newcomer to the industry. Unlike Noel, who had been killed during his first year as a topdressing pilot, Ernie had been in the industry for nearly four years.

So how does a shy young fellow, often uncertain of his own abilities and opinions, cope with the sudden loss of friends and mentors, and undeniable evidence which all seemed to support the claims made by those who insist that flying is a dangerous career? How did I do it? By sitting back and trying to make a logical and philosophical assessment.

We learn from other people's mistakes, and I now knew of several pilots who had paid with their lives to prove that the laws of physics apply to everyone, regardless of personality, rank, or qualifications. Safety margins and accepted safe procedures are there for a purpose and no pressures, economic or whatever, must ever be allowed to whittle these away.

I became an avid reader of aircraft accident reports – not in any way to gloat over other people's misfortune but always to answer two questions: What went wrong? And what would I need to do to be sure I didn't get caught the same way?

It took us nearly three years to get the first prototype PL 11 to the stage where it was ready for its test flight, although it had left the ground for a few feet during fast-taxying trials on 27th April 1960, just to prove that the two tail booms would not go into flutter, but that could hardly be called a proper test flight.

I do not know of any words in the English language to adequately describe the feeling of awe and excitement – almost of unbelief – that overcame me as, on Wednesday 3rd August 1960, we stood and watched this ungainly monster, created by our own hands, roll two or three hundred feet down the runway at Te Kuiti airstrip then lift off and climb steadily away on its first flight.

Yes, I had built a number of model aircraft, some of which had flown extremely well, but this one was a "real" aeroplane. This was "the real thing" and there was a real pilot on board! And I considered that man to be a personal friend. His name I have already mentioned – Axel Neil Johnstone; normally known as *Johnny* Johnstone. An entry in my diary states that the test-flight of that day, which was the first of many for the PL11 prototype, lasted about 35 minutes.

Photo, taken as the PL11 passed back over the airfield on its first flight, shows the plan shape in silhouette.

August 3rd 1960. Historic photograph – *Johnny* Johnstone taxies out in the prototype PL11 for the first test flight.

1959 The team who did much of the work in building PL11 prototype #1. From left: Roger Young, Wally Dowman, Ken (Blue) Langtry, Jack McCleay, "Snow" Bennett (Chief Engineer), Bob Goding, Bryan Buzby. It was mostly a different team who worked with Geoff Young in the building of prototype #2, but I had left Te Kuiti by then and have no photographs or knowledge of who was actually involved in that project.

The end of the PL11 Prototype #1

1963, Oct 8th 11:30 am.

The newspaper headline read "Owes Life to Plane's Design." The cause of the crash may forever remain a mystery, but the pilot, John Worthington, reportedly woke up to find himself in the wreckage of the aircraft. There was some talk that he had suffered a temporary blackout just as he became airborne with a fully loaded aircraft. But he has no memory of how the accident happened. He was admitted to Te Kuiti hospital suffering from head injuries and bruising to his chest.

Photo credits: Geoff Young

A second prototype PL11 was eventually completed under the supervision of Geoff Young, an aeronautical engineer who, at the request of CAA, also did a complete check of all of Pellarini's design calculations ... and found they were all correct. Unfortunately the PL11 never got to the production stage. Predictably there were rumours about political advisors who, it was claimed, had vested interests in other companies that were selling aircraft for aerial topdressing. Pellarini's next design, the PL12 *Airtruk* was successfully manufactured in Australia. Snow Bennet and Johnny Johnstone worked with him on that project.

Chapter Four

A CALL TO THE WORK

Even the thrill of the Airtruck's series of test flights could not negate a strong feeling that I had to move. And there was only one place I wanted to move to. This urging directed my thoughts in only one direction, to a place I had never seen – to New Plymouth, to work with Rural Aviation, a firm which at that time held the sole New Zealand agency for Cessna aircraft. But they had not been advertising for staff, so why...?

Like a swimmer testing the water with his foot before he jumps in, I wrote to "Rurals" merely asking if they had any staff vacancies in their aircraft maintenance section, and briefly mentioned my own experience in the industry. The reply was prompt and precise advising me that "[we] have vacancies for aircraft tradesmen. Please advise us when you wish to begin work." Nine days after that historic first flight of the PL11 I told Snow that I would be leaving at the end of August and moving to New Plymouth to work with Rural Aviation.

It was not easy leaving Bennett Aviation. I had enjoyed the work and especially working with the fellows there. Both Snow and Luigi had a wonderful gift of passing on lots of valuable and helpful information and this was done with a healthy deal of affirmation. And Johnny Johnstone, our test pilot, had even done his best to try and persuade me to go to university and study for a degree in Aeronautical Engineering. But the urge to move had been strong, and as soon as I had settled in New Plymouth I felt very much at home, as though this was the place where I was always meant to be.

A significant part of my life in New Plymouth was spent, of course, in dealings with people outside the workshop. Coming from a church-going background I naturally went to Church in order to meet people and form new friendships. And again it was only on the strength of my church-going background that I was approached and asked if I would be prepared to teach a Bible Class group for young teenage boys. I could not really find a good excuse to say "No" and so it was on that basis I accepted the task, with no great enthusiasm!

My Christian experience at that time consisted only of Sunday School lessons and that rather vague decision to accept Jesus as Saviour when I was about eight years old. I had not really understood what that meant. However, particularly as a result of my parents' involvement with the Billy Graham Crusades in New Zealand during 1959, I had become conscious of differences in the lives of several people I knew. This difference did not apply to all church-goers by any means, but a few, whom I considered to be real Christians, seemed to have unlimited resources of love, of joy in spite of grief and sorrow, and of peace and patience in spite of great frustrations.

The lessons with the boys of that Bible Class produced a lot of heart-searching on my part and also searching of the Scriptures. I discovered why these Christians were different. I learned that it is the Spirit of God, the Holy Spirit, who produces these worthwhile qualities in the life of a Believer and that only those people whose lives are controlled by this Spirit belong to Christ and are "real" Christians.

It became my desire to know this Jesus – to know Him as a real person. His life had been given for me and by the power and guidance of the Holy Spirit my life should be lived for Him. But did that have to affect my chosen career?

On the job scene my love for aircraft was as great as ever. I decided to attend lectures when the New Plymouth Aero Club began a series of lectures for pilots interested in sitting written examinations for the Commercial Pilot Licence. Eventually I attempted (and passed) these exams, although still not with any real intention of doing flying as a full-time job. Several people asked what I would do when I obtained a Commercial Pilot Licence. "I don't really know" I would answer. "It's just a ticket I thought may be handy one day, and this opportunity was too good to miss."

During this time I also gained Aircraft Maintenance Engineer Licences in both airframes and engines. After all, for a quiet young fellow living away from home, this was the golden opportunity for doing study!

Having read Nevil Shute's book *A Town Like Alice*, the concept of the Royal Flying Doctor Service in Australia really appealed to me. But when I discussed this idea with friends I was told that the RFDS would basically only take ex-airline pilots. I realised that any hope of working for such an organisation would always be beyond even my wildest dreams. But then, by a chance meeting with a fellow employee, I came to hear about an organisation known as Missionary Aviation Fellowship – a world-wide fellowship of Christians who use aircraft to provide transport for Christian missionaries working in remote areas where there is little or no alternative means of transport. I was interested to learn about such a work but not sufficiently interested – not at first anyway – to become personally involved in any way. It was several months later that I began to wonder if perhaps God had allowed and enabled me to obtain the qualifications that I now had in order that I should be involved in a ministry such as that provided by MAF.

The subject of guidance, particularly vocational guidance, seems to be a question mark for Christians both young and old. There is no fixed pattern that applies to everyone because the Lord deals with us as individuals. It is exciting when His timing is shown to be so perfect that it cannot be continually written off as just coincidence. It was during this time in my search for guidance that Des Oatridge, a linguist working with the Summer Institute of Linguistics in New Guinea, sought me out and told me of their jungle aviation service, known as JAARS. (Jungle Aviation And Radio Service). He also left me with a couple of booklets on guidance.

The analogy used by one writer was that of steering a ship. In order to steer a ship it must be under way. So long as the vessel continues to just drift on the surface of the ocean the Captain has no control over where it drifts. However, once a boat is moving through the water the Captain can steer it on to a certain course and even change direction as he wishes. And in a similar way God can guide or direct a Christian only when he has prayerfully set out to pursue a certain goal or purpose.

I had written to the MAF office in Auckland expressing my interest in their work and as a result had received a reply which detailed the technical qualifications needed for a MAF pilot. But the letter also explained that a personal call from God into this work was essential. I also wrote to JAARS in New Guinea but I received no reply, and concluded that maybe sometimes there could even be a purpose in things like mail going astray.

Of course a single young fellow who is just 21 years of age cannot be expected to spend all his spare time with his head in a textbook. And it is also a fact of life that in the area of friendships and romances we can still experience God's guidance. But he has given us a free will. We are not robots, and so by our own obstinacy we can confuse the guidance. This is where misunderstandings occur and people get hurt.

Not all of my social life was involved with Church related activities. The local Aero Club also featured fairly prominently in my circle of friends.

For some months I had been very friendly with a Christian girl who encouraged me constantly to press on with my goal of service with MAF. But then one day another friend invited me to make the fourth member on a foursome date. The girl who was my partner that evening was one whom I had met several months previously, but something about that evening was different. There was something about Pat that affected me very powerfully. I now found it difficult to concentrate on my work. I didn't care about things like eating or sleeping, and my thoughts about missionary flying were no less confused. One evening, when I had almost decided that perhaps it was only the adventure promised by jungle flying that had attracted me to MAF, and maybe after all I should stay put in a well-paid job that I enjoyed and possibly even marry a girl whom I absolutely adored, I came home and prayed for an answer.

"Lord, I've got to know your will and your plan for my life. I would give anything, leave anything, if I can just ***know***!" The reply was as clear as a spoken voice. "Anything?"

"Yes Lord, anything." Then suddenly, perhaps predictably, a name flashed into my mind.

"Even her?"

"No, that's too much, please!"

You see what I mean? God gave us a free will and certainly I was not beyond being selfish enough to want things my own way. I should have known that God had better plans for both of those young women, better plans that did not include me, and neither of these people, wonderful and lovable as they were, fitted into His plans for my future.

The next day the mail brought a letter from Peter Bissett, secretary for the New Zealand Council of Missionary Aviation Fellowship. It was just a friendly note of encouragement and a suggestion that if I could complete the flight test for my Commercial Pilot Licence before the end of the year it would be worthwhile my considering a one or two year course at a Bible College, beginning in the new year – 1963. The timing of the letter was too perfect to be coincidence, but the idea of full-time Bible College somehow did not appeal. I was secretly just a little bit pleased when it became obvious that I could not arrange for my Commercial Pilot flight test in time to commence Bible College the following year.

An advertisement for an *Evening Bible College* course came to my attention and I thought, "Aha, perhaps I can get around this hurdle rather than over it." But to attend this course would mean living in or near Auckland, which is a long way from New Plymouth. Then a few days later the manager of a small aerial topdressing firm based in Auckland brought his Cessna 180 aircraft into our hangar to have some work done on it. John Barr was looking for a maintenance engineer and so offered me a job in Ardmore, only about 40 kilometres from the heart of Auckland city. Everything fitted together so neatly, even, as it turned out, the provision of board with a Christian household only a few kilometres from Ardmore aerodrome.

The lectures at Evening Bible College made me realise for the first time what a tremendously interesting and exciting book the Bible is. Instead of being a heavy and hard to understand document, written in archaic language that I could scarcely comprehend, it now suddenly became a vitally interesting book about people – real life characters with all the subtleties and problems of people we meet today – and about God's marvellous dealings with people!

In August of the same year (1963) I was invited to move across to Ballarat, in Australia, to work with MAF-AIR Services, with a view to being considered for service with Missionary Aviation Fellowship.

I had always been under the impression that all of Australia was hot, dry, and dusty. So I was somewhat surprised when at a farewell service arranged by MAF in New Zealand, I was presented with a beautiful thick woollen rug and was told, "You will need this in Ballarat. It gets cold there!" I have since seen fairly heavy falls of snow in Ballarat in both May and October, and even a light sprinkling of sleety snow in December (the first month of summer).

MAF-AIR Services was a subsidiary Company of Australian Missionary Aviation Fellowship and had been established to serve several functions in the overall work of the organisation: Pilot-Engineers, as candidates for MAF, could get both flying and engineering experience at MAF-AIR Services. Besides assembling and modifying new aircraft for a number of church-oriented aviation concerns, MAF-AIR Services also carried out major overhauls and refurbishing of Australian MAF aircraft and engines. The company also provided a spare-parts and engineering back-up service for mission aircraft operating in the areas to the north of Australia. During the mid-to-late 1960's this support included MAF-USA aircraft operating in West Irian [now known as Indonesian Papua].

I arrived at the Ballarat railway station after dark on Sat 31st August 1963 and was met by John and Joan Harverson. As I would be staying in a small two-bedroom flat next door to them at the Ballarat airport they did their best to make me feel welcome and provided me with meals until such time as I was able to get myself organised. Although his father was a missionary in Viet Nam John had done his aircraft engineering apprenticeship with National Airways Corporation in Christchurch, New Zealand, so I considered them to be fellow "Kiwis".

Although my finances were somewhat limited I decided I needed a motor car of some sort. So, when I discovered a 1937 *Austin Seven* advertised for sale I reasoned that in spite of its age, a vehicle such as this should be able to serve my modest needs, chugging between the airport and town eight kilometres away. A discarded FRAGILE label from a crate of aircraft parts seemed an appropriate decoration for such an ancient little machine so I stuck this across the bonnet. After that the vehicle was always known (affectionately) by the name *Fragile*.

During discussions with Alex Jardine, the manager of MAF AIR Services, it was suggested that I should seriously consider doing a one-year course of study at a Bible College in the coming year (1964). I was free to make my own choice of either returning to New Zealand (NZBTI) or to attend Melbourne Bible Institute. After the taste for such study, doing Evening Bible College in Auckland, I was only too keen to agree, and after praying about it I felt very strongly that God's will for me was to attend the college in Melbourne. After one year of wonderful fellowship with other MBI students I was sorry I could not do a second year.

1963 - 64. Staff at MAF-AIR Services, Ballarat, Australia.

Back row (from left):
Dave Tadman, Bill Waters (Chief Engineer), Alex Jardine (Manager), John Harverson, John Johnston, John Seddon.

Front Row:
Jim Lindsay, Roger Young, Ruth Grey, Ray Chapman, Rex Wills.

I had seriously wondered how old *Fragile* would handle the 120 kilometre trip to Melbourne and the city traffic. But I found that the Lord can undertake even in mechanical things and that amazing little vehicle made many trips between Melbourne and Ballarat, chugging faithfully up the 1,500 ft climb over the Pentland Hills every time. The only mechanical failure was on one trip when the generator failed just on dark. I had to drive the next 30 kilometres with the headlights on and by the time I turned in at the Ballarat airport the lights were so dim that the only purpose they really served was to warn oncoming motorists that I was on the road. Fortunately it was a bright moonlit night!

After 12 months of faithful service *Fragile* was sold to a fellow student at Bible College, for the price of £12 ($24).

When I returned to Ballarat in 1965 I had the privilege of sharing accommodation with Ivan Wilson. Ivan had been working at Rural Aviation, in New Plymouth, when I arrived there in August 1960, but he had left at the end of 1961 so he could do a two-year course at NZBTI before offering his services to MAF as an aircraft maintenance engineer. And also during the early part of that year Doug Hunt, who was the first New Zealand pilot to serve with MAF, spent some time in Ballarat and was able to give John Harverson and myself some very worthwhile dual instruction on jungle flying. With all these New Zealand accents around the place I was feeling quite "at home". Doug did have some experience as an aerial topdressing pilot and what he taught us about short, sloping airstrips and mountain country flying was invaluable.

Then during March and April (1965) I had the privilege of going on an extensive deputation tour with MAF Field Leader Max Flavel throughout South Australia and the southern part of West Australia. We took a Cessna 180 which had been retired from service in Papua and New Guinea and was soon to be sold. The itinerary had been carefully arranged beforehand by Stan Fairfull and, almost without exception, every place we called at had an airstrip fairly close to the township. We would arrive at each town about mid-morning and the aircraft would be available for joy flights for the rest of the day. I was surprised at the considerable number of customers we had, even although most of this was on regular week-days, not weekends! On some days, arrangements had also been made for one or more of our group to speak to students in the local Primary Schools where those in the class had a chance to hear some first-hand stories about life in New Guinea. Each evening there was a meeting, usually arranged through the local Ministers Fraternal, where we showed films and slides of the work of MAF.

The problem for me came on Sundays when I was expected to take my share of speaking at church services. This was all very well but I had, at this point in time, no first-hand experience of MAF work. I overcame this by borrowing one or two illustrations that I had heard Max use and also made liberal use of examples and statistics from Harold Morton's book *Below Me the Mountains*, but without specifically stating that I was quoting from Harold's book. After a church service one evening several members of the congregation stopped to talk to me at the end of the service and I took notice that more than one of them mentioned, in a very casual sort of way, something like, "I also enjoyed reading Harold's book."!

Sometime prior to this tour I had actually been able to do some flying with Harold. Back in February 1964 he had been in Ballarat on a visit and it was decided that this would be a good opportunity for him to give me a few clues about some of the flying techniques used in a mountainous country such as New Guinea. We took the faithful old Cessna 170 VH-BUX out to the Grampians (an outcrop of mini-mountains to the west of Ballarat) and Harold demonstrated the standard technique for crossing a mountain ridge.

When attempting to cross a mountain-ridge at low level a pilot must never fly straight at it but always approach at an angle of not more than 45 degrees to the main line of the ridge. This allows the pilot to "feel" if there are any winds that may be creating updraughts or downdraughts over the ridge, and it also gives him an opportunity to see what the weather is like on the other side before committing himself to crossing over. By approaching the ridge in this way it is possible to turn away quite safely if turbulence is encountered or if, at the last minute, it becomes obvious that the valley on the other side is filled with cloud or rain. This is particularly important where a low overcast of cloud makes it impossible to cross the ridge at a higher level. We then flew to the airfield at Ararat where we tried a few short-field take-offs and landings. But, apart from a few general principles such as these, the only way to really learn mountain-flying techniques, or flying techniques for tropical mountainous country, is to actually do some flying in that country. The conditions cannot really be properly simulated anywhere else.

At Sydney airport 31st Aug., 1965. My fiancée Rose turns to say a last word of farewell before walking across the tarmac to board her plane to Melbourne. In those days there was no regular telephone link from Wewak to the rest of the world, so it was more than twelve months before we saw or spoke to each other again.

I also included this photo just to show how different Sydney airport was in those days to what it is now.

Chapter Five

A COLD SHOWER?

The evening of Tuesday 31st August 1965 found me waiting in the rather bleak and chilly Sydney Airport terminal (a far cry from the huge air-conditioned complex you will find there nowadays!). In those days the flight to Port Moresby was an all-night effort. The Lockheed Electra left Sydney about 11 pm and, after a brief stop at Brisbane in the early hours of the morning, we went on to Port Moresby, arriving there just after first light – about 6 o'clock in the morning.

At Sydney Airport I had said farewell to my fiancée, as she was returning to Melbourne to complete her second year at Melbourne Bible Institute. We had announced our engagement just ten days previously and Rose had been able to get across to New Zealand to spend a week with my family before I left for my first-ever period in New Guinea.

After the cool evening in Sydney the 6 am weather in Port Moresby was just pleasant; warm but not hot, and the sky was almost cloudless. After a brief stop-over, during which time the passengers who were continuing their journey on the same aircraft did not even get into the shelter of the terminal building, we took-off again for Lae. There I was allowed to collect my luggage and go through Customs formalities. We landed at Lae at about 8 am and had to wait for a DC3 aircraft for the flight to Madang and Wewak. Sitting inside the terminal building it seemed hot and stuffy so I decided to go outside and get some fresh air. The moment I walked out into the sun it was worse! Of course, I was in the tropics now! I would have to learn to put up with this, 24 hours a day, every day, without a break.

When the boarding call was finally given for the Madang and Wewak flight, I felt relieved. At last, I thought, I'll soon be out of this heat. It will be cooler when we get in the air, and in Wewak I can have a cold shower.

Our next stop, of course, was Madang, a place that definitely looks very attractive from the air. As our aircraft came in to land I saw a beautiful scene – azure-blue sea with borders of white surf along the many coral reefs, and shorelines well protected with coconut palms. This could have been a picture of the perfect tropical paradise except that the rusting hulks of several ships and landing-barges presented an unintentional memorial to the bitter fighting that had taken place here towards the end of World War II. Here the awesome wonder and beauty of God's creation was contaminated by evidence of man's propensity to violence. In spite of that, my first impressions of Madang were of beauty and wonder; but then … with the harsh reality of standing on the asphalt tarmac in the tropical midday sun because our aircraft was unserviceable and there was not enough space to sit in the grossly inadequate passenger terminal, the place lost a lot of its charm! Although it did give me an opportunity to find out if my attempts at speaking in *Tok Pisin* were intelligible, and I was greatly encouraged when the man I had spoken to obviously understood what I had said and made a friendly reply.

I do not recall how long we had to wait before taking-off again for Wewak, but my one consolation was that it must have been even worse for the mechanics working on the engine of the aircraft. The heat radiating from the engine, plus the pressure of knowing there was a load of passengers waiting, gave them a job I did not envy.

Wewak at last! It was now late afternoon and most of the MAF staff were at the Airport to meet me. After the usual round of greetings and introductions I was taken by car to my new home – a small three-roomed dwelling – which I later learned had originally been used for storing air-cargo, but some very capable carpenters had converted it into a two-bedroom house. Nevertheless, it was a welcome sight to me because now, at last, I could enjoy a cold shower.

"A cold shower? Well, you see this bucket here with the shower rose on the bottom? You fill the bucket with tank water, then pull it up on the rope, like so, and hop under before you've lost all the water. And don't waste the water; we've only got a few rungs of it left in the tanks. We're hoping for rain every day."

There were two other houses in the compound where I was to be living, but mine was the only one with a "laundry" – which also partly explained why my tanks were nearly empty, because the families from the other two houses used "my" water for washing their clothes. But the word *laundry* may be misleading, for it consisted of little more than a carport-like structure containing what my parents would have referred to as a "copper". This was a large copper bowl, capable of holding about 25 gallons (100 litres) of water and supported in such a way that you could light a fire underneath and heat the water. This, incidentally, was my only source of hot water – apart from boiling a kettle, which meant lighting the kerosene stove … and *that* was not the sort of task you would give to an untrained person (unless you really wanted to set the whole house on fire!). The refrigerator was also powered by kerosene and required a fair bit of TLC. My washing machine was the "Armstrong" variety … a wooden paddle used to stir the clothes in the copper while the water boiled.

Perhaps I need to emphasise that up until this point in time the electricity supply in Wewak had been so unreliable that most things used an alternative form of power – hence the kero fridge and kerosene stove, and there was no running hot water. Even the water supply I did have was gravity feed, so while water in the tanks was at a low level the two taps in the house would not run and I had to go out to the "laundry" to get water from a tap that would work.

Such were my first impressions of New Guinea, but these minor problems were certainly not going to stop me looking forward enthusiastically to the many new challenges ahead.

1960s. Town of Wewak (from the air). The Wirui airstrip is visible as a clearing between the trees in the background.

Main street and main shopping area of Wewak town in 1965

Chapter Six

WEWAK

At the time I arrived there Wewak was a small, very dusty, town. Most roads were still paved with coronus (crushed coral) and every motor vehicle I saw seemed to be riddled with rust. A brand new vehicle could be rusted out in two years. Since those days a lot of tarsealing of roads has been done and this has improved the durability of vehicles somewhat, but rust is still a big problem.

The main residential area was on a small, almost circular peninsula, probably only one kilometre across. A walk right around the road that circled the peninsula just made a pleasant afternoon stroll. At the neck, where Wewak point joins the mainland, was the main street where there were several stores, mostly owned by Chinese and catering for trade with the native population, plus three larger stores – Burns Philp, George Seeto, and Tang Mow. Besides supplying the needs of those in the immediate town area, these three stores also catered for the equally large expatriate population - Mission and Government employees - working throughout the vast Sepik district and several of the Highland areas which were, at the time, served by air services out of Wewak.

At the western end of the shopping centre was an open market where it was possible to buy locally-grown produce such as pawpaws, pineapples, cucumbers, *moulis* (similar to a lemon, but much more sour; these made a most refreshing drink) and, if you were very adventurous, smoked fish or even sea turtle – I was not quite that adventurous.

It was necessary to be at this market by 6 am on Saturdays to get good fruit as the demand was high, but the supply fairly limited.

About one kilometre from the shopping centre was the Wirui airstrip. In those days MAF had their hangar and facilities at the western end of this airstrip, and the Roman Catholic Mission of the Divine Word had their hangar and facilities at the eastern end. The Control Tower was at the Wewak International Airport, five kilometres by road further along the coast. At that time, the road between the two airstrips ran along the back of the beach. (This has since been closed – when the wharf for coastal and overseas shipping was built and a new road made further inland.) The Hospital was on a peninsula near the main airstrip at Boram, and beyond that again was Point Moem where the Army (No. 2 Pacific Islands Regiment) had a large establishment, probably as large as the town of Wewak itself. In more recent years MAF have built new facilities at the Boram airstrip and the Wirui airstrip has been closed.

My first six weeks in New Guinea were spent working in the hangar completing the Annual Inspection on the Cessna 185 VH-MFB ("Mike Foxtrot Bravo"). I was also asked to do an "annual overhaul" on an old Holden Ute operated by the Fellowship. Salty conditions had had their effect on this vehicle and it was so badly rusted that if more than two people sat in the thing it all sagged so badly that the cab floor actually rested on the drive-shaft! The solution was to design and weld an angle-iron chassis beneath the rotting superstructure.

I was asked to keep this vehicle going "for six weeks if possible." By then, so I was told, we should have a new vehicle. Several months later this same rusty Ute was used for an emergency dash to the hospital after a child had drunk some kerosene. It developed such a tremendous tremble in the front-end that the whole vehicle must have nearly shaken to bits. After that it remained parked near the side of the airstrip and was only touched again many months later when the engine was removed prior to dragging the remains to the local tip.

The six weeks in the hangar gave me the chance to get used to the tropical climate and also gain a better working knowledge of *Tok Pisin* – also known as Pidgin English. Although Chinese traders were, reputedly, the ones who introduced this language it has become the common trade language of Papua New Guinea and it is now widely spoken throughout the country.

Tok Pisin is a recognised language with a set of rules that should be applied to sentence structure and grammar, but many expatriates made the mistake of just adding a few "...ims" to the odd verb, and prattled on, still using normal English thinking and syntax. The national folk called this *Tok Masta*, and the term was not a compliment! However, as with any other language, *Tok Pisin* is subject to constant change and what was condemned as *Tok Masta* in 1965 may even be accepted as legitimate Pidgin English nowadays.

Before we started work each morning it was the practice to gather the staff together (those who had not already gone flying) and take a few minutes for a short Bible reading and a time of prayer. For the sake of our New Guinean employees this was always done in *Tok Pisin.* I had only been there three weeks when the book was handed to me one morning with the comment, "Your turn to read tomorrow."

"Go on, you've got to be joking!"

"I'm not joking. You give it a go. The boys will appreciate you making an effort." So I took the book (a translation of the four Gospels in Melanesian Pidgin), selected a passage I knew well in English and read through it in *Tok Pisin.* I kidded myself that everyone knew what I was reading about the next morning.

Of course the cargo-handlers and other hangar staff had heard people speaking the English language for long enough they probably would have understood most of what I said if I had done my little talk in English. But most of them would never attempt to speak English. In fact I challenged one of them one day by pointing out that he obviously understood what people were saying when he heard them speaking in English, so why didn't he use that language when talking with people who did not understand *Tok Pisin*? He told me that the reason he could not speak English was because he had the wrong colour skin. And he said it with a dead straight face! I hope he was joking, because I certainly took it as a joke.

To give a more complete picture of mission flying in Papua and New Guinea during the 1960's I should mention that there were a number of other Christian organisations operating aircraft in the country at this point in time. I have already mentioned the

Jungle Aviation and Radio Service (JAARS – now known as SIL Aviation) serving Wycliffe Bible Translators. Their base was (and still is) at Aiyura, in the Eastern Highlands. The New Guinea Lutheran Mission (Lutmis) had aircraft based in Lae, Goroka, and Madang. In fact they were probably the first to provide an aviation service to missionaries in this part of the world as they had a six-seat, 270hp Junkers F.13 monoplane operating in New Guinea as early as February 1935.[1] The Anglican Church (Australian Board of Missions) had an aircraft based at Oro Bay, near Popondetta. There were a significant number of places where different branches of the Roman Catholic Church had pilots, maintenance engineers, and aircraft based throughout the country, and the SDA mission had their own aircraft. There were possibly others that I am not aware of.

In September 1965, when I arrived in New Guinea, the total fleet of MAF aircraft consisted of seven single-engine Cessnas. One was based at Wasua, a mission station beside the Fly river, about 100 kilometres north of Daru; there were two aircraft based in the highlands – one at Banz, and the machine which had been based in Tari (as described in Harold Morton's book *Below Me the Mountains*) was about to be relocated to Wapenamanda. The rest of the fleet was based in Wewak on the north coast, where MAF had their only maintenance workshop in New Guinea at the time.

Most of the flying out of Wewak was made up of regular

---

[1] Unfortunately, when World War 2 started (Sep., 1939) their pilot and engineer, who were merely contracted workers and not members of the Lutheran Mission staff, took the aircraft and flew it across to Dutch New Guinea where they abandoned it and eventually made their way back to Germany. So their aircraft was effectively stolen. When Harry Hartwig arrived in Madang with the Auster aircraft in April-May 1951 it was a joint effort between Australian MAF, MAF-USA, and the Lutheran Mission.

The Lutherans have a significant history of work in the area. In 1885 the Neuendettelsau Mission Society in Germany commissioned Rev Johannes Flierl to work in what was then a German administered territory known as Kaiser Wilhelmsland. Flierl, one of the first Christian missionaries in this part of the world, arrived at what is now known as Finschhafen in July 1886. In 1887 two more Lutheran missionaries, Rev Friedrich Eich and Rev Wilhelm Thomas, commenced work in Astrolabe Bay, just south of present day Madang.

flights known as "freezer runs" and, although these were by no means scheduled services, they were done on a regular basis. For example: on Monday morning a MAF plane would always leave Wewak taking mailbags and perishable goods, such as freezer supplies, to Apostolic Church mission stations at Laiagam and Porgera in the highlands and then backload fresh vegetables to Wewak. On Tuesday morning one aircraft would go to Australian Baptist Mission stations in the Baiyer River area, while a second plane would go to the Christian Missions in Many Lands stations at Koroba, Pori, Kelabo and Auwi (all in the highlands), and in the afternoon would take similar supplies and mail to CMML airstrips in the much lower country of the West Sepik area. And so it continued through the week, each day having its allotted freezer runs. Where possible the various mission societies endeavoured to arrange their personnel movements around these regular flights, so the order in which the various airstrips were visited was variable, depending on the requirements of the people involved.

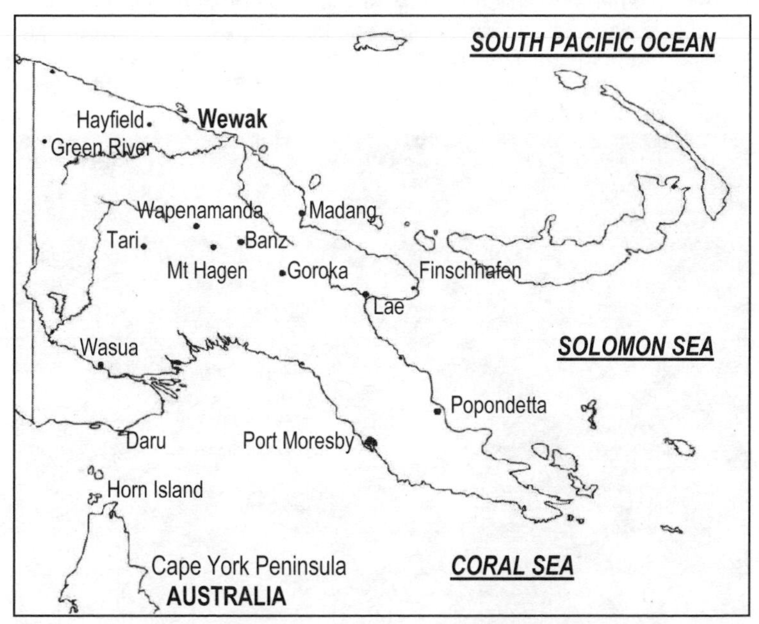

Map of Papua and New Guinea – showing location of places mentioned in the foregoing and next chapters of this book.

1965: Building roads and airstrips in a country where machines, and even wheels, were unknown only a few years previously – when we say, "The work was all done by hand" you can take that quite literally.

Above: Women and children carry rocks as part of a project to create a road between Nipa and Kar, in the Southern Highlands (a government project). [photo credit: Don Whittingham]
Below: Work on the airstrip at Auwi, also in the Southern Highlands (a mission sponsored project).

Chapter Seven

FAMILIARISATION

On October 18th 1965 I had my first flight in a MAF Cessna aircraft in New Guinea, but only as an observer, sitting in the front right-hand seat just to see the country. Regulations at that time required that the pilot of an aircraft on charter operations in the Territory of Papua and New Guinea must fly over any route at least five times before being allowed to fly over the area solo. The first of these flights was done as an observer (hence often referred to as a "familiarization flight"), then there were two flights under dual instruction but sitting in the captain's seat, and finally two flights when the check-captain supposedly just looked on and made certain that the new pilot knew where he was going. My first flight was to Green River, near the West Irian border in the Sepik District, a flight of one-and-a-half hours each way in a Cessna 185.

Soon after this I was officially checked into the old wartime airstrip at Hayfield, just 20 minutes flying west of Wewak. Now perhaps I should mention here that apart from walking or flying, the only other possible method of travel available at the time between Hayfield and Wewak was to travel by "road" from Hayfield down to a spot on the Sepik river and then by boat down to the mouth of the river and back along the coast to Wewak. There was no wharf in Wewak in those days and barges had to be used to move all cargo and passengers between ship and shore. The "road" at the Hayfield end was definitely 4-wheel-drive only, and virtually impassable in wet weather, which was most of the time. The Assemblies of God Mission had several tons of trade store supplies to be flown into Hayfield. So I was given the use of an aeroplane to build up a few hours' flying experience in shifting these goods into Hayfield, and to get a taste of the peculiarities of New Guinea weather. I was soon to begin finding out what this meant.

After the six weeks on the ground I was very keen to get on with the flying – perhaps too keen! An older pilot had warned me always to plan to be home by 5 pm until I became really familiar with the airstrips and the weather patterns, and the country in general. One afternoon I left it almost too late.

After take off from Wewak I headed out over the lowest part of the mountains to the southwest, and flying at about 2,000 feet to keep below a heavy overcast, set course toward Hayfield. However, several extensive and heavy rain showers throughout the wide Sepik valley prevented me from getting to my destination so I decided to turn back to Wewak. But by this time the cloud had settled down right along the ridge behind me and there was no way back. It seemed that I had nowhere to go! I could not go west because of the rain, to the north and east were mountains, mostly hidden in cloud, and I dare not go south or southeast because that was flat swampy country, which I knew was only inaccurately mapped and I was not familiar with any of it. I was beginning to get worried.

I have vivid recollections of circling and sneaking up as close to the top of the mountain ridge as I dare, in a desperate attempt to find even a chink in the weather's armour, and fervently praying, "Lord, I've got myself into this corner but only You can get me out of it!"

I was too low to make direct VHF radio contact with Wewak Control Tower so I tried calling Madang Flight Service on the HF radio. I guess my voice betrayed my concern but perhaps fortunately, as it turned out, Madang did not hear my call. A few miles west of my position the mountain ridge rose up to the 4,000 ft peak of Mt. Turu, and at the foot of Mt. Turu was the Yangoru airstrip. I had never landed on this airstrip, although I had heard that its surface was undulating and tricky. But it was my only hope. I headed west again to Yangoru, and as I circled the unfamiliar airstrip and wondered if I should attempt a landing, I glanced in the direction of Hayfield and miraculously, like the curtains drawing back on a stage, the rain showers parted and I was able to see through to Hayfield, 16 miles away!

What if I had been faced with the additional problem of fading daylight? I was to live through one of those experiences within the next two years, but for now I was beginning to have a growing respect for the advice given to me by more experienced pilots!

Living as a bachelor in Wewak had a few problems. I was continuously being approached by native teenage lads who wanted to do my housework for me. I did not feel that I could afford this and neither did I believe I had enough work to justify the expense.

As I have already mentioned, most of our water tanks were fairly empty when I arrived in Wewak at the beginning of September. After a couple of weeks I noticed that my drinking water was starting to have a peculiar smell about it, not to mention the taste! A quick inspection revealed a dead frog in one of my two water tanks! There was no alternative but to remove the offending remains and then empty and scrub the tank. It hurt to pour all that precious water out onto the ground, but what else could I do? A few days later a suspicious splashing noise in the second tank took my attention. This time it was two frogs, one alive and one dead. I knew that this particular type of frog was able to climb trees, and that in some parts of the country they were known to make themselves at home in bush-material buildings, so I assumed that these two had climbed in through the overflow pipe on the tank. Anyway, I now had to drain all that precious water out of the second tank! Fortunately a shower of rain the night before had put two or three inches of water back into the first tank. Because of these frogs I took to making daily inspections inside my water tanks. Then a few nights later, in the middle of the night as I lay half asleep, I thought I heard soft voices and giggling outside. Next morning, sure enough, there was a frog in the tank! Maybe there was no connection, but soon after that I did employ a "houseboy" and had no further trouble with the water supply. A few weeks later, when the northwesterly winds began, the tanks were merrily overflowing every day.

For the next six months checkouts continued into the various airstrips throughout the Sepik district. Very few airstrips were straightforward level aerodromes on flat country. Most of them were either scraped into the side of a mountain, some with a considerable degree of slope, or, though level in themselves, ran into the foot of a mountain at one end so that it was only possible to land in one direction and take-off in the opposite direction, regardless of the wind. A further problem with these one-way airstrips was that many of them were in the bottom of a small valley and, as the aircraft descended into the valley, a point would be reached where it was not possible to make a comfortable 180 degree turn either left or right, or to climb out of the valley straight ahead. In such cases, once an approach had been commenced, the pilot was committed to make a landing regardless of people or animals suddenly walking out onto the airstrip. The only alternative being to go into the trees! There was no room for error or hesitation. Even airstrips which were level and allowed for two-way operations often had their traps for the unwary.

One such airstrip was Lumi, at a Government Patrol Post, 2,000 feet up in the Torricelli Mountains and about 120 nautical miles west of Wewak. The place was noted for its crosswinds and turbulence during approach and landing, and the red-clay surface used to become soft and very slippery after rain. It seemed that it rained at Lumi almost every afternoon. In addition to this, the ground dropped away very steeply at both ends of the airstrip, and while a pilot may be tempted to land as close to the strip threshold as possible so as to be sure he would not skid over the far end, he had to be very careful not to bring his aircraft in too low. It would have really spoiled his landing if the wheels hit the cliff just short of the airstrip threshold! There were many other airstrips similar to Lumi throughout Papua and New Guinea.

As far as the weather was concerned I soon found that it was often possible to fly quite safely below the cloud base, dodging rain showers if necessary and, once familiar with the area, the large number of airstrips gave plenty of alternate landing grounds. On many of my flights, as I criss-crossed over the country between the mountains along the coast and the Sepik River inland, I could look to the south and see, nearly 100 miles away, the rugged blue outline of the Central Ranges. Beyond them again were the mysterious highland valleys, which I had heard so much about, but never seen. The thought of exploring those valleys fascinated me. Were the highlands, I wondered, so much different from this area? I longed to find out.

After six months of familiarisation in the low country of the Sepik district my introduction to the highlands began. The first area to which I was introduced was the Baiyer River valley, where the Australian Baptist Mission Society was working.

Some 25 minutes south of Wewak we crossed the Sepik River and from there on for another 25 or 30 minutes followed approximately the line of the Yuat River up to the Yuat Gap. This is a very distinct pass in the mountain range through which the Yuat River flows on its way out from the mountain valleys to join the Sepik River to the north. Continuing to follow the river we flew down a smooth-looking grassy valley with the mountains on either side of us rising up to something over 9,000 feet above sea level. Suddenly the river was joined by another, the Jimi River, and our valley made a sharp right-hand turn before it opened out into the Baiyer Valley. The floor of this valley is 4,500 feet above sea level. Ten minutes further south, situated at the western end of the beautiful and fertile Wahgi Valley and 5,300 feet above sea level, is the town and airport of Mount Hagen.

Route checks throughout this area, as in all of the highland areas, involved learning to recognise the different valleys and remembering which valleys ran into a dead-end and which of them joined into yet another valley system. In addition to showing me the layout of the country and airstrips, my checkpilots, Max Meyers and Harold Morton, drew my attention to the normal daily weather pattern and were careful to point out the places where we would be most likely to find a way through, even in comparatively poor weather. Only in exceptionally fine weather is it possible to climb and fly directly over the mountains in a straight line from A to B. The airstrips in these Highland areas were going to be another new experience for me. I was told, and later agreed this was true, that we were starting in the easiest area first. Perhaps it was just as well that we did!

We flew across to Kompiam, tucked in a small cove at the side of the valley – just large enough to make a close right-hand circuit for our approach to land. Standing on the strip at 4,000 feet above sea level, the mountains seemed to tower all around us. It was explained to me that to get out of this place we would have to commence a gentle left turn very soon after take-off. This would bring us over the river, just to the north of the airstrip, and then we would follow the river down to our next port of call at Lapalama. The airstrip at Lapalama appeared to stand almost vertically on the wall of this steep-sided valley directly in front of us, where the river and the valley made a sharp right-hand turn. Actually the slope was only 12 percent (or 1 in 8) but it always looked a lot steeper than that. Once again the approach had to be made off a right-hand circuit and our port wing-tip seemed to be skimming awfully close to a steep rocky outcrop on our left-hand side as we turned on to final approach. Below us the Lai River was a mass of white foam as it churned and tumbled over its rocky course on its way to eventually join the Yuat River. Once on the ground at Lapalama we lost speed very quickly on the steeply sloping airstrip and actually had to apply almost full power to keep the plane moving in order to reach the parking-bay at the top of the strip.

On most Tuesdays a MAF plane would spend almost a full day in the Baiyer area doing shuttles between the Baptist Mission airstrips. It was never difficult to persuade the pilot to have lunch at Lapalama as these people had cows with fresh milk and real cream – a luxury almost unknown in Wewak.

After unloading most of our freight and adding a couple of passengers who were booked to go to Kumbwaretta airstrip we climbed aboard for our next 'hop'. As we lined-up for take-off from Lapalama I looked with some apprehension at the ground, which dropped away steeply in front of us. "I guess it's been done before," I thought, and opened the throttle for take-off. Several years later one of the passengers from that flight admitted to me that he had been horrified to see me push the control-wheel forward at the start of the take-off roll in an attempt to raise the tail of the aircraft (a perfectly normal practice on a level airstrip). I certainly remember my check-pilot commenting very emphatically, as we sped down the hill on that occasion, "Don't raise the tail or we'll go over on our nose!"

Several months later I was flying on and off these airstrips with little more concern than the average motorist might have when he is parking his car in the garage, especially when compared to places like Porgera with its very deceptive slope. The airstrip at Porgera was more than 7,000 feet above sea level and its surroundings of sheer rock faces and jagged mountain peaks, extending up to 12,000 feet, created a rather awe-inspiring scene. Or Laiagam, Oxapmin, and Tekin, with their frightening down-draughts on take-off and landing. And Pori! Pori was situated on the side of a steep V-shaped valley and, like most highland airstrips, was about 5,000 feet above sea level. The landing approach was made down the valley, at right angles to the airstrip, while airspeed and rate of descent had to be monitored very carefully. At the last minute a left-hand turn put the aircraft just a few hundred yards away from the airstrip threshold. Pori did have one advantage – its steep slope made it possible to fly the aeroplane right onto the airstrip as much as 15 knots above the stall, and even without touching the brakes, the machine would come to a stop before the top of the hill.

My first take-off from here was a memorable one. From the parking bay, a level section at the top of the airstrip, it was only possible to see about 50 metres of the airstrip surface before it disappeared over the brow of the hill. Max Flavel, who did my checkouts at Pori, was careful to point out some significant features on the not-too-distant mountain range across the river from the end of the airstrip. "Aim straight at that point," he said, "and then, as you go over the hill, you will find you are right down the centre of the strip". I found he was right. But I never really did learn to relax when operating in places like that.

Typical airstrips:

On a mountain plateau: Lumusa – 4750 ft (1448 metres) AMSL

Or tucked into the corner of a valley: Tekin – 5600 ft (1707 metres) above mean sea level, surface slope is 11.3%

Chapter Eight

ONLY A SINGLE ENGINE

"There's one thing about this Roger Young fellow, he doesn't seem to mind getting stuck out away from home overnight." "Hah," replied the missionary's friend, "You wait till he gets married. He'll be as anxious to get home as the rest of them!"

It was probably true. There had been a number of times when I'd been only too pleased to spend a weekend out in the bush so that the aircraft could be on hand for an early flight on Monday, or had been happy to fly all Saturday to do taxi service for weddings etc. Mention of Saturday flying reminds me of an amusing story I heard.

Some 30 nautical miles southwest of Wewak was the small mission station of Wingei. There was no airstrip at Wingei and in those days it was fairly isolated from the rest of civilisation. However it did stand out fairly noticeably on the top of a small hill, and it was not unknown for pilots returning to Wewak with the relaxed feeling of a Saturday afternoon ahead of them, to get down lower than usual so as to fly close to the house on the hill at Wingei and give the missionaries there a friendly waggle of the wings. On this one occasion a couple of elderly ladies were visiting missionary families in the area to give some practical help with household chores, like sewing and darning, and perhaps helping with the children's education, just to give the mothers a bit of a break.

Now one Saturday the family at Wingei were sitting at lunch when one of the children, for some reason, left the table without asking. So "Aunty" proceeded to instruct the child that this was not good manners. "It is more polite," she was explaining, "to ask first if you need to leave the table during a meal time." Now "Aunty", being elderly, was a little hard of hearing but just then everyone else suddenly became aware of a familiar noise – the kind of noise that grows rapidly louder and that stirs a strange excitement. Without one word being spoken, except perhaps shouts of delight, the entire household, all except "Aunty", threw back their chairs and raced outside to wave frantically and happily at the MAF plane as it roared past with an exaggerated rocking of its wings that said, "You are not forgotten." Oblivious to the domestic confusion he may have just created, the pilot flew happily on home to his own family, and probably an afternoon on the beach in Wewak.

I had been in New Guinea for just on 12 months and was now planning the longest flight I had yet undertaken – from Wewak in New Guinea to Melbourne in Australia, a distance of some 2,000 nautical miles. I would be flying the MAF Cessna 185 VH-MFB to Ballarat for its 3-yearly overhaul, and returning in the same aircraft three weeks later with my new wife! By my planning I expected to be in Melbourne by Friday 16th September 1966, and our wedding was planned for one week later, Saturday 24th. There were three passengers travelling with me on this flight. John was travelling to find a wife, or at least to confirm arrangements for the day – I think he had already 'asked the question'; Alan was travelling to visit his wife who had gone south for hospital treatment; Len Creek was returning home to his wife and family after several weeks of voluntary missionary work in the New Guinea highlands and I was travelling to marry a wife. So we were a happy foursome!

Armed with piles of maps, sandwiches, documents for HM Customs, and flasks of drink for our expected two days of flying, we departed from Wewak at 6.40 am on Thursday 15th September. Just before 7 am there began a series of events that would make this flight even more memorable. The first I heard was a radio call from Madang Flight Service on 5498 kHz. "Mike Foxtrot Bravo, this is Madang. Have you heard anything of Bravo Victor Kilo on this frequency this morning?"

"Negative."

"Could you try giving him a call? He was due to report in the Yuat Gap two minutes ago." I complied with this request but received no reply from the other aircraft. Then I received another message from the Madang operator:

"Mike Foxtrot Bravo ... it's all OK. We have contact with

the aircraft on 5666 kHz. Apparently Bravo Victor Kilo has had an engine failure and is making a forced landing on a sandbank in the Yuat River. Can you proceed to the area for a search?"

"Affirmative," I replied. Then after a bit of quick mental navigation added, "Estimate the Yuat Gap at time three zero (ie: 7:30 am)." I passed all this information to my passengers and their reaction helped me to grasp the significance of what I had just heard. At 7:30 we were in the Yuat Gap area but on top of what appeared to be a solid layer of cloud. It took me another ten minutes to find a break and descend underneath it to begin following the course of the river downstream. A few minutes later we spotted the aircraft VH-BVK on a sandbar at the side of the river, several thousand feet below. Apparently the only damage suffered was a blown tyre, and as the radios were still working I was able to communicate with Alan Collecutt, the pilot of the other plane, and confirm that he was not injured.

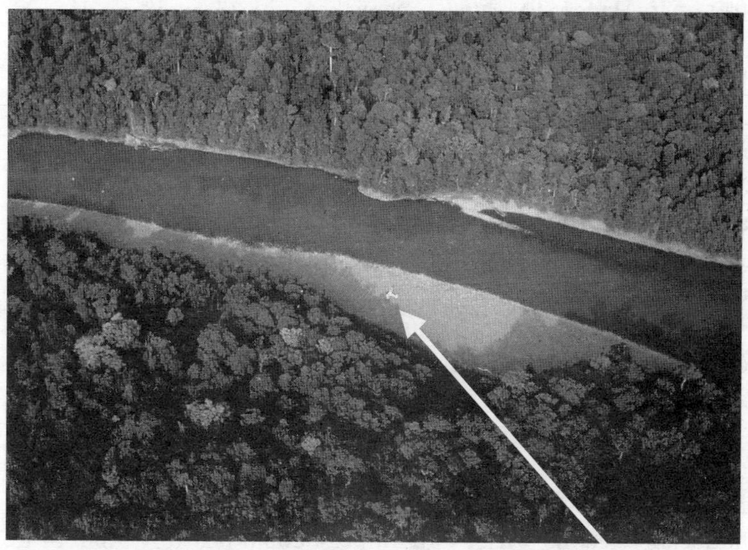

Successful forced landing on a sandbar of the Yuat River

I found out later when talking to Alan that he had been on top of that same cloud layer in the Yuat Gap area when there was a loud bang and he lost engine power. Of course he had no time to look for a hole in the cloud for his descent and barely had time to give a "Mayday" radio call then set the aircraft up for a descent through the cloud on instruments. Miraculously he not only managed his descent without flying into any mountains but also came out from the cloud layer right over the top of the Yuat River. A further miracle was that the water level in the river was well down and he found there were several sandbanks from which to choose for his forced landing. When we saw the aircraft on the sandbank that morning, I was immediately reminded of the words of the Psalmist: "*He shall give His angels charge over you to keep you in all your ways*." (Psalm 91:11).

During the next 40 or 50 minutes, while we waited for a second aircraft to arrive over the "crash" site (which meant that we could then be released to continue our journey southward), I confess that I had many anxious thoughts. Considering the circumstances of this situation some people may think my thoughts were rather too concerned with self-interest. But I was satisfied that Alan was safe and that a helicopter was on the way from Mt. Hagen. My fears were that with the possible loss of VH-BVK, the management of MAF may decide that the aircraft I was flying would now have to remain in New Guinea, and with my own wedding in eight days time I would suddenly find myself desperately trying to find (and pay for) a seat on an airline flight to Melbourne. But no such order was forthcoming, and although we had to stop at Mt Hagen to take on more fuel, my passengers and I spent that night in Cairns, Australia. Later that morning a helicopter rescued Alan from the sandbar, and several days later BVK was dismantled and floated down the river on canoes to a proper airstrip where the machine was re-assembled and a new engine fitted before being flown out to Wewak.

But our adventures were not over yet. The next day, Friday, at about midday, when we were still about 40 miles north of Bourke in New South Wales, the engine of MFB started running noticeably rough. I tried everything I could possibly think of to get the engine running smoothly but without much real success. We managed to get to Bourke safely, although I did take the precaution of following the Mitchell Highway at an altitude of at least 6,000 feet all the rest of the way.

After landing at Bourke I taxied over to the parking area in front of a large hangar. Over recent months several operators had been having trouble with a modified design of piston, which had been fitted to new engines in the Cessna 185 aircraft. An engine check on the ground at Bourke indicated that the same problem of scuffing pistons was probably the cause of our trouble on this occasion also.

In those days there was an aircraft maintenance engineer and a maintenance workshop in Bourke, so after shutting down the engine I walked into the hangar and asked the engineer, "Can I please borrow a couple of spanners? I would like to remove some spark-plugs so I can check something on my engine." The engineer, understandably not too happy about pilots who fiddled with aircraft engines, responded with, "When I have finished what I am doing I will come and have a look at your problem myself." Fair enough, I couldn't really complain about that, so I walked back to where I had parked the aircraft. But then the engineer came over, and having recognised the Missionary Aviation Fellowship name painted on the side of the aircraft, gently asked, "You guys are also qualified maintenance engineers as well as pilots, aren't you?" I told him that, although this was not always the case, I did have the necessary aircraft maintenance engineering licences to do work on the aircraft that I was flying. He thereupon apologised for his previous brusque response to my request, and when I explained to him what I suspected was the cause of my engine problem, he said, "My workshop is yours to use as you need. If you need any further help please do not hesitate to ask."

One look inside the cylinders and a check of the oil-filter element confirmed what I had suspected. I made a telephone call to Ballarat, explained the situation to Alex Jardine, manager of MAF-AIR Services in Ballarat at the time, and insisted that the only acceptable course of action would be to install a replacement engine before we could continue our flight to Ballarat. The now very helpful Bourke-based engineer arranged the equipment we would need to do a complete engine-change, including a hoist to lift the engine out of the aircraft. He also gave us an invitation to have dinner as his guests at the local RSL Club. However we did not take him up on that offer as none of us could match the jacket-and-tie dress standard, which seemed to be the norm when we peeked in at the door of the club later that evening.

While Alan, John, Len and I worked to remove the engine from MFB at Bourke, the fellows at MAF-AIR Services in Ballarat worked late into the night to prepare a replacement engine. They did this by removing a serviceable engine from another Cessna 185, which was in the hangar in Ballarat at the time. At 10 am on Saturday morning Gordon Chisholm arrived in a Cessna 180 from Ballarat bringing our replacement engine, which we then installed into MFB. We had that task almost finished before we returned to our Motel room that night – but it was a late night!

The rest of our flight to Ballarat and Moorabbin was without incident and even the weather was good to us. After leaving Alan and Len at Ballarat I then flew the aircraft on to Moorabbin, where, although I had completed some Customs formalities in Horn Island, I now had to hand certain other documents to an officer of HM Customs in Melbourne for our final clearance into Australia.

Our failure to arrive in Ballarat on the Friday afternoon had caused some unexpected confusion for my fiancée Rose and her family. Unbeknown to me, Rose and her father had left their farm on Friday and driven through to Ballarat, in those days a trip of three-and-a-half to four hours each way, expecting to meet us there. They had arrived at Ballarat airport some time after 5 pm but found the hangar locked. Eventually they managed to find Bill Waters, the Chief Engineer, at his home and were then told, "Oh Roger has had to do an engine change at Bourke. We will be flying a replacement engine up there for him but he will be a few days away yet." So they turned around and drove forlornly all the way back home. When they arrived, Rose's mother met them with the obvious question, "Where is Roger?" "He's not coming," she was told. Her first reaction, as mother of the bride-to-be, was to interpret this as meaning not that I had been delayed but that I had changed my mind about the wedding. They had no sooner resolved that confusion when a car load of young people from the local Christian Endeavour group arrived, all excited to meet Rose's future husband. When Rose told them, "He is not here," they would not believe her and insisted on searching the entire house – under every bed and in every wardrobe as well as all of the surrounding yard, even climbing the trees to ensure that he was not just hiding somewhere.

When I finally did arrive in Moorabbin that Sunday afternoon (Sept 18th) I would have to admit that it was with a rather strange mixture of emotions. In those days there was no direct telephone service between Wewak and Australia so, although we had written many letters in the interim, it was nearly 13 months since we had spoken to each other. Rose now smilingly admits that she did have some fluttering of uncertainty when she saw this sun-tanned stranger walking towards her at Moorabbin airport that afternoon.

Saturday, September 24th 1966

In spite of the pessimistic forecasts from some prophets of doom, we enjoyed a lovely fine Saturday for our September wedding. However I was quite unaware at the time that the day we had chosen may have been seen by many Australians as an intrusion into what they considered to be a sacred day. It was many years later that our son David handed me a small package with the words, "Dad, this is a video recording of your wedding day. Please note carefully, I said 'wedding ***day***' not 'wedding service'." What he had handed me was a video recording of the VFL Grand Final game of September 24th 1966. And I have to admit that it was a ***very*** exciting game. With less than one minute to go to the final siren, the score was even. The winning point was kicked by a St Kilda player less than thirty seconds before the siren sounded. So The Saints defeated Collingwood! It still is, as I am writing this, the only time St Kilda (The Saints) has ever won a Grand Final!

Rose and I spent most of the following week packing wedding gifts for shipment to New Guinea and showing members of my family, who had come over from New Zealand for the wedding, some of the beauty spots of Victoria. Honeymoons cost money. We had not given any thought to such an extravagance. So little more than a week later, on Monday 3rd October we set off for New Guinea. For me it was a return to work – for Rose it was the beginning of a totally new adventure.

That Monday at Moorabbin airport dawned with a clouded sky and drizzling rain, and I had doubts that we would even get to Ballarat where we were to collect another MAF pilot, Ed Lumsdaine, who was on his way back to New Guinea after furlough. However, by the time we got to Ballarat the sun was actually shining and we had no further weather troubles until we reached Torres Strait and Daru.

The fellows at Ballarat did not want to feel left out of our wedding festivities and as soon as I walked into the hangar they grabbed their chance. By the time I came back to the aeroplane it was well decorated with toilet paper streamers and "Just Married" signs had been sprayed on with dye-check developer (a form of spray-on white chalk). I knew that the dye-check developer could be easily removed, and would probably wash off in the first rain shower, so was quite happy to leave it there. But the paper streamers had to go. Ed and I shared the flying on this trip so he was actually in the pilot's seat when we commenced descent into Charters Towers, in Queensland, later that afternoon. As this was a much hotter climate than we had left behind at Ballarat, Ed reached up and opened an air-vent to get some cool air into the cabin. As soon as the vent came open the cabin was filled with confetti and Eddie copped a face-full of it. We all laughed.

Alan Collecutt's experience on the morning of my departure for Australia was not the only occasion when one of our aircraft suffered an engine failure. But I can honestly say that none of these failures ever resulted in the loss of an aircraft. In every case there was a suitable forced landing area available, and I believe it is also fair to say that these provisions were from God, who honoured the prayers of the many people who pray daily for the safety of our pilots and passengers.

A few months before I arrived in New Guinea, Eddie Lumsdaine had suffered an engine failure while on a flight between Wewak and Telefomin. He also landed on a sandbar – in his case it was in the Leonard Shultz River. And then on the 14th October 1966, about two weeks after Rose and I arrived in Wewak, Alan Collecutt suffered a second engine failure. On this occasion Alan had come in to Wewak to do his first oil change on the new engine fitted to BVK, and late in the afternoon departed again for his home at Wapenamanda in the highlands. The weather over the mountains was unusually good for late afternoon and Alan was on the direct track from Wewak to Wapenamanda, which took him over some very rough country 20 to 30 miles west of the Yuat Gap. He was just about to cross the highest mountain ridge on this route when his ever watchful eyes noticed his engine had lost oil pressure. Without hesitation he turned and headed back towards the flat country he had just left behind. Selecting the best looking sandbar available he planned his approach for another forced landing, this time in the Karawari River. Only seconds after selecting his landing area the engine seized completely. The Lord's protection was again evident in the timing of this second failure. If Alan had not noticed the loss of oil pressure when he did – if it had been just three minutes later, then the aircraft would have been too far over the mountains to get back to a suitable forced landing area before the engine seized. Once more, we were all thankful for God's enabling in that Alan made another perfect landing, this time with a fully loaded aircraft, which again suffered only relatively minor damage.

The Department of Civil Aviation immediately dispatched an aircraft from Mt. Hagen to locate the downed aircraft and drop some storepedoes containing essential survival equipment for the pilot to use, as it was not possible to get a helicopter into the area until the following morning. Fortunately the crew of the search aircraft located BVK very quickly but for some reason, when they made their drop, the pilot elected to fly across the river instead of down the length of the sandbar. The storepedoes landed perfectly – in the middle of the river! However MAF aircraft carry basic essentials of survival gear so Alan was not greatly dismayed but made use of the equipment from his own aircraft. He spent the night in the aircraft, his only major cause of concern being that the level of water in the river rose significantly during the night and he was a little fearful that the aircraft, with him in it, might be swept away downstream.

Alan's second forced landing, again with only minimal damage to the aircraft, was in even more formidable looking country

Once again the machine was salvaged by using canoes to float it down the river to the mission station at Timboli (on a tributary of the Sepik River) where we did some repairs before the aircraft was flown back to Wewak. Exhaustive investigation revealed that the shell of the front main bearing on the crankshaft had moved slightly and cut-off the oil supply, causing the bearing to seize completely. But there was some dispute as to the exact chain of events.

Returning to Wewak as a married couple, Rose and I had to go through the same process of patiently explaining to the many hopeful job-hunters that we did not need a "houseboy". Rose felt she would prefer, for a start at least, to run her own house. So it was a surprise to me when a young man with an irrepressible smile came into the hangar one morning and told me, in *Tok-Pisin*, that my *missus* had said he could work as our houseboy. "Seems strange to me," I said with a shrug "but if she says so then I guess it's *something belong her*." I looked forward to getting home that afternoon to find out just what was going on!

That same morning Rose had been interrupted in her household chores by a young man with a bright smile who managed to make her understand through the language barrier that her *masta* had sent him to work as her houseboy! "Seems strange" she said. "He knows I don't want any house help. But if he said so, all right, you come inside. I'll find you work." The smiling man told her his name was Wanpis. It sounded like "one piece" so that was how she remembered his name.

"Wanpis, can you iron clothes?"

"*Yes missus. Mi savi*," (I understand). So Rose left him to do the ironing while she went next door to talk with Joan Harverson about something. Half an hour later she returned to see how Wanpis was going. He had apparently only ironed one shirt and that could hardly be called ironed! So she was about to show him how to iron a shirt when she noticed the face of the iron was covered with a sticky black mess. Obviously Wanpis had put the hot iron onto some synthetic material.

A few questions later Wanpis, still as cheerful as ever, produced a pair of damaged synthetic shorts from a wardrobe in the bedroom. Apparently our new helper had spent his time going through the house to find a suitable place to hide the damaged shorts! Our smiling houseboy did *not* know how to do ironing. Rose then decided to try him on cleaning shoes. Having been given a pair of black leather work shoes and a tin of polish, Wanpis proceeded to cover the shoes, soles as well as uppers, with a thick layer of polish and then placed them out in the sun "to dry", he explained! "Good grief," thought Rose. "Well perhaps I'll try him on gardening." After explaining that she would like Wanpis to put some compost around the pineapple plants Rose again left him to it. A little later she looked out the window and saw all the pineapple plants pulled out and thrown on the compost heap! This was too much. Roger would have to be disappointed. Rose paid him and told him to go. At least Wanpis had given us something to laugh about, and I wished him the best of luck — the cunning young fellow!

The imaginative approach tried by Wanpis may have been somewhat unique, but the attempts used by some young hopefuls desperately looking for work, sometimes went beyond the humorous. Many of them realised that it was helpful if you had a reference from a previous employer. But it soon became quite obvious that the few who did possess such a trophy were making their letter, or *pas*, freely available for others to copy. It was not at all uncommon to find a smiling young man at the door enthusiastically flourishing a piece of paper as he said, "*Missus, you gat wok*? *Mi gat pas*." ("Madam, do you have any work? I do have a reference."). On investigation the *pas* always turned out to be a pathetic forgery, sometimes a painstaking attempt to copy a letter, but obviously produced by someone who was illiterate. But you really had to commend them for at least trying very hard.

By the end of 1966 it was becoming obvious that MAF's fleet of Cessna 185 aircraft was barely keeping up with the workload. It was not many years since they had started replacing the Cessna 180's with 185's, capable of carrying (supposedly) another 250lbs (115kg) of payload. We now had a fleet of 8 Cessna 185 aircraft and two Cessna 180's. The next four new aircraft MAF purchased were Cessna Turbo 206 *Super Skywagons*. These aircraft were supposed to carry about 100lbs (45kg) more payload than the 185, and had a longer and wider cabin. However, because they actually weighed more than a Cessna 185, they didn't really carry much more weight. But, with their flat cabin-floor and large doors at the back of the cabin they soon proved to be an excellent aircraft for handling cargo. And they were significantly more comfortable than the 185 when there was a full load of passengers.

With a growing number of mission stations putting up permanent buildings, loads of roofing-iron were becoming very common. There was also an increasing demand for fuel to run powerplants, sawmills, tractors etc. and the Cessna 206 proved ideal for carrying 44 gallon (200 litre) drums. A further advantage with these new aircraft was their turbo-supercharged engines. This system makes full sea-level power available to the engine up to 19,000 feet, and there have been several times when these aircraft have got through by flying over the top of weather where aircraft with normally aspirated engines have had to turn back.

There was also expansion in the areas in which MAF Australia was now operating. The Anglican Mission (Australian Board of Missions) had approached the Fellowship asking them to take over the operation of their Cessna 185 aircraft based at Oro Bay, near Popondetta. Agreement was reached, and this aircraft was subsequently based in Port Moresby with Rev. Doug McCraw as pilot.

With hopes of providing a service throughout the Solomon Islands an aircraft was based on the island of Buka (just to the north of Bougainville), with Harold Morton operating this base. When the Highlands Highway was opened from Lae on the coast through to Mt. Hagen in the highlands, then Mt. Hagen became the obvious centre to base an aircraft. So the aircraft that had been based at Banz was moved across to Mt. Hagen.

By this time, Christian Missions in Many Lands (CMML) believed that they had enough work in the West Sepik district to keep an aircraft and pilot fully occupied if these were based at their head station of Anguganak, 90 nautical miles west of Wewak.

Rose and I were the ones chosen to move to Anguganak, so we started packing for our first of many moves.

According to what we were told, the house we lived in at Anguganak had been built as temporary accommodation some eight years previously and was only intended to last one year. But we were just very grateful to have a house to ourselves.

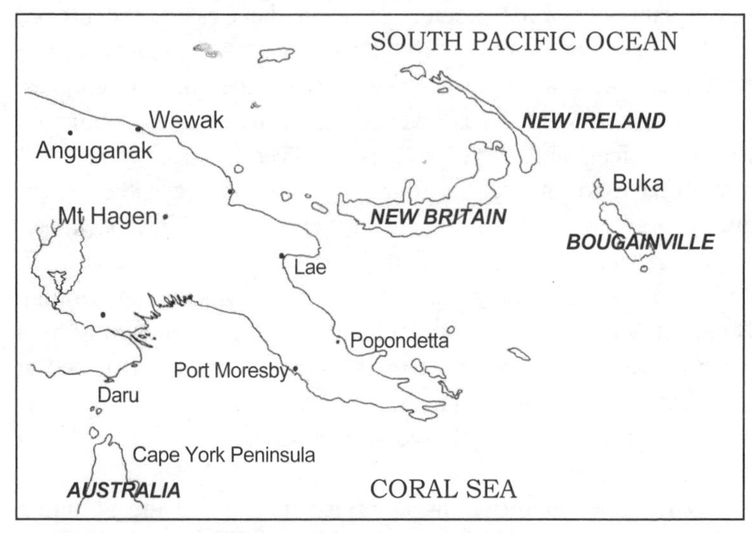

Map showing approximate location of Anguganak and other places mentioned at the end of the previous chapter

Anguganak mission station, “out in the bush” 90 n. miles (160 km) west of Wewak. In the background can be seen part of the Opan River as it heads south, towards the mighty Sepik. When we lived here in 1967 there were no real roads. The only access to the outside world was by plane, or walking. (This photograph was taken in January 1970)

Chapter Nine

ANGUGANAK

The afternoon of 28th December 1966 was shocking weather in Wewak. We were now well into the monsoon season and the constant moisture-laden northwesterly winds brought lots of cloud and rain, especially along the north coast, and much of this spilled over the coastal ranges into the broad expanse of the Sepik Basin. But this Wednesday was particularly bad, and yet this was the day for our big move to Anguganak. We had planned to leave soon after lunch, but after pacing around waiting for an improvement in the weather we only just made it to our new home by teatime! We found a very warm welcome among the brethren at Anguganak, and soon began to feel much more actively involved as part of a missionary team.

Our Anguganak house was built entirely of bush materials; had a thatched roof, plaited bamboo walls, and bark floors covered with sea-grass matting. The teatowel hanging on the wall shows, in cartoon form, a kiwi bird sitting in a pilot's chair and bears the question "*Who said Kiwis couldn't fly?*" It was among our wedding gifts. The table has been set for guests.

With an expatriate population of about 25, including children, Anguganak was probably the largest mission station in the West Sepik district. There was a hospital, whose staff included doctor John Sturt and two or three nursing sisters who were also responsible for Maternal and Child Health clinics in the area, and several national aid-post orderlies in training. There was a boarding school for students in grades five and six, which meant that many students from the surrounding CMML Mission Schools would come to Anguganak to do their final two years of primary school. But the only "shop" was a trade store, which sold such items as rice, salt, tinned fish, bush knives and axes, torch batteries and kerosene. Most of the missionary families did their grocery shopping by mail-order from Wewak, and it was the responsibility of the MAF pilot to ensure that these goods, together with the regular mail bags, all arrived safely and in good condition.

Perhaps I need to emphasise that in 1967 there were no real roads into the place. Everything that was not locally grown or born had either walked there or had been carried in by aircraft – in most cases in a little MAF Cessna. This included all the roofing iron on the houses, the rainwater tanks, the diesel generator which produced our electricity, the X-Ray machine and operating table in the hospital, the station tractor, and all the equipment in the sawmill. Much of this equipment had arrived in stripped-down condition and was then reassembled on site. Of course there was a continuing need to supply fuel and kerosene to keep all this equipment running. So the aircraft was definitely essential for the existence of any centre such as this, and it was a very logical place to base an airplane.

The isolation that some folk felt out here in the bush was brought home to me several months after our move. I was busy doing some of the necessary paperwork associated with my job as a pilot when I became aware of crowds of school children running past our house excitedly shouting and repeating the word "Landrover". Then Rose called out to me, "Roger, come and see. There's a Landrover!" "Big deal," I said, "I see them every day." She came and poked her head into my office and said, "Don't you realise that this is the first vehicle to ***ever*** drive into this place!?" Truly a momentous event!

Every month the nurses from the hospital had a regular program of village visitation for Maternal and Child Health clinics and the aircraft was very much involved with these. The usual procedure was that I would drop one of the sisters off at an outstation airstrip where she would conduct her clinic and often a Bible study as well. She would then walk on through the jungle for two or three days visiting villages on the way to the next airstrip where I would collect her and return her either to Anguganak or to Lumi, where there was a Government Hospital staffed by CMML workers.

On one of these outstation visits Sister Heather McIntosh greeted me with a question: "Do you think we can possibly do anything for these?" She stood with her hands held out in front of her and one tiny baby in each hand. They looked like two little dolls, and at first glance that is what I thought they were. One was just over one kilogram and the other was one-and-a-half kilograms! They were twins, and had already survived for at least six weeks.

In these swampy, malaria-ridden areas food was poor and sometimes in short supply, so it was not uncommon that mothers of twins simply did not have enough milk for both babies. It was quite normal for our nursing neighbours to have 2 or 3 such infants to care for in their "spare" time. Heather brought these two back to Anguganak and in a few weeks they were both healthy and well, putting on weight fast.

This problem of the young baby's fight for survival was not peculiar to the Sepik swamps. Several years later I was flying throughout the islands of Buka and Bougainville when MAF had an aeroplane based there. One day at the Rotokas airstrip I was given a small woven basket and asked to give it to Sister Esther Watson at Kekesu, a United Church airstrip where there is a hospital. I had just loaded several bags of potatoes on to the aircraft and this basket was the same kind as was frequently used for carrying vegetables such as tomatoes and cabbages. As the contents of the basket did not feel like vegetables I sneaked a look inside and saw a tiny baby!

Along with their other charges Sr. Esther and her staff of nurses fed and loved this little bundle of life and only two months later little Paula Hoi was a very healthy and chubby baby girl.

I believe it is fair to say that if it was not for the services of MAF Paula Hoi may not have survived. It was only because there was this small aircraft flying regularly in the area that the Rotokas people had been encouraged to build an airstrip. In those days the only other air service on Bougainville was a twice-weekly DC3 flight from Rabaul and even that was notorious for being delayed or cancelled.

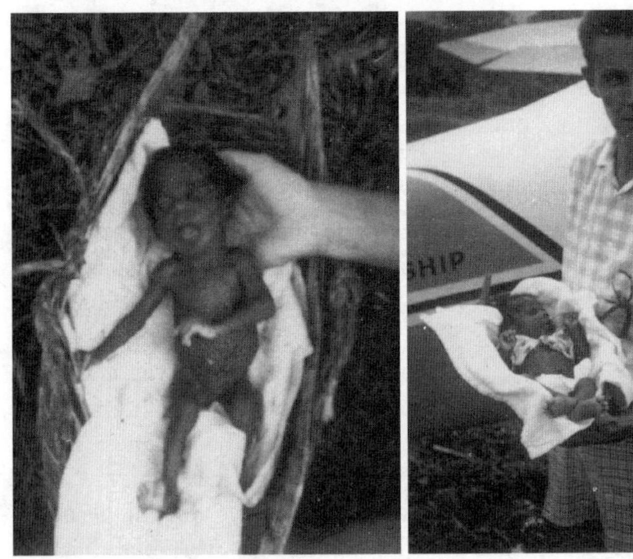

Picture on the left shows the baby as she was when delivered to Kekesu mission station on October 18th. Photo on the right is the same infant (held in the same basket, for the sake of the photo) eight weeks later. [Photos taken by Sr. Esther Watson]

As we had been moved to Anguganak in the middle of the wetter northwesterly season we often had as much as four inches (100mm) of rain in 24 hours, and once nearly 2½ inches (60mm) of rain in one hour. On several occasions I was grounded for most or even all of the day because of the water-logged airstrip surface. One morning we looked out the window and saw that our house was completely surrounded by water. The airstrip was several inches under water and some of the schoolboys had great fun chasing empty fuel drums, which had floated away down the airstrip.

In spite of these frustrations, the Anguganak base still recorded 76 hours of flying in its first full month of operation, with 201 passenger movements and 17 tons of cargo moved. For the 76 hours of flying there were 187 landings. So, quite apart from the paperwork involved with accounts and scheduling flights, as a MAF pilot I often spent more time loading and unloading the airplane than in actually flying the machine.

Internal toilets were virtually unheard of in these temporary bush dwellings such as we were living in, and our house was no exception. Out the back was a small square building raised over the necessary deep pit dug into the ground. We referred to this as the "sentry box". Because we knew there were snakes around, we were always careful where we put our feet when stepping into it.

One day, after one of our overnight floods, Rose went out to the "sentry box", opened the door, looked, … then stopped half way through her step in unbelief. There was no floor and no seat! Just a gaping hole about six feet (two metres) deep and the seat down at the bottom of it! Apparently the continual rains had restarted an underground stream, which passed right through this area and had created what we now call an "automatic self-flushing outdoor dunny". Needless to say we decided that the system was too effective, so that site was abandoned and a second "sentry box" was built on another site.

Passengers were by no means the only living things MAF carried in their aircraft. During our 10 months at Anguganak, besides the usual grocery items, mailbags and trade store goods, I had loads including drums of water with live fish, goats, fowls, dogs, pigs and cattle. One missionary even talked about a hive of bees in a sealed container. On at least two occasions MAF pilots have unintentionally had a snake included in their load of cargo, and a pilot with another company found a one-metre crocodile running free on board his *Skyvan* aircraft.

On one memorable trip I flew down to Madang to collect four calves and bring them back to Lumi. The Madang to Lumi section made a leg of about two-and-a-half hours of flying. I was told the calves were quite young and should only be about 75 kilograms each. As this would be well short of a full load, even with full fuel tanks, I decided to take Rose to have a look at the town of Madang. The calves, when they arrived, were bigger than I had expected and it was difficult to get the four of them into the relatively small cabin of the Cessna 185. The animals had their legs securely tied and, by stacking them with each calf's head on the rump of another we finally had them all on board and tied down. It was fairly obvious from our sluggish climb-out from Madang that these animals weighed somewhat more than the estimated total of 300 kilograms. Although these beasts had their legs tied they could still wriggle and squirm, and before we were much more than half an hour on our way one of them had wriggled itself upside down. The creature then began vomiting and finally drowned itself in its own vomit. It was a most unpleasant experience! In my first hour of flying I passed over only one airstrip, but I knew I could not take-off from there even with a normal fully loaded 185 and certainly not with a machine that I suspected may be overloaded. I decided to keep on going and hope that the other three calves would survive the trip.

On arrival at Lumi we were met by the local *didiman* (agriculture officer). I warned him that the three surviving calves should be carried to a properly fenced paddock, or at least securely tied with a halter before having their legs unbound. But no, this man was quite sure the calves would be too stiff to run around and should be unbound as soon as possible. So he proceeded to untie the first one there and then on the airstrip. Once unbound the calf soon proved that it was still frisky enough, and frightened enough, to avoid being caught and led off to her paddock. So a halter was fitted around the neck of the second animal and a local boy asked to hold the other end of the rope while the *didiman* unbound its legs. As soon as the calf realised its legs were free it carefully got to its feet and gave a gentle tug on the rope around its neck. The native people of this area had never seen animals like this before, and if it be possible, were probably more frightened than the calves themselves. As soon as number two gave a tug on its halter the boy at the other end let go and a delighted calf charged playfully at a group of bystanders! Screams of fear were mingled with squeals of laughter as brown bodies took off like startled gazelles! One excited young man, finding suddenly that there was no tree within easy reach, shot up a basketball pole and sat himself in the hoop at the top! Of course by this time some brave assistant had managed to free the third calf. What pandemonium! And I was now becoming anxious about a different problem. Daylight was running out, and if this nonsense continued for much longer Rose and I would be stuck at Lumi and would be dependent on some friendly person to offer us a bed for the night. Fortunately, with still a few minutes to spare, we finally managed to round up those three frisky animals and I was again able to use the airstrip for its appointed purpose – to take off for Anguganak and home.

I may not have previously mentioned this, but the beautiful girl that I married was a farmer's daughter. Rose had grown-up on a market-garden and berry farm not far from the Silvan Dam, beyond the Dandenong Ranges, east of Melbourne city. Their normal water supply was from rain-water tanks, although she could remember the days before they had this luxury, when every morning, her father had to walk a half-mile each way to collect two buckets of water from a stream on their property. Rose was at least 15 years old before they had the luxury of electricity, so she was well prepared for life in the bush where kerosene was the normal source of power for things such as lamps and the refrigerator.

Work on a farm can also be very seasonal, and this had meant that her father, Don Whittingham, had often been available to travel to Papua and/or New Guinea and offer some voluntary help to mission societies during the winter months when work on the farm was "quiet". During the year I was living on my own in Wewak, Don (Rose's father) did some work with the Christian Union Mission at Kar, in the Southern Highlands of New Guinea. On one occasion he contacted me and asked if I could purchase and send him some film for his camera. Out of deference to a man I respected greatly and also out of recognition that he was my "father-in-law elect" I addressed the package to, "Rev. Father D. L. Whittingham." Apparently my touch of humour caused quite a stir. When the American missionaries on the station where he was working saw how this item in their mail bag was addressed, they held Don in even higher esteem than they had before. Then on another occasion, when he was "out bush", men in the village were very keen to persuade him to come and live with them as their own personal missionary. They not only offered him land on which to build a house but also offered to provide him with a wife. Don thereupon showed them a photo of his wife and ten children. The men gazed at the photograph, open mouthed. "*Em olgeta pikinini b'long yu*?" they asked. "Yes," Don cheerfully replied, "Those are all my children." The men now looked at him with an attitude that showed great respect and said, "*Yu wanpela man tru*!"

During the year that we were living at Anguganak, Rose's father again made a visit to the country to give some short-term help – this time with the Unevangelised Fields Mission, specifically at Pangoa (Lake Murray) in the Western District of Papua. We made some enquiries and found that MAF were planning a flight from Wewak to Pangoa and thus managed to arrange for Rose to visit her father while he was there. The only possible problem was that she was beginning to suffer from bouts of morning sickness, but Rose chose to try and ignore this because the chance to see her father again was just too good to miss.

When she passed through Balimo, on her way back "home" to Anguganak, she mentioned her morning sickness problem to the doctor there. In response to this she was given a package of medication with the comment, "You could try this. It was sent to me as a sample, but I will never use it. Papuan women do not know what morning sickness is, or would never admit it if they did." The name on the packet was *Debendox*. Rose thought little of it at the time, she was just grateful for anything that might help to ease that nauseous feeling at the start of every day.

Chapter Ten

WEATHER

Everyone who is interested in flying in New Guinea probably knows that weather is one of the pilot's biggest uncertainties. Weather changes do not seem to conform to the fairly predictable text-book systems of areas further from the equator.

When checking a new pilot it is as important to try and describe to him/her the more common weather patterns as it is to familiarise him with the valley systems, mountain passes and airstrips in the area. But to a certain extent the feeling of the weather patterns has to be developed as a sort of sixth sense.

On one occasion a pilot and his three friends who were doing a flying tour of the country in a hired light aircraft had planned to visit Anguganak. Wisely, the pilot decided to land at the Government airstrip at Lumi and they had then flown the seven minutes down to Anguganak as passengers in a MAF Cessna.

Anguganak is a grassed airstrip 850 feet above sea level. It is about 700 metres long and at the bottom of a basin-like valley. Just south of the station an almost sheer bluff rises to nearly 1,000 feet above the airstrip, and to the north the Torricelli Mountain Range rises to a peak of 5,500 feet above sea level. The Opan (or Nopan) River flows down from these mountains, turns and flows alongside the Anguganak airstrip then at the end of the airstrip makes a sharp left hand turn and flows southward through a gorge at the western end of the Anguganak Bluff. Under conditions of medium to low overcast cloud the usual air routes to and from Anguganak are through a saddle in the hills off the east end of the strip, or via the Opan River to the southwest.

Although Anguganak airstrip is level it was at that time only licensed for one-way operations. Landings were made to the east and take-offs towards the west. The only reason for this seemed to be that those men with their theodolites and measuring tapes considered that the hills off the east end of the strip rise too steeply to permit safe landing-approach and take-off gradients. I certainly agree about the take-offs.

On the day that Phil and his three tourists planned to return to Lumi to collect their aircraft I was also expected to be in Wewak fairly early so that the aircraft I was using could be used for a flight in to the highlands. I therefore decided to do a quick shuttle to Lumi and back, as soon as possible after sunrise and then leave for Wewak.

At the time of our departure there was broken cloud at about 3,000 feet but the valley was otherwise quite clear. We took off from Anguganak and began to climb out straight ahead towards Lumi, eight minutes away to the northwest. Before we arrived over Lumi I had to climb for extra height to get over a bank of fog that is typical in the Lumi area, although this must have formed since I had received the weather report only 15 minutes or so beforehand. As there was no way to get under the fog from the east, I decided to keep going because there is often a hole in the cloud over the top of this airstrip or just to the west of it. However, on this morning there were no such breaks. A solid sea of white extended over the entire Lumi area and for miles beyond it, so we had to return to Anguganak. But by the time we should have been able to see the Anguganak airstrip there was just a great white expanse below. We had left only 15 or 20 minutes earlier, and there had been no fog in the area then. As I peered down, trying to see some recognisable feature, a hole appeared and I suddenly saw part of a building beside an airstrip, which I recognised as Ningil, a Roman-Catholic mission station east of Anguganak. That meant I had already flown over the place I was looking for! Like a widespread group of stealthy hunters moving in for the kill, the cloud above us was now thickening and descending and the mountains to the north were rapidly disappearing in the all-enveloping mists. I turned back towards where I knew by dead reckoning my home airstrip must be, and although still remaining above the fog, commenced a descent into what I estimated was the downwind leg of the Anguganak circuit. Peering intently down through the rapidly thickening mist I was desperately trying to see something to positively identify my position, when through the second hole that morning I saw the village of Wulukum. By familiarity with the area I knew it was right over this village that I normally turned on to the base leg in the circuit and reduced engine power when landing at Anguganak. A tight turn over the spot on this occasion allowed me to see that I could just make it to the end of the airstrip beneath the fog layer. The only alternative to this rather precarious landing approach would have been to enter cloud in an attempt to climb over the Torricelli Mountains and hope the weather was better out on the coast. But I had no way of knowing what the cloud was like on the north side of the mountain range and in any case, our aircraft were not properly equipped for flying in cloud. They did not have the necessary gyro-stabilized instruments, nor did they have any radio navigation aids. On top of that, research has shown that the average pilot who has never been trained in instrument flying can become disoriented and lose control of his aircraft within three minutes of entering cloud! It would have been very foolish to take that risk.

I believe in a God who answers prayer. Those two holes in the fog were just where they were needed! A glimpse through the cloud of a few acres of jungle-covered hillside would have been no use whatsoever but in each case I had seen just enough to specifically identify my position. So we dived down through that hole and 'plopped' down onto the airstrip, very relieved to be back on the ground. Once safely back in the parking bay I was met by Colin Cliffe who had come down to tell me that Max Meyers had been on the radio demanding to know what time I would be in Wewak, and if I was not already on the way then I must leave immediately because he considered that I should already be there. Yes, of course, he was anxious to get the highlands flight done before the afternoon weather built up over the mountains. As if I didn't already know that!

Even early in the morning, weather over the mountains of this country is often unstable and quite unpredictable. By eight or nine o'clock the weather has usually decided what it is going to do for the day, but then soon after midday the cloud builds up over the mountains, bringing the afternoon rains. This deterioration can sometimes be fairly rapid – a pilot in the tropics must always be watching the weather, very closely.

Problems with the weather at the other end of the day are even more likely to give a pilot ulcers because of the added fear of being caught in the dark. Darkness comes very suddenly in the Tropics and the twilight lasts only a couple of minutes. This, added to a pigheaded determination to keep pressing on, with the attitude that "I've never been caught yet" can add up to a dangerous situation, as I found during my second year of New Guinea flying.

I had, as was so often the case, been held up during the day and did not leave Wewak until about twenty past five. But I had planned only one stop on the flight to Anguganak. The weather conditions had reportedly been fluctuating through the later part of the afternoon, although I had no trouble getting into my first port of call at Sibilanga, on the inland foothills of the Torricelli Mountain Range. After unloading the aircraft I frantically threw on board some bundles of food for the patients at Anguganak Hospital, and at 6.10 pm was airborne again for the 12 minute leg home. Before landing at Sibilanga I had taken note of the weather further west and had noticed particularly that I could see the Anguganak Bluff. So I was not greatly concerned when, after the departure from Sibilanga, I found that an amount of cloud had moved across my direct track and was now obscuring the bluff, which was my normal landmark for home.

Although the Sibilanga mission station was located on a mountain ridge, the actual airstrip then in use was on a river-flat in a valley – almost a one-hour walk away from the security of the mission station, and I guess this thought affected my decision to keep going and try for home! Besides, the Anguganak weather report passed to me by radio while I was still on the ground at Sibilanga had indicated there was clear sky to the west. Knowing this, and finding that I was unable to get through the usual saddle in the hills at the eastern end of the valley, I simply revised my ETA Anguganak and proceeded to fly further west, south of the cloud-covered area, and then follow the Opan River in to my destination. This would mean an approach from the west, where the sky had been reported as clear. But this proved to be an unwise move and I soon had to admit that I was really in trouble! When I was less than two kilometres from the airstrip my route was completely blocked by teeming, heavy rain. It was like a black wall preventing any further advance into the valley. I would never be able to see where I was going if I flew into that stuff! I now had little more than ten minutes to go before it would be dark. And there were not many airstrips within a ten-minute radius of my present position! In desperation I headed towards Lumi, switched the radio to the channel used by our mission stations, and in the faint hope that someone at Lumi might be listening, gave them a call.

"Kilo Charlie, Kilo Charlie this is Mike Foxtrot Echo. Are you standing by?" Amazingly I got an immediate reply.

"Mike Foxtrot Echo this is Kilo Charlie. Is that you Roger, I was wondering who was flying out here at this time of night".

"Affirmative, Don. What's the weather like at Lumi? I can't get into Anguganak and there's nowhere much else to go."

"Stand By", then a few seconds later, "Outside it's pitch black and raining!" Apparently they had heard what they thought might be an aircraft in the area so had switched on their radio just in case!

I switched back to the Flight Service frequency and explained my predicament to them. It was just possible that I might make it to Yellow River airstrip, ten minutes to the south, before it was too dark to identify the airstrip. But apart from that, the only alternative was to return to Wewak. But Wewak was nearly 50 minutes flying time away.

Then a third voice entered the discourse. "Mike Foxtrot Echo this is Madang. From Senior Operations Controller, return to Wewak". This, of course, was the only sensible decision and once again the men-behind-the-voices in those Flight Service Units had proved that they were taking a real interest in their work of keeping tabs on all the aircraft flying in Papua New Guinea. As a pilot I really appreciated their cooperation.

By the time I had skirted back around the storm area and set course for Wewak it was completely dark. But this was where I noticed a miraculous thing. Whereas there was heavy cloud and torrential rain around Lumi and Anguganak, and I had been dodging cloud all the way from Wewak, the mountains ahead of me now stood out in sharp, black silhouette against a clear moonlit sky! Amazing! I headed northeast, towards the coast and, once I had gained a bit more altitude, I could see the moonlight reflected off the sea to the north. So I continued on out to the coast, where the surf gave a phosphorescent glow, and followed the coastline back to Wewak. Apart from that, the rest of the flight was uneventful and I landed back at Wewak at 7.35 pm - almost one hour after official last light – where the airstrip was properly lit for night landings.

On this occasion several people had been aware of my predicament and had prayed for the safety of the aircraft, my two schoolboy passengers, and me. And God answered those prayers.

No pilot is ever happy to admit that he is the victim of familiarity breeding contempt, such as was probably the case in the story I have just told. However, I have mentioned these two incidents to show how easy it is to get caught.

A few weeks later I was on my way to Wewak in VH-MFE for a routine oil change and service check on the aircraft. It was planned that the aircraft would be used for one more trip for the Wewak flying program, after which I could return home to Anguganak. Experience had shown that on such occasions it was wise to bring an overnight bag, just in case of delays.

The radio receiver in MFE was not the best, especially when we depended on the loud-speaker in the cabin-ceiling to hear what was being said. So, when I heard Wewak Flight Service calling one of our aircraft, I reached for the headphones and put them on.

"Mike Foxtrot Golf, Mike Foxtrot Golf, this is Wewak. Do you read?"

VH-MFG was our most recently purchased Cessna 185, although not a new aircraft. It had been bought second-hand from our USA-MAF colleagues who had been using it in Irian Jaya [now Indonesian Papua]. MFG was in fact the only serviceable aircraft that the Wewak base had at the time.

But what had happened to MFG? Wewak Aeradio was still calling him. Then again it is not uncommon to have to call some aircraft several times before they answer. Radio conditions may not be good in that area – the pilot may have turned the receiver volume down while talking to his passengers and forgotten to turn it up again, or possibly he had landed and forgotten to report before landing. This problem was not uncommon, especially where a pilot had been pre-occupied with getting the aircraft down on the ground in poor weather conditions. There could be several reasons why John was not answering the radio calls.

15 or 20 minutes later, after I had landed at Wirui, I decided to phone DCA and ask what the story was, and whether MFG had eventually answered the radio calls. It was then I learned that the last they had heard from the aircraft was at 10.50 am when he reported "In the Olsobip area" but weather was poor and the pilot had said that he would call again at 11 o'clock. He had been on a flight from Telefomin to Olsobip, a trip of normally 20 or 25 minutes. He had not been heard from since. Perhaps he had landed at Olsobip and forgotten to call Flight Service before landing? There was no way of finding out, unless the Government officer there was listening to the ABC news at 12.30 and heard the request for him to call Kiunga or Port Moresby on the teleradio. The flight from Telefomin to Olsobip, although it appears as only about 20 miles on the map, involves a climb from the Telefomin airstrip in a valley at 5,500 feet above sea level, to at least 9,000 feet to cross the mountains enroute to Olsobip. Often when there is cloud over these mountains it is necessary to climb considerably higher. On the southern side of this mountainous ridge is the Hindenburg wall. This gigantic wall, a sheer drop of several thousand feet, curves around the northern end of another valley, the floor of which slopes down to a point where the Olsobip Patrol Post and airstrip are situated at 2,000 feet above sea level. The route is notorious for its unpleasant weather.

About halfway through lunchtime one of the hanger staff came down to the house where I was having lunch and asked, "How much more of the servicing on MFE is still to be done?" I guessed why the question had been asked and, as I had just finished my meal, I returned immediately to the hangar. We had the aircraft ready to go again in about 40 minutes. After filling the fuel tanks and collecting some Search and Rescue equipment from DCA, five of us bundled into the aircraft and set off for Telefomin. While we were still on our way we learned from DCA Flight Service that MFG was not on the ground at Olsobip. Also Ed Lumsdaine, who had been operating in the Upper Fly River area that morning in VH-BVJ, had already arrived at Telefomin and checked all the mission airstrips in that area and reported that MFG was not on the ground at any of them either. Our hopes sank lower.

At first, after reaching the Telefomin area, we were unable to get through to Olsobip because the cloud was utterly impassable. However after waiting an hour or so, all of us in MFE, plus Ed Lumsdaine with some other observers in BVJ, were able to take off for the Olsobip area. A helicopter was already searching.

All our MAF aircraft at that time were painted yellow – *Shell Yellow* #4, to be precise. And it is amazing how much yellow there is in a tropical rainforest. We investigated several patches of yellow, but they all proved to be part of the jungle vegetation. In one village we noticed a flashing mirror, so quickly flew in closer, but after a good look through binoculars from a low level we were satisfied that we had only seen a villager playing with a mirror, and there was no sign of a European. However this did give us the idea of sending a helicopter with an interpreter into the area to ask if people had heard an aeroplane on Friday morning. During the afternoon of Friday 23rd June 1967, the day of the incident, we were only able to search some valleys and the sides of some of the mountains. All the tops were still hidden in cloud, but even so it looked frightening country, with sheer cliffs rising several thousand feet from the valley floors. And the valleys themselves could be treacherous. Even though some of them appeared flat and level the valley floor was actually on a very deceptive slope. More than one pilot, thinking he was flying over level ground, suddenly found that he was running out of airspeed and the ground was coming up to meet him. At 6 pm, as the cloud was rolling down the mountains again, we landed at Olsobip.

The Patrol Officer there suddenly found he had 11 overnight guests, including one lady, to squeeze into his little two-bedroom house. We managed to find enough floor space, and the lady slept in the bath. This lady, incidentally, was a photographer for National Geographic magazine, and I understand that some excellent photographs of her tour through Papua New Guinea did appear in a copy of that magazine a few months later. As we curled up on our mattresses, kindly loaned by the local policemen, I wondered how to pray for John Harverson and his two passengers. Would we find them tomorrow? Who could tell? For his wife and family back in Wewak, we could only pray that God would give grace for the trial.

On Saturday morning, as soon as it was light enough, we flew over to Telefomin again, because the search was to be organised from there. Some more aircraft arrived, some with DCA officers to organise the search, some with drums of aviation fuel. An SIL plane arrived with their special "Rescue Squad" (a well-equipped team of trained bush walkers including a doctor) and a powerful portable radio-transceiver set up to keep contact with search aircraft as necessary.

It was not long before things were organised. The Department of Civil Aviation Searchmaster turned out to be Brian Thurckle, the same man who had been Senior Operations Controller at Madang on the night I had got caught with weather near Anguganak and had flown back to Wewak after dark. Brian drew up a search-plan, briefed all of the pilots, and then one by one the aircraft took-off for their appointed search areas. Considering the normal weather for this area, which includes the Star Mountains where there are peaks over 13,000 feet above sea level, the first few days were reasonably fine and allowed for a good look at the higher peaks in the early mornings. The typical daily weather pattern in tropical mountain areas, even on a fine day, is for cloud to form on all the mountain peaks and higher country during the morning and then spread into the valleys. By mid-afternoon it is normal to have rain showers everywhere. Brian had taken all of this into consideration when he had prepared his search plan.

Other operators made pilots and aircraft available, and people from all walks of life came to act as observers. Most aircraft carried a crew of at least three observers. The Army provided a complete kitchen and facilities including the all-important cook. The CWA ladies in Madang sent in several plane-loads of pre-cooked food – pies, cakes, roast-chickens – the work of their own hands, not just a heap of tins. The encouraging spirit of helpfulness, where the whole community cooperates, has also been a characteristic of other searches where aircraft have been lost in this country.

Day after day the planes came and went, eyes got tired with looking ... looking ... trying to see a sign of yellow that might be part of the missing aircraft, or broken trees that might mark the spot where the plane had gone down. Dozens of broken trees were seen, but no sign of the missing aircraft. Reports from people who said they had heard the aircraft flying around Olsobip that Friday morning were all considered to try to work out where he was last heard. Helicopters constantly stooged over the most likely areas. In all, something like 27 aircraft covered an area of 8,000 square kilometres, but nothing more has ever been seen or heard of the Cessna 185 VH-MFG and its three occupants.

One explanation offered by a native youth, in his simple faith, is that God just reached out his Mighty Hand and took them, aircraft and all, right up to Heaven.

After ten days the search was abandoned.

POST SCRIPT to "MFG"

It was probably in 1980, when we were living in Mt Hagen, that one of our pilots, Paul Hutchinson, passed on to me what may be a very significant comment. At the time Paul was living at Telefomin.

The pilot of an Army helicopter was talking with Paul on one occasion and mentioned that he thought they had seen the wreckage of an aircraft at the base of the Hindenburg wall. Paul immediately showed real interest and started asking for more details. The Army pilot had never heard of the saga involving the Cessna 185 MFG and even offered to go back and try to relocate what he thought might have been the wreckage of an aircraft. But, although they flew over the area again and again, they could see no evidence of what they thought they had seen on the previous day. We can only guess that the wreckage may well be there but can only be seen when the sun is in a certain position and the wind moves tree branches in a certain direction at the same time.

Chapter Eleven

MEDICAL EMERGENCIES

Not all our medical emergencies were exciting, although some were unusual, and on those occasions where weather is a significant factor, it has been my experience that the pilot is so preoccupied with the problems of navigation and weather that he is unfortunately, or maybe fortunately, unaware of the associated drama taking place from the medical point of view.

One of my greatest fears, before moving to Papua New Guinea and commencing flying with MAF, was that I might one day have a baby born in my airplane.

One Tuesday at 2:42 pm I had just landed at Wirui after doing the last Koroba-Pori freezer run for the Wewak program when Jim Charlesworth came running out of the hangar to tell me, "There is a medical emergency at Balif, requiring immediate hospitalisation." My cry of "*Kargo bois*" brought the usual lack of response from our cargo handlers. It was our normal policy to avoid flying an empty airplane if we could possibly make use of the flight to move stores or supplies that were already in the aircargo store. So with help from two other pilots we had the aircraft loaded, refuelled, and the load securely tied down when the first cargo-handler shuffled around the corner some ten minutes later. I was airborne at 2:55 pm and 26 minutes later (3:21 pm) landed at Balif to find that this emergency was a case of obstructed labour — a New Guinean woman. It took us five minutes to unload the aircraft and put the woman and her husband on board. At 3.50 pm I was on final approach to land at Wirui when the husband, by excited and agitated pointing, indicated that the baby, a breech presentation, was half born. This was the very situation I had so often feared, and to add to my concern the ambulance I had ordered, with instructions not to be late, was nowhere in sight.

I made a short landing, spun the plane around and taxied back to the hangar. Almost before the engine had stopped, I was out of the plane and running to find someone who knew something about midwifery! The suggestions from the office were, "Ask Jo, she's had four of her own," and, "Ask Bessie, she's a nurse." I don't know if I broke any world records for the 200 metre sprint down to Flavel's house, but I certainly wasn't stopping to pick daisies! I gasped out my message to Bessie that a baby was being born in the plane, and we both ran back to the aircraft. The whole process had taken perhaps four or five minutes at the most, and by the time we got there the ambulance had finally arrived. But for the new-born baby, still with his head jammed inside his mother, the mystery that means life and breath had gone! I felt physically sick with frustration. Even as I re-read this, 40 years later, I still feel the gut-wrenching sickness of that frustration. "If only ... If only ..." My first reaction was to blame the ambulance driver and his nurse for being tardy. Then I wondered if I could have done anything myself. … If only I had done a medical orderlies course as part of my training

Many years later, when MAF were seriously looking at plans to develop a comprehensive Orientation and Training Program for potential staff, I was asked if I had any suggestions as to what subjects should be included. Of course I mentioned my experiences of having babies born in the plane. The second case for me had involved a child who was already presumed to be dead, so there was much less drama when the (stillborn) infant was delivered, about three minutes after we became airborne. Nevertheless I was happy to continue that flight just to save the mother's life.

I knew of a number of other pilots who had also experienced the trauma of a woman giving birth while still on board the aircraft. So I put in a recommendation that a properly trained Ambulance Officer, or perhaps even an Obstetrician, should be asked to give all pilots a thorough briefing on how to deal with this situation.

On a subsequent Orientation Course I noticed that a St John's Ambulance Officer did appear and gave a lecture to all candidate pilots on the course. The next day I asked one of the pilots what he had learned from that particular lecture. He told me that they had been given an illustrated lecture on how to deal with a patient who suffers cardiac arrest and an opportunity to practice CPR. I was surprised to hear this, because in all of my experience in Papua New Guinea I had never heard of a pilot who had ever had to deal with such a case. But not one word had been mentioned about dealing with pregnant women or patients who give birth while in the aeroplane. I was *not* favourably impressed!

But most medical emergencies have happier endings.

One Saturday afternoon several Anguganak families, ourselves included, had been sharing a barbecue tea down by the river. Shortly after 6 pm, as the mosquitoes were starting a picnic of their own at our expense, we were packing up when Colin Cliffe, who had shortly beforehand gone up to the radio for the afternoon *sched*, returned to say there was a medical emergency at Yebil.

Although Yebil was only 11 minutes flying from Anguganak there was not a lot of time left before dark, so on this occasion the aerial ambulance driver's uniform was bathing shorts and bare feet. I was back at Anguganak with the patient by 6.35 pm scarcely twelve minutes before dark and the baby, a boy, was delivered safely in the Anguganak hospital at 9.30 that evening.

A couple of weeks later I moved another expectant mother from Yebil, this time to the hospital at Lumi. The next morning on the 7 o'clock radio sched, Dr Lyn Wark of Lumi Hospital advised that this patient would have to be moved to Wewak Hospital for a caesarean operation as soon as possible. Unfortunately the 7 am weather report from Lumi was "fog on the ground," but as the report at 7.30 indicated some improvement, I took off from Anguganak where the weather was reasonably clear. The fog between Anguganak and Lumi was, as usual, too low to get underneath so I had to climb to 3,000 feet and go over the top, again hoping to find a break around Lumi airstrip. Fortunately, or should I say miraculously, there was a hole about a mile across just off the western end of the airstrip and the strip itself was clear. Except where the fog broke up miles away to the west I could not see any other break in the fog.

Apart from this low layer of early morning cloud (fog) the weather was fine and we had no problems getting to Wewak. The baby, again a boy, was safely delivered in the Wewak hospital.

****

With their loss of one aircraft and pilot in June, I was now being asked to do more flying to help out our Wewak program. This of course meant a lot of early starts to be in Wewak before 8 am in order to fit in with their flight schedules for the day. To save time in the mornings I often loaded my plane the night before. On one of these occasions I was given a large oxygen cylinder to be taken to Wewak for refilling. Because any gas cylinder is classed as dangerous cargo I slipped this one into the cargo pod of the aircraft but then left it there for the night.

Next morning was one of those mornings when the cloud seems to hang down all around and can't seem to decide whether to lift and dissipate or come down and start drizzling. The kind of weather that has me sitting on the edge of my seat watching it like a hawk. To add to my anxieties that morning, as soon as I commenced a turn after take off the whole aircraft gave a faint tremble, which I interpreted as engine vibration. It settled down again almost immediately and as I couldn't get a repeat of the trouble by any amount of fiddling with mixture control or ignition switch, I decided to carry on with my flight to Wewak. But, just to be sure, I elected to cross the Torricelli Mountains through the Tadji gap and fly down the coast. The aircraft rocked slightly in mild turbulence as I flew through the gap and again I felt that disconcerting tremble go through the machine.

On arrival at Wewak I taxied up to the hangar and reported to the Chief Engineer that the plane was unserviceable due to an intermittently rough running engine. Max Meyers and I took off in another aircraft to continue my check-outs into the Telefomin area. When we returned in the afternoon, Bruce and Ray were still puzzling over the reported problem with MFE's engine. They had been unable to find any fault in the ignition or fuel systems.

“Oh well,” I said “it must have been a couple of spots of

water in the fuel," and proceeded to open the cargo pod to begin loading the aircraft for my flight home to Anguganak.

With the pod door open I saw, and stopped, and remembered! One large round oxygen cylinder was still there where I had put it the night before. A light push and it rumbled obligingly from one side of the pod to the other. I didn't quite know whether to laugh or not. Somewhat sheepishly I approached the Chief Engineer, "Er, ah ... Bruce, I … ah … think I've found the cause for that 'engine vibration'."

With increasing demand for me now to do flights from Wewak, after 11 months of very enjoyable life in Anguganak Rose and I were moved back to Wewak and our place taken by Peter and Florence Holmes. Peter was then the latest addition to the MAF team in Papua and New Guinea and had broken my record of being the youngest pilot to serve with MAF in that country.

Seven weeks after our move back to Wewak I had a medical trip with a difference. This was by car and was simply to take Rose out to the Wewak Hospital at 7 am before I went flying for the day. At 4 pm I had just returned from the day's work at Telefomin and was climbing out of the aircraft as the hangar phone rang. It was Dr Risto Gobius, to advise me that Rose and I had a fine healthy son. However, he added, "Please come to the hospital immediately as there are some things I need to talk to you about."

When I arrived at the hospital Dr Gobius was at the front entrance waiting for me. He began talking as I followed him along a corridor. Suddenly he stopped, reached into a bassinette and almost thrust a baby at me. My immediate reaction was to step back out of the way. "I have just come from work," I said. "I haven't even washed my hands."

"He's your baby," said Risto, "you hold him." And he carefully placed our son into my arms. "Now, let's go and see your wife."

I looked down at our baby as I gingerly held him in my arms. He seemed to be looking back at me – hair so fine he appeared to be bald, but the smile in his eyes was beautiful! Now, as we walked to the ward, the doctor was talking much more seriously.

"You will notice that he has a double hare-lip. That can be fixed easily. It is a simple operation. He also has a cleft palate. But once again, with modern surgical techniques, that is no real cause for concern. There are plastic surgeons in Australia who can fix that so you will scarcely even know he ever had the problem. Apart from that he is perfect. You have a very healthy son. I have checked everything else, thoroughly."

By this time we had reached the room where Rose was in bed. But, even though Dr. Gobius had done a magnificent job in removing any undue concern from my mind, I was not prepared for what I was about to learn in the next few minutes.

Rose was almost in tears. After a very difficult labour, our son, David, had finally been delivered just before 3pm – more than one hour previously. Rose had expected that the midwife, or the nurse, would give her the baby to hold. But instead they had taken him out of her sight. When she asked, "Can I see my baby? Is it a boy or is it a girl?" the nurse had allowed her less than one second to view a small bundle wrapped in a white sheet, told her, "It's a boy," and then left the room, taking the baby with her. For Rose the past hour and a half had been one of indescribable anguish as she struggled with the question, "What is wrong with my baby?"

Dr Gobius was certainly not pleased with the way this situation had been handled. But he had been powerless to do anything different because, like me, he had only arrived back in Wewak at about 4 pm. He had spent the entire day many miles away, doing medical clinics at Maprik. The first thing he did after arriving back at the Wewak hospital was to check the two babies born that day. Immediately after that he had grabbed a telephone and called the MAF hangar to get in touch with me. He had not even had time to visit Rose in her room.

Although he may not have had any direct control over events in the maternity ward of the Wewak hospital on that day, his quiet, positive and helpful counsel for two young, first-time parents, who were still struggling to come to grips with the unexpected in this part of the world, was excellent and ***very*** much appreciated.

It was a few years later that I saw an article in a magazine about the drug Debendox and its possible connection with birth defects. Although we were not interested in suing anyone, for years I passionately believed that this drug had caused the defect in our child. It has only been in very recent years that a paediatrician friend has shown me several well researched medical papers which all present very convincing evidence that I was most probably wrong all along.

However, regardless of that, one thing that has impressed me about children who suffer from these kinds of problems, whatever the cause, has been the courage with which they tackle life! Our son David has most certainly been no exception.

After a further six months of routine flying out of Wewak we left as a family in the Cessna 185 VH-MFE, taking the aircraft to Ballarat in Victoria for its three-yearly overhaul and refurbishing. Our first priority was a visit to the Royal Children's Hospital in Melbourne, where a skilled plastic surgeon did the necessary work on David's lip. We then travelled to New Zealand for a period of deputation meetings and furlough before returning in October to relieve Harold and Hope Morton at Buka (Bougainville), while they took a much-needed furlough in Queensland.

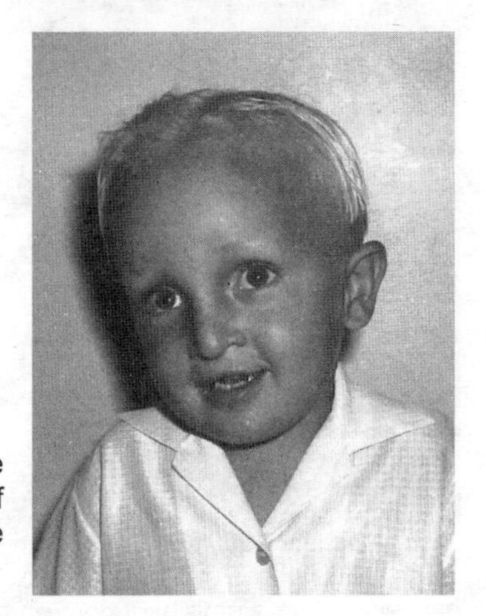

Photo of our son David, taken late 1971 when he was three-and-a-half years old. As you can see, the surgeons at RCH did their job well.

1968 MAF staff in New Guinea – taken in front of the Wirui hangar when we were all in Wewak for a pilot's meeting, April 1968. Left to right:

Standing Max Meyers, Jim Charlesworth, Ed Lumsdaine, John Seddon, Peter Holmes, Wal Job, Gloria Penberthy, Max Flavel, Bruce Lindsay.
Squatting: David Graham, Ted Crawford, Roger Young, Ian Stacy.

Other staff, such as Alan Collecutt, Laurie Darrington, John Johnston, Harold Morton, were not present when this photo was taken.

During the late 1960's MAF experimented with using a float plane to reach some areas accessible only by river. Note that there are no doors on the hangar. In those days security was not a problem – only the office, cargo store, and workshop (where the tools were stored) had lockable doors.

Chapter Twelve

BOUGAINVILLE

'The Land of Wait-a-While'

Readers who want to know where Buka and Bougainville are in relation to the mainland of Papua New Guinea should refer to the map on page 78

We arrived at Buka airfield by TAA DC-3 aircraft around mid-afternoon on October 9th 1968 and shortly afterwards I was sitting in the front right-hand seat of the Cessna 180 VH-BVR on my first check-out ride around the island with Harold Morton.

Some three years previously, MAF had decided to base an aircraft in this area with hopes that they may soon get permission to extend their work into the British Solomon Islands where there was a great need for a service such as MAF could provide. Nobody could have guessed then that it would be nine years before permission would be granted for the B.S.I.P. work, nor could anyone have guessed how the Buka-Bougainville operation was going to grow beyond all expectation. It was not until MAF's third application, on the third day of the third month of 1975, that permission was granted for them to operate throughout what was then the British Solomon Island Protectorate. By then the thinking had changed from considering the use of a light twin-engine aircraft, to actually operating a single-engine Cessna amphibian aircraft. But even this type of aircraft proved to be unsuitable for the work because so many of the alighting areas were on the open sea. After two years of "experimentation" the attempt to provide an air-service in the Solomon Islands area was abandoned.

As for the Bougainville work: over a period of nine years this grew from a one man (pilot/engineer) operation, using a four-seat Cessna 180 aircraft, to a minor Airline operating two twin-engine, ten-seat BN-2 *Islander* aircraft plus two six-seat Cessna 185 aircraft. In 1975 the entire operation was sold to the Bougainville Provincial Government as *Bougainville Air Services,* and the operation of the aircraft on that island had become as vital to the community as any suburban bus or tram service is to any city in Australia or New Zealand. In fact more vital, because there were only two private aircraft on the island of Bougainville, whereas there are a lot more than two private cars in any city suburb.

However, this situation was by no means the case when Harold and Hope first arrived in 1966. The island and its people had been completely oriented to the idea of boat travel, accepting delays of several days as perfectly normal and unchangeable. When the Morton's first arrived in the area there was only one airstrip on Buka Island and only three on Bougainville. In only two-and-a-half years the existence of a light aircraft on the island, and Harold's encouragement, had inspired the building of a further eight airstrips. In 1969 I opened another one, and in the following five years another three were opened.

The work and flying conditions in this operation were different from those I had experienced in Wewak. Here we were essentially operating an aircraft charter company available to anyone who wanted to use the service. Work for church and mission organisations usually amounted to perhaps one or two passengers in a day, or a few kilograms of freezer supplies or medical goods. Very rarely enough work on its own to justify the expense of an aircraft. But as the commercial charters had aircraft moving around the island I found it was possible to meet nearly all of the transport needs of church and mission folks, and to do it fairly economically.

One of the first things I discovered in this area was a new type of medical emergency. Whereas in the Sepik area these had been mainly maternity cases with one or two cases of food poisoning, and in the highlands many of the medivac flights had been for patients with battle wounds, here on Bougainville I found a different kind of “battle wound”. In a number of spots around the island there were still some ammunition dumps containing live rounds of ammunition left over from World War II. Many of the coastal villagers were aware that an explosion under water could kill, or stun, any fish in the area and of course these live shells proved to be very tempting for this purpose. On more than one occasion I was called on to do a medical evacuation flight where a man had seriously injured himself when one of these shells had exploded in his hands as he was tinkering with it.

But there were also other things that were peculiar to operating a light single-engine aircraft on a relatively small island, with miles of open sea in every direction. Perhaps if I quote from one of the letters I wrote during this time, while we were living on the island of Buka, it will help to give a better picture:

[Dec 1968] "On two days running, Thursday and Friday, I arrived back at Buka thinking I had finished flying for the day only to find that there was an urgent medical flight to be done. Thursday was for a man whose foot had been crushed under a full 44 gallon (200 litre) drum of fuel when it had been dropped. Then on Friday there were two medical trips, one of them a stretcher case but both out of Wakunai. On Friday evening Rose and I were commenting on the coincidence of three-in-a-row emergencies when the telephone rang. It was the doctor asking if I could do a charter to Rabaul the next morning to take two patients to the hospital there. The cases were too urgent to wait for the regular airline flight on Sunday.

So on Saturday morning, shortly after 10 am, we were about to leave, with life-jackets and life-raft, one sitting patient and one stretcher patient, plus a medical orderly to watch over both, when a DC-3 aircraft arrived on its way from Rabaul to Honiara. I asked the pilot what the weather was like between Rabaul and Buka and he replied that it was much as forecast, but the most significant feature was a large area of low cloud and heavy rain in the vicinity of Nissan Island. This was not good news, because Nissan, which is little more than a coral atoll, had to be my first landfall and navigational reference point on what would be a one-and-a-half hour flight, most of it over the sea.

As soon as I set course after take-off from Buka I could see that the weather was as bad, or even worse, than it had been when the TAA aircraft had come through. But I was still wondering about whether or not I should continue with the flight when the medical orderly became concerned enough about his stretcher patient that he asked me to return to Buka. By 10:52 we were back on the ground with one dead patient. It was as quick as that, and suddenly people appeared from everywhere, weeping and howling long before they reached the aircraft. It was rather uncanny really, as they all seemed to know what had happened, and the patient himself had insisted that the flight was a waste of time because he knew he would be dead before we reached Rabaul, and he did not want to be buried in a foreign land.

Soon I was left alone with the one patient. Rose, who had driven down to the airstrip as soon as she saw my aircraft back in the circuit area, had gone off with the medical orderly to try and find the doctor, and friends had come and taken the body of the dead patient. Now I was wondering whether to have a second attempt to get to Rabaul, but was not at all happy about the weather for such a long over-water flight. While I was still waiting for Rose to come back with word from the doctor as to whether he still wanted to pay for a charter to Rabaul for only one patient, I casually watched as a twin-engine Piper Aztec aircraft flew overhead, fairly high and obviously heading for Rabaul. Suddenly "the penny dropped" and I realized what a provision this might be. I switched on the aircraft radio and called the pilot of the Aztec. Within ten minutes his aircraft was on the ground and my second patient was placed on board. And by then Rose had returned with word from the doctor confirming that he still wanted this patient taken to Rabaul today if at all possible.

As the Aztec pilot was about to get back into his aircraft I said to him, "Thank you very much for stopping, John. You saved me a sticky battle with the weather out over the water – and only one engine at that." His reply may be worth recording: "I think anybody who flies that far over water with only one engine deserves a medal. I think you fellows put too much faith in your patron"."

Now I have read a number of the stories and books written about the exploits of men who fought in this part of the Pacific during WWII, and I do know that often they were expected to fly single-engine aircraft over the sea for distances of 150 miles, or possibly even more. But most of them were operating at altitudes above 20,000 feet and in many cases there were seaplanes or motor launches specially assigned to rescue any pilot who had to parachute into that shark-infested ocean. But I did not have those advantages, and in the event that I did have to put down in the sea as the result of engine failure I had serious doubts as to whether it would even be possible to extract our life-raft before the aircraft sank.

Legally, it is permissible to fly a single-engine aircraft out of Rabaul and over the sea to Buka and Bougainville, and then to proceed all the way down the chain of islands that make up the Solomon Islands, because it is possible to plan the route so that you are never over the sea for more than 50 miles in one stretch. Well, theoretically it is possible, if the weather is fine all the way! But I was beginning to discover that the weather in this part of the world could change even more rapidly than it did over the mountains in New Guinea.

I remember one time when a business man chartered the aircraft for a trip to Rabaul. On this occasion the weather was fine and he was the only passenger, so I asked if he would mind if I brought my wife and child along – so that Rose could do some shopping in Rabaul. He was perfectly agreeable to this idea, but by the time we had finished our brief shopping sortie in Rabaul the weather over the sea had changed dramatically. There was no way I was prepared to take-off into that kind of weather for a one-and-a-half hour flight over the sea. So Rose and I, with our infant son David, were faced with an unplanned overnight stay. We had been so confident that this would be a straight-forward trip out and back again that Rose had not even brought a replacement diaper (nappy) for David. Fortunately, as I was wandering around wondering where we might find some beds for the night, I was recognised by a lady who had visited one of the plantations on Bougainville a few days previously, and she remembered that "this pilot" had been particularly helpful to her. She was more than happy to drive us to a guest house and, as a bonus, she and her husband gave us a guided tour of many of the scenic spots in Rabaul.

The problem of totally unpredictable changes in the weather is again well illustrated with a flight I had undertaken for a Government Patrol Officer. He had chartered the aircraft to take two loads from Wakunai (on the east-coast of Bougainville) across to Boku, a Government patrol-post down on the south-western corner of the island.

The run from Buka down to Wakunai was without incident and on the first flight over to Boku the weather was so nice that I had actually enjoyed the opportunity to fly an almost direct track over the Crown Prince Range. However, after I had unloaded the aircraft at Boku – and that took a bit of time as it was not easy cargo to handle – and started on the flight back across to the east coast I noticed that there was now a build-up of cloud along the top of the mountain range. So I proceeded with caution, and by the time I had reached the edge of the mountain range it was obvious that I would not be able to get over the top. Instead I would have to divert all the way down to the southern end of the island and then fly up the east coast in order to remain below the cloud. But before I even reached the southern end of the mountains I could see a line of tremendously heavy rain storms sweeping in across the island from the eastern seaboard. They appeared to be travelling so fast that I doubted it would even be possible to return to Boku before the storm front beat me. In fact, I judged that I might barely make it to the airstrip at Buin, so I had no choice but to make a straight-in approach there, as there was not enough time to fly a routine circuit over the airstrip first. As my wheels touched the ground at the northern end of Buin airfield the first rain-squall reached the parking bay on the eastern side of the airstrip, and before I had even finished the landing roll visibility was reduced to only a few yards. As I sat in the aircraft waiting for the rain to ease off my shivering was not so much from cold but from fear. If that squall had beaten me, and obliterated my view of the strip before my wheels had touched the ground, then it would have created a very frightening situation, with literally nowhere to go! I did not fancy a crash landing into any of the jungle around here!!

Communication problems in the developing nation of Papua New Guinea involved far more than the simple problem of language differences. Something like 850 different native languages throughout this country gives an indication of the continued isolation in which many of the tribal groups have lived, but I am referring to communications in a slightly different field. For example, take the case of the not uncommon medical emergency. The expression "Hurry up and wait" must have been born in such a situation.

The following description refers to the scene as we so often experienced it back in 1968 …

On the island of Bougainville something happens … it may be an accident or a complicated maternity case, but medical attention is needed, urgently. The patient is walked or carried to the nearest mission station or government patrol post where a nurse or medical orderly makes an assessment of the problem.

If evacuation was required, this involved firstly a radio call to the District Medical Officer to obtain permission for evacuation. Then, once this had been granted, someone needed to make a further radio-phone call to MAF to organise an aeroplane.

Even to this point things were by no means straightforward, as radio communications on the island in 1968 were a far cry from the STD microwave telephone system that was operating between main centres throughout PNG in the 1990s.

Assuming the caller was able to get through to MAF they were likely to find the pilot was out flying, so we had to get a message to the aeroplane. Pilot's wife would telephone the DCA groundsman at Buka airfield, and he would then contact Rabaul Flight Service by radio. The Flight Service operator would pass the message on to the pilot of the MAF plane, who then usually asked for details about the nature of the emergency. But as the operator had often not been given this information the pilot had to decide whether to divert in flight (and possibly leave passengers stranded somewhere they did not wish to go) or continue with his planned flight and then attend to the medical evacuation. Some emergencies are more desperately urgent than others, but even as the pilot involved, I often had no way of knowing how urgent each situation was until I was able to see the patient for myself.

Of course all this business of one person contacting another with a message to be passed on to someone else took precious time, and this was for emergency conditions! And even when we finally did get the patient to Buka airfield, it was not “the end of the story”. Having brought the patient to Buka he would then have to be taken by Landrover to the wharf at Chinatown, about a mile away. From there he was loaded onto a boat and taken across to Sohano Island, at the entrance to Buka Passage. Then from the Sohano wharf to the hospital was a walk of a few hundred yards. This was the best we could do, even in an emergency!

Buka Passage and Buka airstrip. The point of land on the left is the northern tip of the island of Bougainville. The triangular shaped island at the far end of the passage is Sohano

This apparently ridiculous situation was perhaps not so crazy when you realize that for many years the people in these islands had been completely oriented to travelling by boat. Some of the old-timers told me how in times past, even in the case of a medical emergency, they would send someone down to stand on the beach – sometimes for more than just one day – in the hope that they could catch the attention of a passing ship. But with the arrival of a light aircraft on the island this situation began to change. In December 1968 the 4-seat Cessna 180 aircraft was replaced with a 6-seat Cessna 185. Then, soon after Harold Morton returned in June 1969, he employed a second pilot to cope with the work, and shortly after that a full-time aircraft maintenance engineer was added to the staff. When we returned to Bougainville for a few months at the end of 1973 the people of these two islands had become so adjusted to the idea of air-travel that the service was very much taken for granted.

The problem of communications of course affected every aspect of our operation on Bougainville.

The end of January, with hundreds of students returning to boarding school is always busy for MAF, and flight schedules had to be arranged for days or even weeks in advance. Bougainville was no exception! In the middle of this rush, on Friday 24th January to be exact, I received an urgent request: Sixteen passengers – two pastors with their families who were moving to work in the New Guinea highlands, and eight students who would be attending high school in Rabaul – had to be collected from Tonu at the far end of the island to catch a boat leaving Buka Passage on the following Tuesday morning. This was because there had been some unexpected changes in the plans for transporting the Pastors between Rabaul and Mendi, in the New Guinea highlands.

The United Church had no planned radio contact with their station at Tonu until Monday midday, and even a telegram would not get there before then. So it was decided to send a message through the Roman Catholic Mission radio network to one of their stations, which was only 45 minutes walk from Tonu. The essence of this message was that the 16 passengers should be ready early Monday morning. We expected that a runner would take this message through to Tonu on the Friday evening, and this would then give those passengers the weekend to organise their packing. Of course the flying program also needed a few major changes!

On arrival at Tonu on Monday, as you can guess, no one was ready. Yes, the message had been sent through by runner, but he had not arrived at Tonu until Sunday evening. The nearest Pastor lived several hours walk away. So that was Monday's trip wasted! Frantic changes were made to delay the boat departure until Tuesday night and Tuesday's flying was changed again to fit in these urgent flights.

Back at Tonu on Tuesday morning I found five students ready and was told that the second Pastor would be ready by 1.30 pm. I took the five students to Buka and returned at 1.30. There was no sign of the Pastor and his family, but I was told they had a long way to come. After making some enquiries I discovered that the message had not been passed on to the second Pastor until this same Tuesday morning, and nothing at all had been done about it on Monday!

"Well," I said, "If he is not here by 4.30 I shall have to go without him. I cannot afford to upset Wednesday's flying as well." At 4.30 exactly, a tractor returned with the message, "the Pastor cannot come as one of his children is sick in hospital." There was still one high school student ready to go, so we both scrambled aboard the Cessna and at 4.45 we were airborne and heading for Buka – due there at 5.30 pm. But our problems were not finished yet….

I had already had one memorable lesson on the dangers of operating close to 'last light' in all but the finest weather, and as it usually gets dark on Bougainville before 6 pm I had made it my policy to plan to be on the ground by 5.30 pm. There were no lighted airfields on Bougainville. The nearest such aerodrome was at Rabaul, one-and-a-half hours' flying away, over the sea! My route between Tonu and Buka took me up the west coast of the Island. In those days there was only one other airstrip on this side of the island and that was Moratona, which I flew over ten minutes after leaving Tonu on my way back to Buka. Apart from the then abandoned wartime airstrip at Torokina, there was scarcely even a suitable forced landing area anywhere along the west coast. It was all either swamps covered in dense rain forest, or extremely rugged jungle-covered limestone mountain ridges. On my left was the sea, stretching for hundreds of kilometres before the next landfall, and on my right were mountains – the Crown Prince Range, covered in the usual late afternoon build-up of cloud. Impassable.

And so it was that I was flying merrily along, fully aware of the two factors I have just mentioned but trying to concentrate on thoughts about Wednesday's flying and how it would be affected by these two disruptive and unfruitful days of confusion, when I was suddenly given a further problem….

"Mike Foxtrot Alpha, this is Rabaul. Special weather Buka: Moderate continuous rain, visibility half a mile, cloud ..."

I did not register the rest of the report, that was enough…and he repeated the words, "visibility half a mile" at the end of the report! Two alternatives were possible: either we could return to Tonu immediately or, by quick mental calculation I estimated I could continue on for another ten minutes and still make it back to Moratona with a safe margin before last light. By continuing for another ten minutes I should be able to just reach the northern end of the mountain range and it might then be possible to see across to the east-coast side of the island. If I could do that, then I would have the choice of three airstrips all within 15 minutes flying time from Buka. This would mean that I could get much closer to Buka before having to abandon the attempt to reach that place. And knowing the local weather, this could well be an isolated squall that would clear as suddenly as it had arrived. I acknowledged the call from Rabaul and advised that I was continuing towards Buka.

The next seven minutes were long and anxious ones, and I found myself checking that the clock was still going, checking my position on the map, and I also did another check on my calculations of the time for last light at Buka.

George Anderson, the DCA groundsman at Buka, had actually knocked off work about 4.30 that afternoon and gone home, but when this storm hit he knew that I was still out flying so he had driven back to the airstrip where he was able to contact Rabaul by radio. He was obviously taking an interest in my progress. He also knew that, because I only had a limited amount of daylight left I needed to know that the weather at Buka had turned nasty.

There will be those who, when reading this story, would simply quote their favourite ditty, "If in danger or in doubt, turn around and chicken out". They will ask, "Why didn't you simply return to Tonu for the night?" Firstly, I had one passenger who was supposed to catch a boat leaving Buka Passage that same evening. And secondly, I had already thrown two days of my flying program into chaos and to spend this night away from

Buka would put Wednesday's flying into even further confusion. But I was also aware that compulsion is one of the greatest dangers in flying. Although I believed this action was a calculated risk, if it be called a risk, it was a risk worth taking.

Yes, there was still the nervous strain in knowing that my attempt to reach the east coast may be a complete waste of time, or that if I reached my decision point with still no clear route open to cross the island I could be tempted to keep trying for just a few minutes more and thus erode the safety margins I had left myself. If that happened, then I would not have enough daylight left to return to the airstrip at Moratona, and we would be in ***big*** trouble! And so I was anxiously counting the minutes, and anxiously checking my progress on the map. Then, right on the deadline – there, yes, I could see across to the east coast.

Now, with Dios as an alternative destination less than five minutes away off my starboard wingtip, I would have time to fly right up to Buka and back to Dios with a comfortable margin before last light. In fact the weather in this area now looked so good I found it hard to believe the "special weather" on Buka, which the Flight Service Officer in Rabaul was just now repeating. I could even see both sides of the island (which at this point is only about six miles across) and could see to within two or three miles of the Buka airfield, so simply acknowledged this last report from Rabaul with "Mike Foxtrot Alpha, Roger".

Three miles from Buka I was able to make out the airstrip through the rain just as Rabaul came back on air with "Buka reports the rain has eased off, wind has dropped, but the airstrip is very wet". I thanked the operator and five minutes later reported, "Mike Foxtrot Alpha on the ground Buka. Cancel Sarwatch. Thankyou, and goodnight".

Nerve-wracking? Well, I certainly found it so at times, with messages that didn't get delivered, passengers who had to change their plans but couldn't let me know, unpredictable weather – the only predictable thing was, "nothing will go according to plan". And when people asked for confirmation of a flight booking and I replied with something like, "I'll be there about 10 am on Wednesday", I wonder sometimes why they ever believed me! It is "the land of wait-a-while".

The need for patience and a resignation to accept the unexpected is further illustrated in a wedding, which was planned while we were at Buka. A nursing sister who had been working with the United Church was to be married to a plantation manager whom she had met during her time in this "tropical paradise". The date of the wedding was set for Saturday, 16th November, with the service to be held in the Hutjena United Church building, which was next to our house and not far from the Buka airstrip.

On Monday 11th I collected Sister Beverley from the mission station at Tonu and flew her to Buka – that was about the last thing that happened according to plan! On Wednesday 13th, Peter, the groom, and the matron of honour were supposed to arrive on the weekly Fokker F27 "Friendship" aircraft from Port Moresby, but as the flight was fully booked Port Moresby to Munda it did not even stop at Buka – so ... no groom! The regular Thursday TAA flight arrived from Rabaul, but still no groom. Then on Friday the plane from Rabaul was cancelled due to unserviceability. With little more than 24 hours before the wedding, poor Bev was, of course, getting rather anxious! Finally, the groom and the matron of honour arrived on a specially chartered Piper "Aztec" aircraft from Rabaul at 1 pm on Friday.

Meanwhile I was frantically flying around the island getting people to Buka for the wedding. When Peter arrived he asked where his best-man was. I had never even heard that the person he named was supposed to be coming to the wedding. I certainly had no booking and no spare seats on any flight to bring him in to Buka. Peter immediately arranged a radio conversation with one of the plantations in an effort to contact his friend. It turned out that his letter asking David to act as best-man had never arrived at its destination, even though it had been posted nearly one month previously. By some reorganising of passenger loads we did manage to get the best-man to the wedding – but barely 15 minutes before the service was due to start!

Then, to add to this great occasion, the cream cakes and salad vegetables ordered for the wedding breakfast did not arrive as expected on Saturday morning's plane from Rabaul! Still, nobody really seemed to mind. We had all learned to accept these things as part of the unexpected joys of living in this wonderful "tropical paradise", and at least all the members of the bridal party had made it to the wedding!

And perhaps I should mention that in the midst of all this busyness of bringing folk in from all over the island for the wedding at Buka, I also received a request from someone down at Buin to do a charter and take him to Rabaul because Friday's TAA flight had been cancelled. Now that would have involved yet another five hours of flying – absolutely out of the question! The answer to that request was a polite but emphatic "No way!"

I found I was often reminded of the Scripture verse, which says "We have need of patience ..."

January 1969 began with not only the worst weather I had ever encountered in this part of the world but also looked like being even busier than December had been with its 522 passenger movements. But then on Wednesday 15th January we received a letter from the Royal Children's Hospital in Melbourne, advising us that our son David was booked in for an operation on Monday 20th. This was to be a follow-up on the plastic surgery of June/July 1968. But this gave us a mere five days, which included the weekend, to organise everything – not only accommodation for Rose in Melbourne, but all the necessary airline bookings in between. When we went to see our friend Peter Wong, the local TAA agent in Chinatown (Buka Passage), he told us that there just happened to be a direct flight from Buka to Port Moresby "tomorrow morning" (Thursday 16th) and he was able to arrange all the airline bookings and issue the necessary tickets. We did some frantic packing that night, but when Rose got to Port Moresby she found that there had been an airline workers' strike of some sort and there was a tremendous backlog of passengers waiting to get onto any possible flight to Australia. One person she spoke to had been waiting for six days to get a seat on a flight going south. So she placed David on the check-in counter and announced to all-and-sundry, "This child is booked in to hospital in Melbourne for an operation on Monday. So you've got to do something to get us there!"

"He looks healthy enough. What's the problem?"

"He has no roof in his mouth! But some doctors in the

Children's Hospital are going to do some very clever surgery and make one. So he can eat and drink and learn to speak like any other child!"

They were given a seat on the next flight, but by the time they arrived in Melbourne it was nearly midnight. "Where am I going to stay for the rest of the night?" Rose wailed to one of the airline attendants. Again the airline staff were very helpful and she spent the rest of that night in the same classy hotel where all the hostesses and pilots normally stayed overnight. It cost a bit (!!) but at least she was in Melbourne, and was there in time for the Monday appointment at RCH. But when she arrived at the hospital on the Monday morning there seemed to be much confusion. It seemed that they weren't really expecting David to be there, in spite of the letter we had received the previous week. Rose heard some other mother loudly complaining, "We have come all the way from Warragul, and now we are told we will have to wait a few more days because some child has arrived unexpectedly from New Guinea – wherever that is. Now we have to go all the way back to Warragul!" Warragul is about 100 kilometres from Melbourne (less than 1½ hours driving time). Rose and David had just travelled something like 3,000 kilometres and overcome many other difficulties enroute in order to keep that appointment.

After eight very busy months flying around Bougainville we moved again, this time to Mount Hagen, in the Western Highlands of Papua New Guinea. Our trip with the airlines to Mt. Hagen was quite normal – quite normal for this country that is! We arrived in Lae to find that our confirmed bookings for the Lae to Mt. Hagen sector were on a flight that did not even exist!

A MAF pilot does not only act as pilot, but also sometimes as an engineer and often as Traffic Officer. As a pilot I have sometimes had to cancel or abort a flight due to problems over which I had no control, such as weather, and as an engineer I have had to cancel a flight because of unserviceability of the aircraft. But to convey this information to tired, irritable, or impatient passengers is always the hardest and most thankless task of all. Abusing an airline traffic officer cannot change the facts – it only shows the measure of the passenger's own lack of self control.

The traffic officer on duty that day in Lae was a living advertisement for The Friendly Way (a common TAA slogan) and we actually got to Mt. Hagen that same day. He found us two seats on an aircraft going to Goroka, and then squeezed us in on a flight that was taking a party of American tourists from there to Mt Hagen. Well done!

We were just getting settled in at Mt. Hagen, where we were really enjoying the cooler highlands climate, and our boxes had just arrived from Buka, when we were asked to move again – this time to Port Moresby, the administration centre for Papua and New Guinea. However, the few weeks in the cooler highlands had been a refreshing change and had provided an opportunity for me to become familiar with airstrips and 8,000 square kilometres of country in the Southern Highlands, which were all new to me. The highlands weather patterns and moods are quite different from those of the relatively small tropical island of Bougainville, and the few weeks in Mt Hagen had been a valuable time of re-adjustment.

Chapter Thirteen

PORT MORESBY

Compared with other areas and towns in Papua New Guinea in the late 1960's, we found the city of Port Moresby to be remarkably different. A distinct dry season for about eight months of the year and monsoon weather from Christmas through to Easter gives this area a vegetation that is most unlike the rest of the country but very similar to parts of Northern Australia.

The nearest areas of dense tropical rain forest are in the foothills of the Owen Stanley ranges about 20 miles (30-35 km) from the city. What with sealed roads, supermarkets, service-stations where you could buy petrol or get the car serviced, and even policemen controlling traffic at some of the intersections, I found it hard to believe we were still in Papua New Guinea. The brightly coloured trees, which line so many of the streets (especially colourful in the southern spring) and stunted little gum-trees on the surrounding hills added a lot to this feeling that we were somehow back in Australia.

However, in spite of its apparent sophistication in some respects, there were other aspects where I felt worse off than we had been in "isolated" places like Anguganak. All other MAF bases on the mainland of New Guinea had radio contact with the various mission stations and so could obtain weather and airstrip reports before beginning a day's flying, as well as make last minute changes to a planned flying program where necessary. But in Port Moresby we did not have this facility, so all flights had to be arranged by mail or by personal discussion on the airstrip several days in advance. In fact, in those days we could not even conveniently make telephone calls from Port Moresby to anywhere outside of the city. To make a "telephone" call to anywhere else, even to a major town such as Wewak, still involved the use of HF radio and often had to be booked as much as one or even two days in advance. The HF radio network operated by Christian Radio Missionary Fellowship (CRMF) was so efficient and so well run that we actually had far better communications with the rest of the country when we were "out in the bush" than we had from the city of Port Moresby.

When it came to checking the weather at my destination before leaving on a flight, the Meteorological Office at the Moresby airport could provide me with a weather forecast, but this was often based on guesswork, or on reports of yesterday's weather. I could not even call a mission outstation to check the weather at my destination until I was already airborne and well away from the airport, when I could then use the HF radio in the aircraft. So, in practical terms, for weather information I found it necessary to rely very much on local knowledge. Even reports from other aircraft were of limited value because so often when this information was most needed, there would be no other aircraft in the area where I wanted the weather report. And the flying itself was quite different from that of any of the places I had worked before. On Bougainville the average flying time between landings had been only five to ten minutes, whereas here it was common to set out on a flight of one-and-a-half hours or even three hours before my first landing.

On one occasion I had been asked to do a flight to Esa Ala, on Normanby Island, two hours' flying to the east, just to bring one mission official from Esa Ala back to Port Moresby. This would involve an almost empty flight of four hours. So, in order to try and reduce the cost to the mission involved, I asked a number of the fellows in the Flight Service office in Port Moresby if any of them might be interested in a trip to Normanby Island and back, just to have a look at the country. They would be expected to pay a regular one-way airfare. Of the three who gladly took up the offer one worked in the Meteorological Office – and just out of interest, his name was Mark Forecast

My most direct route was to fly from Port Moresby in an almost straight line to Cape Vogel (Baniara), then across Ward Hunt Strait to Fergusson Island enroute to Normanby Island, where the Esa Ala airstrip was located. However, when we arrived in the Cape Vogel area there was low cloud and rain showers out to sea, so I chose to divert and track along the coast of the mainland as far as East Cape and then we only had a ten-mile hop over the water to Normanby Island. As a professional weather forecaster Mark expressed interest in this decision, and particularly in the reason for it. He asked, "Is this kind of weather normal for this area?"

"Oh yes, definitely." I assured him. "This is typical weather for this part of the country during the south-easterly season." "Wow," he said, quietly. "I have been writing weather forecasts for this area every day for the last I-don't-know-how-many months, but this is the first time I have ever seen what it really looks like."

The simple fact is that when the southeasterly trade winds are blowing (the so-called dry season in Port Moresby) any coastal area exposed to the southeast and/or the east is often enshrouded in low cloud with almost continuous rain.

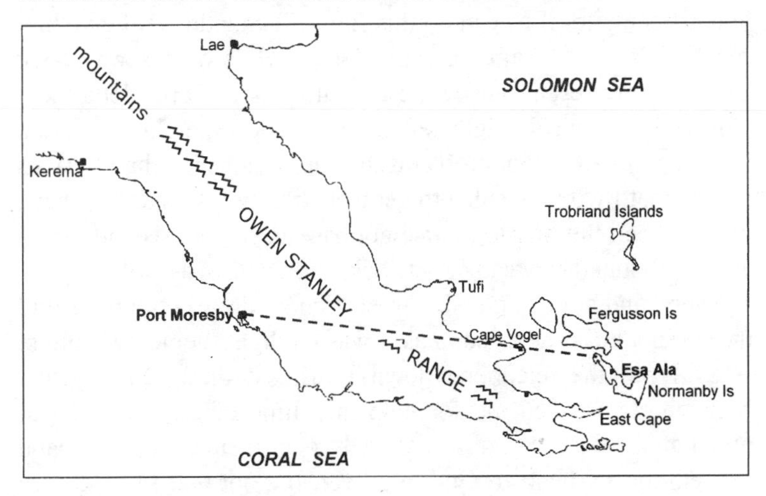

As I think back over the two-and-a-half years we spent in Port Moresby I now realise that, as far as I was concerned, requests to do medivac flights were relatively rare. This was probably because other operators in the area mostly had more than one aircraft and so they were more readily available to do this sort of work. But there was one request I did receive that stays in my memory. It was some time after 4 o'clock one afternoon when I received a phone call, through the Post Office radio network, from the nurse at the Sakarina Mission Station asking if I could come immediately and take a woman with child-birth problems to the hospital at Popondetta.

I knew that by this time in the day the cloud build-up on the mountains would make it almost impossible for me to fly over to her station. I said I would make some enquiries and asked her to call back in another half-hour. First I phoned the control tower at the airport. "What does the weather look like over the mountains, and what might be my chances of getting through to Popondetta?" The reply was predictable, "The normal – rain and storm-clouds floor to ceiling right across the horizon." And the term "storm-clouds" definitely implied those with the full sound-and-light show – lots of thunder and lightning. I phoned the Flight Service office and explained, "I have had a request to move a patient from Sila down to Popondetta. I know that Macair have a Cessna based in that area. If he is airborne could you ask the pilot if he can do this flight?" "Standby, I'll give him a call." And then after a short delay, "He's on his way back from Lae at present but by the time he gets to Popondetta there won't be enough daylight left for him to do the flight." And, quite apart from the problems of the weather, I had serious doubts that I would be able to get there before it was dark either.

So when the mission nurse got back to me the second time I asked about the weather at Sakarina and was told, "Rain showers, and a lot of cloud." So all I could do was to promise to try and get airborne as soon as it was daylight the next morning. After I put the telephone down I just sat there feeling sick. Someone had asked me for help in a time of crisis and I had given an answer, "It can't be done." I sat there in the chair and poured out my heart to God in prayer. It's not that I could have changed anything, I guess, but I felt I had failed to do the job I was expected to do. But then it was almost as though God put his hand on my shoulder and quietly spoke to me, "Its okay. It is going to be okay. I have it all under control."

About 9 o'clock that evening the phone rang and again it was the nurse from Sakarina: "Roger, I just called to let you know you can cancel that flight for tomorrow morning. The baby has been delivered and the woman is doing fine. We don't need that flight any more." Do you know what it is like to cry, with relief, because you have just heard some good news? Yes, God does answer prayer. But sometimes I still wonder how, or **if**, it is really going to work out. Thank you God, for answered prayer!!

Have you ever played that game called "Cluedo"? It is a family-oriented board-game in which the players have to solve a "crime" mystery – who committed the crime? The fact that Rose's parents had now moved to Port Moresby – in fact they had bought the house next door to where we lived – meant that we often tried to make time for activities which involved the whole family. *Cluedo* was one of our favourite games, but I was amazed at the number of times Rev. Green turned out to be the guilty person. Of course it is just coincidence, but what follows is a true story – a noteworthy drama which involved a very real Rev. and Mrs Green:

Amongst the numbers of passengers carried by MAF aircraft are visitors to mission stations. Some are just visiting relatives, or friends of special interest, but many are spending holidays from their regular jobs to do voluntary work for a particular mission society, while yet others are retired folk who have come as associate or temporary workers. In this last category was a Rev. David Green and his wife Susan. They had been working in New Britain for several months and, before they returned home to Australia, it was my privilege to fly them around to see some other areas of Anglican Church work in Eastern Papua. This had been planned as a two-day flying visit. As it worked out it was more than two days and not all flying.

Mr and Mrs Green arrived at the MAF hangar at 6.30 one Friday morning, and after weighing them and their baggage I topped up the load with store goods and supplies for mission stations we would be calling into en route. A large carton of frozen sausages had just been delivered to our hangar and, as this was marked for delivery to Sakarina mission station I included that in our load.

Now, just to give you a passenger's view of this little adventure, many of the following comments are taken from Susan Green's own writing:

"We took off towards the southeast and then turned left to take up a heading towards the Kokoda Gap. Below us the rounded hills with their dry grass and stunted gum trees quickly gave way to steep slopes and razor-back ridges covered in dense tropical rainforest. Ahead of us the Owen Stanley Ranges stood out against a pale and cloudless morning sky. Directly on track ahead of us a broad V shape in the crest of these mountains was the Kokoda Gap. To the West of the gap Mt. Victoria raised its head to 13,000 feet. David showed a lot of interest in the rugged country below us as this was the area of the famous Kokoda Trail, which had become only too familiar to many of our soldiers during World War II."[2]

There are now several airstrips along this trail and, apart from the regular weekly service flights, I also knew that they were not infrequently used to fly out hikers who had found, to their embarrassment, that they were in fact **not** fit enough to walk this tortuous track. Twenty-two minutes after take-off we passed through the Kokoda Gap, made a slight change of course and commenced a gentle descent towards the airstrip at Sila.

"If anything the slopes on the northern side of the Owen Stanley Range are even steeper than on the south. Little streams, foaming white through their rocky course, scramble down the valleys to meet the broad and stony Kumusi River. The flatter country nearer to the coast in this area is rich volcanic soil and supports several plantations, mostly cocoa. The area is also rich in interesting stories. It was near here that the invading Japanese army landed during World War II and the Martyrs High School, near Popondetta, stands as a memorial to the missionaries who were slain at that time."

---

[2] Susan Green has written her own book *Ever a Fighter* ISBN 0 909837 98 8 in which she has described this "adventure". She had given me a copy of her typewritten notes covering this episode, and permission to use them before her book was published.

The remains of something like seven airstrips within a radius of less than 10 miles gave an indication of the concentration of forces located here during those war years.

Almost directly in front of us the smoking cone of Mt. Lamington stood as a reminder of how one Sunday morning in 1951 this volcano erupted unexpectedly and, like Mount St Helens in more recent years the blast had gone out one side rather than out the top. In a matter of seconds several villages were wiped out and over 3,500 people were dead. But even in the records of that fateful morning I have read some fascinating tales of deliverance and escape. It was Sunday morning and many of the local residents were in Church services. As the cloud of scorching-hot poisonous gasses from the eruption swept through the jungle it killed everything in its path. But then at one village it suddenly stopped, just outside the wall of a house where a Christian service was in progress. The people in the house were unharmed.

A change in heading of 30 degrees to the right put us on track for Sila, and we landed there 45 minutes after leaving Port Moresby. This steeply-sloping airstrip, barely 460 metres long, is set on a mountain side 2,500 feet above sea level – just a small grassy clearing on the side of a hill, surrounded by dense tropical rainforest. Nevertheless the airstrip was well marked and well maintained. A few buildings in a clearing at the bottom of the hill made up the Sakarina Mission station. Many village clearings with gardens and another two airstrips within about ten miles (16 kms) of this spot indicated a densely populated area. But this was not the norm for many parts of the country. In many areas I could fly over miles of hot, steamy jungle, which appeared to be uninhabited – nothing more than birds. Well, I guess there were snakes and mosquitoes, and crocodiles in the swampy areas, but all I ever saw was birds – birds and trees – trees so close together that I could never see the ground.

We unloaded the goods for Sakarina – all except for those frozen sausages. These were meant to have been tinned sausages and the staff there had no room in their little kerosene refrigerator for anything like 30 kilograms of frozen meat!

Our next port of call was Wanigela and I left the Greens there for one-and-a-half hours while I took a load of passengers back to Popondetta. This gave David and Susan an opportunity to look over the Wanigela station. Sister Roberts met us on her pushbike and, as always, had a refreshing cold drink of *mouli*-juice for the pilot. She then invited the Greens to her house for a cup of tea and an opportunity to look over the school and hospital.

After I returned from Popondetta I was interested to hear the Green's reactions to their tour of the Wanigela station, and I quote here again from the report that Susan Green wrote:

> "Sister Roberts showed us over the hospital. But I was horrified at the appalling conditions she has to work in. The floor threatened to give-way under our feet. Sure, they have the basic essentials: sterilising room, intensive care, baby clinic … but all made in rough undressed timber or bark. It must be impossible to keep it all clean. And the equipment was so primitive! In the maternity room was a modest plaque, which said that the equipment had been donated by one of our Australian auxiliaries. I feel ashamed to think that we leave a dedicated soul like Sister Roberts there for 22 years in a place that Pentridge prisoners would revolt over!"
>
> "Our next leg was a forty minute flight to Wedau, the airstrip serving Dogura mission station. Our route followed the coast. Below us and on our left side the sea was a beautiful deep blue with patches of a transparent greenish colour sometimes bordered by a white line of surf where coral reefs lay hidden just beneath the surface. On our right the land was low rolling grass-covered hills, the soil here apparently too poor even to grow trees. Further south and inland the dark jungle-covered mountains rose up into a white line of cloud.
>
> "From the air [when we reached Wedau] we could see an impressive array of buildings, some with bright red roofs, and the large grey concrete Cathedral. Yes, they have a Cathedral – and it was built entirely by voluntary labour. A beautifully coloured mural on one of the walls had been painted by Canon Benson, one time missionary and prisoner of the Japanese. In it he has incorporated the

story of Mclaren and King, the first Anglican missionaries to the area[3], together with the massacre of missionaries by the invading Japanese army, and also the Mount Lamington disaster. In the centre is a large Papuan Christ and there are Papuan angels in the background."

"Sister Henderson showed us over the hospital – a teaching one at the time because a Plymouth Brethren doctor had given six months of his time to be on the staff at Dogura. To do this had meant leaving his wife and five children at home. "How wonderful of you," I said warmly. "I don't think so," he replied, "it is a very small thing compared with what my Lord did for me. And if there was a war on I would probably be expected to stay away longer." Sister Henderson has been in charge of the hospital for years. She is completely unflappable, coping with malnutrition, neglect of twins, leprosy, T.B. and obstetrics with equal capability. She told me that they were hoping a lady doctor would come soon and then the nurses could continue their training."

David and Susan stayed overnight at Dogura and I planned to return the next morning to fly them back to Port Moresby, but this was to prove the beginning of an adventure more unforgettable than perhaps any of us had planned, and definitely not in the "operations normal" category.

I arrived at Wedau just before midday the next day, Saturday. At 12.15pm we were airborne again, bound for Agaun and thence Port Moresby. On board we had Rev. and Mrs Green, plus Susan Trek, a 16 year old Papuan schoolgirl and head prefect of Holy Name Girls High School.

Susan was going to Port Moresby to take a secretarial course. Her father and brother were in the Police Force, one sister had trained as a nurse in Townsville, another brother was at an Agricultural College, and her mother worked at the hospital making uniforms for the girls. Both parents had been educated at Dogura. Like most Papuan girls she was polite, quiet and shy, but we were going to be thankful for her knowledge and intelligence later that day.

---

[3] Albert Mclaren and Copland King landed at Wedau in August 1891.

Because the Greens had seen the north coast during our flight to Wedau on Friday I decided to cross the Owen Stanley Range as soon as possible and fly along the southern coastline. Agaun is in a mountain valley 2,000 feet above sea level and in fine weather is easily accessible from either the north or south side of the range.

About ten minutes after take-off we had just crossed the main ridge of the Owen Stanley Range, to the southwest of Wedau, and were descending to get below a layer of cloud ahead of us when I noticed a slight loss of engine power. This was so similar to the slight loss of power usually noted when one magneto is switched off during engine run-up that I immediately suspected the cause of the trouble. One look at the rising indications on the exhaust-gas temperature gauge helped to confirm my suspicion of a magneto failure. Decisions, decisions! Return to Wedau? No. That would involve climbing again to cross back over the ridge behind us. So where was the nearest airstrip? The options were Gurney to the east or Baibara to the west. But to fly to Gurney meant crossing over some very rugged country with no forced landing sites, and Baibara was like the end of nowhere. I did not know who lived there, but at least I could fly straight to the coast and follow the beach to Baibara, if the engine would keep running that long! I looked at the river below me. It was a small stony creek, no room for a forced landing there. The decision was obvious – head straight for the beach and then towards Baibara. If the engine continued to run satisfactorily I might even make it to Amazon Bay where I knew there was a mission station and accommodation for my passengers.

But how long would this engine run on one magneto? Could I even consider the one-and-a-half-hour flight right through to Port Moresby? I thought this over as I again checked the readings on all the engine gauges. The large combustion chamber used in aircraft engines requires two spark plugs to ignite the charge simultaneously and get it to burn cleanly. If full-power is demanded with only one ignition system working then the engine will detonate (ie: explode the charge instead of burning it - like the "pinging" in an overloaded car engine) and this can quickly cause serious damage and a complete engine failure! However, at reduced power the engine may continue to run for some time. But the question was "how much did the power have to be reduced on this particular engine?"

As rising exhaust-gas temperatures indicated detonation was probably occurring already, I increased the mixture and reduced the engine power settings to return the EGT to normal. But still there was a very slight roughness that I did not like. At this stage I was still quite sure the trouble was a simple electrical fault in the ignition system. If this was the case I could land and probably fix it. But then, if the fault was not repairable in-the-bush I would not be able to take-off again. If the engine was happy to keep going at reduced power then why take the risk of getting stuck at a remote airstrip until replacement parts could be flown out to me? This was not an easy decision.

Another quick scan over the engine instruments. How are we going? Should I try for Amazon Bay? Baibara airstrip was just passing under the nose. Temperatures? … OK. Pressures? … pressures! Horrors! Practically no oil pressure! No doubt about that decision now! I grabbed the microphone, "Moresby this is Alpha Whiskey Mike. I apparently have a magneto failure and oil pressure is dangerously low. Landing at Baibara and in the circuit at this time. I will call on the ground."

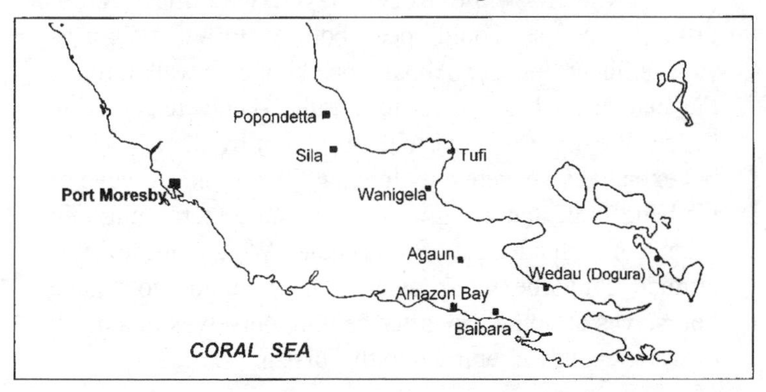

Baibara is a plantation of coconut palms right at the sea's edge. On a few yards of black sandy soil between the trees and the sea there is an airstrip. Since I had not mentioned anything of our troubles up till now, not wanting to cause undue concern or fright to my passengers, I turned and said as casually as I could, "This is not where we were planning to land, but there seems to be a bit of engine trouble so we'll stop here and have a look at it."

After landing and closing communications with Flight Service I climbed out and removed the top engine cowl. To my great surprise I found that the right-hand magneto had completely sheared off at its mounting, and broken pieces of metal had obviously fallen into the oil sump. The oil on the dipstick showed enough metal particles in it that we could almost have used it for glitter on Christmas decorations! I will let Susan take up the story again:

> "As though by the stroke of a wand, a crowd of plantation workers appeared on the side of the strip, and when we asked them where the plantation manager lived, they told us that the manager, a single man, had gone away for an indefinite period – probably for the whole weekend at least. We had a box of mangoes on board the plane but apart from a few dehydrated survival rations, not another thing to eat or drink. And the day was hot.
>
> We decided that David and I should go with Susan Trek up to the plantation homestead and see what could be found there while Roger stayed with the aircraft. Susan, of course, could speak both Motu and Pidgin as well as fluent English. About a one kilometre walk through the plantation brought us to a rather neglected looking house. We were greeted with suspicion by the houseboy, but explained we were only looking for a drink. A wave of his hand indicated a rainwater tank and a metal mug tied to the tap with a length of wire cable. We did not feel this attitude could be interpreted as an invitation to "make yourselves at home" so, after helping ourselves to a drink of water each, we returned to the airstrip."

A little later that afternoon, when it was time for the United Church radio *sched*, I made use of the aircraft radio to contact Dr. Peter Strang, a New Zealander who worked in the Gilkinson Memorial Hospital at Iruna, in Amazon Bay. He very kindly offered to arrange for a dinghy to come to Baibara and take us to

Iruna for the rest of the weekend. He also managed to relay a message to MAF headquarters, then in Wewak. It was arranged that another aircraft would be sent from Wewak on Monday with a new engine.

> "We had expected the dinghy from Iruna to reach us about 4 pm. We waited and waited, but there was no sign of any dingy. At 5.30 Roger was able to contact Dr. Strang by radio again. We then learned that their outboard motor had been found to be out of order and their spare was in pieces. They had then checked with the Government Patrol officer but their boat was not available either. They finally managed to borrow one from an Oil Exploration company. Loana, their Papuan boatman, was now due to arrive at Baibara about 6 pm. He would have some food with him and was game to take us back to Iruna – in the dark, over that treacherous reef-ridden sea. It may seem strange but although none of us had eaten any lunch, neither had we noticed any feeling of hunger."

With the help of some friendly plantation workers we pushed the aeroplane back into a little hollow at the end of the strip, and with the few tools from the emergency toolkit we always carried in each of our aircraft, David helped me to prepare the engine for removal.

> "As 6pm came and went Susan Trek and I were keeping a close eye on the sea, anxiously looking toward the point where we expected Loana to appear. Then suddenly a cry went up and there he was, coming around the headland at the western end of the beach. The crowd on the beach all waved frantically, but Loana just kept on going for about another half mile or so. A bit of time was lost before we realised that he could not land or launch his dinghy from where we were standing. In fact, with the surf on this open beach it was as much as he could do to beach it at the point he did choose. By messages shouted back and forth we were told that we must go to the boat, and by now daylight was fading."

As I've mentioned before, twilight in the tropics is very brief, so we ran down the beach and quickly loaded our luggage into the boat. Having decided that the dinghy would be overloaded if we tried to take the mangoes with us we soon found that the crowd of labourers on the beach were all very happy to accept them as payment for their help. We put the two ladies in the centre seat while I held the stern with Loana, waiting for his signal to push off. At the shout of "Now'" many willing hands pushed our boat out into the surf. David jumped into the bow and Loana and I scrambled into the stern.

We heard an enthusiastic yell of triumph from our team of helpers, then as we ploughed our way into the oncoming waves, they began to run back along the beach. "They're after the mangoes," said Susan Trek, and she laughed, the first laugh for several hours.

The dinghy did look rather overloaded and although I had remembered to bring the lifejackets from the aeroplane, somehow they had got stowed underneath the other luggage. As I looked beyond the bow I saw a thin strip of daylight, the last remains of the sunset, a brief indication of an uncluttered horizon ahead of us as Loana steered us out towards the open sea. The rest of that two-and-a-half hour trip was in darkness. There was no moon, only an occasional star peeked out from behind the clouds, and there were a few light showers of rain – just to keep us cool. As I think back over that little adventure I now realise that Mrs. Green was in real fear that we might possibly strike a submerged reef. Nevertheless, in spite of the comments she later wrote in her version of the story, I had confidence that Loana knew what he was doing and knew exactly where he was going.

Once clear of the more pronounced waves nearer the shore David Green tried to get us all to sing. He claims this was intended to cheer me up because he thought I looked so worried. Well, I admit that I certainly felt a sense of responsibility. Susan Green wrote,

> "As darkness settled down and the waves splashed up, our clothes and spirits became dampened and we sat silently looking towards the shore, barely visible in the darkness."

My memory of that part of the adventure was more of a growing sense of admiration for Loana's navigation. He held a straight course, in the darkness, for nearly two hours. His only visible reference that I could identify, was the shadowy silhouette of the land a few hundred yards away on our starboard side. At times we could see the luminous glow of surf where it crashed against rocks along the shore.

"Do you think you could swim far enough to reach the shore if you had to?" Mrs Green asked me.
"H-m-m, Possibly." I said, not believing I would have to.
"I suppose we'd be smashed against rocks, even if we did make it to shore," she added, watching the phosphorescence of the spray as another wave smashed against the rocks.

After about half an hour there was a scraping sound along the bottom of the boat. The motor stopped. "What was that?" The voice betrayed fear and the question reminded us of the coral reefs along this coast. "Just a palm branch. I think the leaves got caught in the propeller," I said as I watched Loana untangling fronds. Even with the lack of light, from the way Mrs. Green looked at me I doubt that she believed me.

We continued on, the cool rain making spray from the sea feel relatively warm. Then another bump … bump … bump … as something slid under the boat. I looked over the stern and could just make out the shape of a coconut floating away behind us. "Just a coconut," I said, as cheerily as I could manage. But I noticed that one of our passengers felt the bottom of the boat (for water?) and looked anxiously towards the shore.

Along the shore at intervals we could see the lights from village houses. I know from Susan's record of this "adventure" that she looked to every one of these as a beacon of hope, which was subsequently deferred as we went on past. "How much longer?" was the un-spoken question in everyone's mind.

Suddenly the noise of the engine stopped and Loana reached for another jerry can of fuel. Susan Green held a torch, and with considerably less than one hundred percent accuracy due to the constant rolling of this small boat on an unpredictable swell, I poured more fuel into the tank. Loana restarted the motor and we moved off again. I'll let Susan take up the story again:

"At last, after about two-and-a-half hours, so many lights showed up ahead of us that we knew it had to be the mission station at Iruna. But here Loana slowed right down and showed some hesitation. He stood up in the boat and waved his torch from left to right. An answering flash from the shore. Carefully, slowly, we moved forward almost brushing the edge of a coral reef, changing direction, and then turning again towards the lights on the shore. When we were within a few yards of the beach the tall red-headed Dr Strang strode out into the water and pulled our boat up onto the sand. The landing here was easy compared to our departure from Baibara because the waves in this area are broken by extensive coral reefs before they reach the shore.

"Our whole party was made welcome by Doctor Strang, who personally cooked a good meal for us while we all took a shower and changed into dry clothes – borrowed ones where necessary."

The Greens and I slept in the Strang's house while Susan stayed in the Hospital Nurses' Home where she seemed to be happy with girls of her own age.

Next morning we attended a Church service that was conducted entirely by the Papuan people, and most of it in their own language. There was an Australian Minister in this circuit but I remembered with sadness how he had been drowned on patrol only a few months previously. Apparently he had been hiking along the beach and was swept out to sea when he attempted to cross the mouth of a river. His body was found on the beach a few kilometres away. I have seen this river from the air and it normally looks fairly innocent, although a spreading curve of brown water out to the ocean shows what could become of anyone who lost their footing while crossing it with an outgoing tide. And Dr Nick Thompson, the resident doctor at Iruna before Peter Strang had arrived, had told me that one of his main concerns when trying to cross rivers while on patrol was the crocodiles. I had asked him for a little more detail, such as, "How big are they?" "I can't vouch for length," he said, "But one that I saw watching me had eyes about 12 inches apart – and that means a big croc!"

> "The Church bell rang for 15 minutes, during which time the gathering congregation sang hymns and choruses – without musical accompaniment. The Church was a simple building made of local bush materials and doubled as a schoolroom on weekdays. But we were specially privileged as this was a special service of commissioning for five graduate nurses. Every louvre of the windows in that building was decorated with hibiscus and frangipani flowers.
>
> "Although the entire service was a mixture of Motu and the local language the head councillor of the village spoke also in English when he presented the graduate nurses each with a gift in an envelope and wished them God's blessing as they returned to their home lands. Two of them replied, also in English. They thanked the mission and promised to use their training and abilities to help the people in their villages and also for the extension of God's kingdom on earth.
>
> "On the Sunday evening we had our meal with the two mission staff nurses and then afterwards shared together in a good time of fellowship and singing – this, of course, was in English. David closed this completely impromptu time of fellowship in prayer."

Next morning I left early to return in the dinghy with Loana to Baibara. By the time we arrived there the plantation manager had returned, and after introducing myself, I explaining the reason for my unscheduled visit. After borrowing a few tools, I got back to work removing the aircraft engine. Max Meyers and Bert Kater arrived in a Cessna 206 with the new engine at about 11 am. The rest of Mrs Green's story makes interesting reading:

> "As Roger left with Loana early Monday morning we had no idea when we would get away. But while some of us were at breakfast I heard, "They're delivering on the beach." "Aha", I thought, "that's good. I suppose we've been

eating them out of house and home". But it was a baby being delivered! The canoe bringing the woman to hospital had been delayed by contrary winds and they were just in time to wrap the littlie in a sheet. Matron carried it up to the hospital, and David, who had been doing a bit of plumbing for Matron, together with the doctor and two natives, carried the woman on a stretcher up to the hospital. Unlike the last woman, who had nearly died, she was OK.

"Our next news was that the plane, which brought the mechanic for Roger was now at Iruna ready to take us to Port Moresby. Matron said the pilot had better stay for lunch because she was sending two nurses on the plane, and they were not ready yet.

"Our pilot, Max Meyers, was a bright, talkative chap the reverse of reserved Roger. But after our recent adventures I felt horribly uneasy in the Skywagon with its single engine. As we approached Port Moresby our path was blocked by a storm, and when we heard on our radio that a Fokker Friendship had actually returned to Port Moresby, and then we struck some bumpy patches, it wasn't just the pilot who kept looking around to see if there was anywhere to land if necessary. Then we climbed up, trying to get above the storm. No good. "I'll go out over the sea," he said. "Perhaps we can get below it." We flew at four or five hundred feet above the waves but the storm was still with us. At last, to my relief, Port Moresby came in sight. We landed with no further problems and were met by Roger's wife anxious to hear all the details of our forced landing."

Meanwhile back at Baibara, Bert and I had the engine change completed by Tuesday afternoon and made it back to Port Moresby by 6.15pm, about 20 minutes before dark. Perhaps that was one weekend we would not call "operations normal"!

Chapter Fourteen

BUT WHAT IS NORMAL?

On Saturday 26th September, 1970, an aircraft went missing between Kokoda and Port Moresby. The aircraft was a twin-engine Piper Aztec and, from what I had been told, was owned by the South Pacific Aero Club. With all such incidents there is always a great deal of sadness involved, but it was even more tragic on this occasion because the pilot had been trying to get home for his son's birthday party.

In our own family our second child was due about this time so I had deliberately planned a week almost free of flight bookings. Since I was therefore available I offered to help in the search for the missing aircraft at least until the end of the month.

The MAF aircraft, which I had the use of (a Cessna 185) was chartered on several occasions during this search to do supply runs between Port Moresby and Kokoda with food, portable radios, observers and DCA Controllers for the search. For me this was all routine flying and very much "operations normal". But I gained the distinct impression that for some of my passengers, particularly those not used to flying in Papua New Guinea, the idea of circling for height between Kokoda and the narrow valley, which leads up to the Kokoda Gap, then setting course over the top of cloud at 10,000 feet with apparently nothing much more than a compass to show the way to Port Moresby didn't seem to be quite what they expected to be normal.

Perhaps they didn't know, as I did, that in another ten minutes, or less, we would have the cloud behind us and would be commencing descent through the controlled airspace of our destination airport. Had they asked, or rather if I were not so preoccupied with radio communication with the airport Control Tower, I could have explained to them a lot of significant visual clues. Such as: as we passed through the Kokoda Gap, "If you take a look out the left side you may see a large grassy area and possibly a lake [Myola]. But the lake may be hidden by a spot of cloud." Then, shortly after we had passed through the Gap, "Down there on the right you will see a large valley with a river flowing down the middle. Perhaps you might be able to see an airstrip on the right-hand side of that river. That is the Brown River, and the airstrip is called Manumu. If necessary we could follow that valley all the way down to the Brown River bridge, follow the road, which crosses the river and it would take us to the end of the main runway at Port Moresby." "But," you say, "Right ahead of us is a big build-up of cloud." "Not a problem. We just turn a little to the right and follow that valley and that will keep us clear of cloud. We should have the airfield in sight in another couple of minutes." And another little clue that may be worth passing on is to look at the cloud shadows on the ground. This can sometimes give a good picture of how solid the cloud layer is and where to find a clear path between the build-ups.

By the end of the month we had still not located the lost aircraft and, although I had other flying booked, the Searchmaster was very keen that I continue to help in the search at least from 6am till 9am each morning. By this time each day the weather around the mountain tops of the search area had deteriorated to the extent that the search had to be virtually suspended until the next morning anyway. We knew from the missing pilot's last report that he had climbed above 10,000 feet, so expected to find him above that height. As it turned out, the wreckage was located at 7 am on Thursday October 1st. There was no hope of survivors – from what we could see of the wreckage the aircraft had flown straight into the side of a mountain at high speed. During the next seven days I logged just over 29 hours airborne (the legal maximum is 30) and then on Monday 5th, the busiest day of one of my busiest weeks, our second son Stuart was born. In fact the last sector of flying that day had been a late afternoon one-and-a-half hour battle with weather between Lae and Port Moresby, and by the time I arrived home I was just very glad to be back on the ground. I guess my sister-in-law Dawne might have thought I was pretty dense when I asked her what on earth she was talking about as she excitedly thrust a congratulations card in front of my face before I could even get out of the car.

A few days later, Saturday 10th October, I arrived at the airport briefing office at 5.30 am to lodge my flight plan for the day. As the Briefing Officer was looking at the page with my flight-plan on it, the Superintendent of Operations came over to the counter to ask if I could possibly help in another search that was now at a critical stage. Three observers were available if I could supply pilot and aircraft.

The ground party of four men who had gone in to investigate the wreckage of the aircraft found ten days previously, had themselves apparently become lost. Two other aircraft with observers were also involved in this search but by about 8.30 am both had returned to Port Moresby or Kokoda for fuel. By this time we had also been chased out of the highest country due to cloud forming, but then just before 9 am one of my observers shouted, "Down there! Look at that. What is it?" He was pointing out the window just behind my head. I rolled the aircraft over to the left and we all saw a small cloud of red smoke drifting across the trees.

“That's them. It must be.” I continued turning to the left and sure enough in a small clearing at the head of a narrow valley four men were excitedly waving a silvery-white 'space-blanket'.

“Port Moresby this is Alpha Whisky Mike. I think we've found them. A party of four men with a space-blanket. My position is ...” I explained our position as accurately as I could on the rather inaccurate aeronautical charts we were obliged to use in those days.

“Alpha Whisky Mike, remain in the area. We'll despatch a helicopter from Kokoda. Can you direct him to the area?”

“Affirmative.”

Once I knew the helicopter was within a few miles of the men with the space-blanket I left the area. My fuel was getting low and I was rather anxious to get back to Port Moresby and get on with the rest of the flying that I had booked for the day. This, as it turned out, was not a good move because the helicopter observers were unable to actually see the ground party. Nevertheless action was immediately taken to arrange other ground parties to go in and meet the lost group.

Evidently the four men knew, more or less, where they were going but the main cause of concern was that radio contact with them had been lost, and it was known they had been out of food for several days. The next day the helicopter did locate the "lost" ground party and dropped them food supplies. This possibly saved their lives as they were almost collapsing from starvation and had resorted to eating ants! The country where we saw those men was so rugged that it would have been impossible to do a successful airdrop from a conventional fixed-wing aircraft.

I cannot recall exactly how it had happened but someone had given me one of those daily-text calendars – the type that contains only the day, date, and a brief bible text on each page, and you tear off the old to expose a new page each day. This was a compact little design and the whole thing measured only about 5cm by 8cm. I had stuck this onto the instrument panel of AWM, the aircraft I flew while based in Port Moresby, and found that it had an interesting affect on the people who noticed it. One or two of our staff had been critical, claiming that it looked as though I was preaching at my passengers, but in actual fact I never found a passenger who showed any negative reaction and many expressed definite approval. And sometimes the verse gave me just the encouragement I needed for the day.

There was one occasion during the wet season when I had already postponed my flight program for one day due to weather: I had left Port Moresby feeling rather glum and not at all hopeful that I would ever get through the work ahead of me for this day.

I had only been in the air for maybe 15 minutes when I decided that I would have to turn back and wait for yet another day, but just as I was half-way through the turn I noticed a spot where I could cross the range and still stay out of the cloud. Once over the Owen Stanleys the weather to the north side of the range was reasonably clear, but rather turbulent due to a 40 knot gale from the northwest.

As I crossed over the mountain range that morning I felt very despondent and quite sure I would not get back home again before the day was ended. And yet I felt a strange mixture of emotions because the verse for the day read, "*Have not I commanded you, do not be afraid, neither be dismayed for the Lord your God is with you wherever you go*." But as I looked at the weather I was dismayed. "Miserable weather", I thought – and yet there was that strange sense of peace and a conviction that I should just wait and see what the day would bring forth. This was one of those days with a lot of short flights, about ten minutes each way into and out of Sila airstrip, mainly to bring in teachers and school students for the beginning of the school year.

At the first airstrip the passengers just didn't turn up. They were nowhere to be found. At the second place I was told, "A message from the teacher. … He says he is due for another three weeks of holidays and is not ready to come." No good arguing, he lived several hours walk away in the bush. What a start for the day! But … "*Have not I commanded ... do not be dismayed*."

Shortly after midday I asked for a report on the weather from the pilot of an airline aircraft just outbound from Port Moresby. His reply indicated that the weather was definitely worse than when I had left there at 9 am. What a temptation to feel discouraged! But, "*Have not I commanded* …" the verse said, and somehow I was encouraged by that.

It was about 3 pm when I landed at an outstation airstrip for the last load of passengers. There was no radio at this airstrip and, as I had expected, the teacher was not there. In fact he had returned to his village, several hours walk away, because the aeroplane had not come on the appointed day – which was yesterday. However, they did have a patient who needed to be taken to Port Moresby. Could I take him? So we loaded the patient and his guardian on board and took-off for Port Moresby. It was amazing! The weather report from Port Moresby was now quite good and furthermore it was now possible to fly through a gap in the hills enroute to Port Moresby below cloud at an altitude of only 8,000 feet. It was "a little bit turbulent" because of the 40 knot northwesterly wind but it was definitely visual flight conditions. "… *for the Lord your God is with you, wherever you go*." The verse had helped to keep me cheerful throughout an otherwise very tiresome day.

On Friday 3rd July 1970 I had the privilege of taking an SIL/WBT couple (Roger Garland and his wife Sue) into the airstrip at Efogi. Although this airstrip is on the infamous Kokoda Trail (probably the end of your second or third day if you are walking the trail from the Port Moresby end) it is only 30 miles by air from Port Moresby.

Because I was feeling rather weary I had left the local people to unload the aircraft and it was only after I had returned to Port Moresby that I realised the centre passenger seat was missing. Often, when not in use, it would have been folded up and stowed in the cargo pod, but it was not there. So it had obviously been unloaded at Efogi along with the Garland's luggage. As it was now too late in the day to return to Efogi and I needed that seat for an early flight on Monday morning, there was no alternative but to load the aircraft with another full load of luggage for Efogi and make another flight into there on Saturday morning. But when I arrived at the airstrip (on Saturday morning) the place seemed surprisingly deserted. There was normally an enthusiastic crowd of village people to meet the aircraft, but today there was no-one. It was only when I noticed a couple of senior village-elders walking down the path toward the airstrip that I remembered – the Efogi people are mostly Seventh Day Adventists. Saturday is their day of worship – it is their holy day. So as soon as the elders were within speaking distance, I began to apologise for using their airstrip on a Saturday but hastened to explain my reason for doing so. The men were very polite and said, "Well, that's okay – we will forgive you this time. But be sure that you never do it again!" Graciousness, understanding, and forgiveness – we need it every day.

During the time we were based in Port Moresby, Rose and I actually managed to arrange a one-week holiday at the SIL/WBT town of Ukarumpa, which is in the highlands, so the cooler weather was a pleasant change from the constant humidity and heat of coastal living. We also enjoyed the rare occasions when we were able to spend a few days with the SIL folk because their warm friendship was always such a blessing to us.

But on this occasion I had also planned to make use of my location in the highlands to bring two plane loads of delegates in to attend a medical conference in Goroka, which is not too far from Ukarumpa. There was one load of passengers to come from Baimuru, in the Gulf of Papua, and another from Port Moresby. My intention was to collect the Baimuru passengers first as this would involve a flight of only about one-and-a-half hours each way, and I should then be able to get back into the highlands before the usual afternoon weather problems.

So on Monday 10th August I departed Aiyura (the airstrip that serves the town of Ukarumpa) shortly after 6:30 am, but when I was only a few minutes flying away from Baimuru I received a radio message from Flight Service to the effect,: "Baimuru airstrip is closed all day," and then the operator continued, "A message from Doctor Calvert: he will be at Kikori by 11 am." Baimuru was a grassed airstrip, which could become soft and wet after heavy rain but Kikori, although it is in an area that receives more rain than Baimuru, had an airstrip with a sealed surface, so it was not affected by rainfall.

Well, now I was in a quandary. Should I fly across to Kikori and wait for something like three hours, and leave all the rest of the flying until the afternoon when the weather over the mountains could become quite impassable, or should I now go straight on to Port Moresby and hope my passengers there, not expecting me until after midday, would be able to come possibly three or four hours earlier than expected? After a few quick calculations I realised that if I chose the first option – of going directly to Kikori and waiting there for three hours – then I would not have enough hours left in the day to move the passengers from Port Moresby. So the second option was really my only choice. I therefore asked the Flight Service operator if he would be kind enough to phone the United Church office and advise them of my revised ETA for Port Moresby. Of course when I arrived there at 9:45 there was no sign of my passengers. Even a phone call seemed to catch them by surprise.

"But we weren't expecting you until after midday!"

"Yes, I know that was the original plan. But I have had to make some last minute changes, because overnight rain has made Baimuru airstrip unusable. You should have received a phone call more than one-and-a-half hours ago to advise you about these changes."

I discovered later that the Flight Service officer had faithfully passed on my message but the person who received it did not understand its significance and had made absolutely no attempt to pass it on or to even ask anyone else if it meant anything to them. So that cost me another one-and-a-half hours of precious time. We actually managed to get away from Port Moresby at 11:30, and after delivering those passengers to Goroka I finally landed at Kikori at 4 pm. Now spare a thought for Dr. Calvert who, by this time, had been waiting at Kikori for five hours, wondering if his message had ever been passed on to "the pilot" and wondering when, or if, his flight would ever turn up and if he would get to his medical conference on time. Amazingly we did make it back through the weather, Dr. Calvert did get to his conference on time, and I landed back at Aiyura at 6 pm. Rose and I had been invited out to tea that evening and, understandably, our hosts were wondering if I would ever get there. For me that was just another 12-hour day. Next day we returned as a family to Port Moresby – our holiday was well and truly over.

Later that month I had a booking to bring some passengers from Mendi, in the highlands, down to Port Moresby. I managed to arrange for a load from Moresby to Tari, to pay for the forward (or outbound) sector of the flight, but when I arrived at Mendi there was no sign of any passengers and no-one seemed to know anything about the booking. After scrambling back to Port Moresby for an expected additional two-and-a-half hours' flying in the afternoon almost the same thing happened again. When I finally landed at Safia some 60 miles to the east of Moresby, and after the predictable battle with the weather, I was greeted with the news, "Those people went on a PATAIR flight this morning."

Operations normal? Yes, definitely! That sort of thing was certainly just all too "normal".

Not infrequently I was asked to airdrop supplies to a village and mission school in the Owen Stanley Ranges behind Mt. Yule. An attempt had been made to build an airstrip adjacent to this village about 5,000 feet above sea level, but the site was pretty hopeless really. Across a very steep-sided valley, only a few miles by air but eight hours hard walk on the ground, was another airstrip site. A road, of sorts, connected this second area to the long established airstrip at Tapini. But apart from that, the airdrop site at Suesi was very remote and isolated.

Normally the aircraft was loaded at Port Moresby and we made the 45 minute flight to the drop site from there. However on one occasion I was asked to carry out this operation from a relatively new airstrip at Iokea. Now many airstrips in PNG, particularly new airstrips or those in areas where overnight rain is common, were automatically closed at the end of the day. These strips were then re-opened for use the next day ONLY if the Civil Aviation Department received a radio message from the strip reporting agent indicating that the airstrip surface was hard and dry enough for the safe operation of aircraft.

Although I had, as usual, planned an early start, the Iokea strip report did not come in by the usual time. About 9 am I decided to leave anyway and hope the report would be in before we arrived over Iokea. However, by 9.45 when we were overhead and had advised Flight Service of our position, I was simply advised: "No strip report on Iokea yet". This meant I was not permitted to land, and obviously the airstrip was meant to be serviceable. I could see Pastor John waiting there beside his piles of goods already arranged for the various flights he had planned.

After some discussion over the radio it was decided that Iokea was due to come up on the Post Office outstations radio *sched* at 10.30. If MAF was prepared to pay for the radio call, DCA would endeavour to get a strip report from Iokea then. So there seemed to be no alternative but to land at the nearest alternative strip, Lese, and wait until 10.30.

While having a cup of coffee with the lay mission worker at the Lese Roman Catholic mission (who owned the airstrip) another mission worker came in and asked if I could take a woman patient, with childbirth difficulties, to the nearby hospital at Terapo. The baby was thought to be already dead, though not yet born, and there was concern for the mother's health. From even my limited experience I suggested that it may not be necessary to do this, after all she had only been in labour an hour or two. And what usually happens when we put patients in this condition on board an aircraft, the child is delivered very soon after take off. They assured me this woman had difficulties and when the priest, a European man who had lived with these people for many years, also recommended moving the patient I agreed to take the woman to Terapo.

I had with me a young woman who had come to act as despatcher or "pusher-outer" for the planned airdrop operation. As soon as we were safely strapped into our seats I started the engine, taxied out, and after the normal pre-take-off checks, took-off and headed towards Terapo. We had been airborne about two minutes when I turned to see how my passengers were. A smile and nod from my assistant indicated that my predictions had been perfectly correct. In less than five minutes we were on the ground again where we lifted the mother and still-born child out of the aircraft and went off to find the hospital Matron at Terapo.

Incidentally, the strip report on Iokea never was received in Port Moresby that day. It was supposed to have been relayed via the Post Office at Kerema. Sure, the Agent at Iokea had radioed Kerema at 8 am but the operator there had simply forgotten to pass the message on to its destination!

Operations normal? Absolutely!

As part of normal operations I could also tell of experiences where I encountered what could be described as miraculous changes in the weather. Once, after taking off from an airstrip, a sudden and unexpected gust of tailwind caused my machine to sink horribly towards the trees. "If we're going to hit the trees," I thought "I may as well close the throttle just before we hit." Then, uncannily, just before I moved the throttle, the aircraft lifted almost as though an unseen hand had given us a push. My passengers, and people still back on the airstrip, had also thought we were going to sink into the trees.

Of course there were many frustrations. I have already given examples of flights that were made, sometimes through extremely poor weather and to isolated airstrips, only to find the passengers were not ready, or had already gone on another aircraft that just happened to have called in earlier and had space available. Or the patience that was needed when the weather was obviously closing in but some individual at his isolated airstrip wanted to discuss future flight bookings at length and in detail. And it always seemed to be when I was already running behind my planned schedule that someone would want to argue the point. Passengers with no prior bookings would not seem to understand that even though we might appear to have a spare seat, the aircraft was already carrying as much weight as could be lifted off their muddy little airstrip. But there were also many times when things beyond my direct control worked together so smoothly that it was exhilarating to be involved.

* * * * *

The aircraft that had been used for the Port Moresby MAF base since it was first opened had originally been owned and operated by the Australian Board of Missions (Church of England in Australia) and had been blessed, or commissioned, with the name *Saint Gabriel*. I had to admit that the aircraft did fly nicely – “like a homesick angel” as one of our pilots had described it. But it did have limitations. Many people considered the Cessna 185 aircraft (such as the *St Gabriel*, or “Alpha Whiskey Mike” to use its correct radio call-sign title) to be a six-seat aircraft and in their mind this meant six adults. Yes, it is true that when some of the MAF-designed modifications were incorporated these aircraft were capable of carrying six passengers plus the pilot – making a total of seven persons. But these modifications were meant to cater for a pilot with six school children, not five or six adults. Many times I would be asked to carry a load of five hefty adult passengers, but it was simply not possible to put two 80 kilogram adults in the rear seat of a Cessna 185 and still have the aircraft loaded within the design limits for weight and balance. Also, many of the flights I was now being asked to do involved trips into the highlands where I would be flying at altitudes of 10,000 feet or more. But the *St Gabriel* was not fitted with any oxygen system. Civil Aviation regulations required that on any flight above 10,000ft the pilot must have access to supplemental oxygen. Obviously it was time to replace the aircraft with something more suited to the task. With the many long flights that were becoming a normal part of the Moresby program, any aircraft that could fly faster than the Cessna 185 would be a big help. But there was just nothing available that could combine short-field take-off performance with a faster cruise speed. A turbocharged Cessna 206 would be a compromise, but it seemed to be the best aircraft available to do the job. This machine could still handle the short, soft airstrips; it should give some extra load capacity; and with its longer and wider cabin, certainly better passenger comfort.

After many, repeated requests it was finally agreed that the Moresby program could have a Cessna Turbo 206. But the aircraft that was allocated, although the newest in the MAF Australia fleet, was 112 lbs (50 kg) heavier than other aircraft of the same model and it "flew like a pregnant duck". Yes, we had the advantage of improved passenger comfort, but that was about all. Because most of my flights required a full load of fuel at the point of departure I felt it was very unfair that the Moresby base should be given this heavier than normal aircraft. I may need to explain that it is the *gross weight,* which is critical when operating an aircraft and the weight of fuel carried needs to be considered in calculating the all-up weight. Where the aircraft is to be used on a short flight it is normal to carry only sufficient fuel to complete the flight (with a safe margin in reserve, of course) and this then means that more payload can be carried. But as I was now stuck with a heavier than normal aircraft, and had to operate with full tanks on most flights, I felt it was very unfair. The response I heard when I complained about this problem was, "Nobody else wants that aircraft, so you can have it." I was not favourably impressed and hoped that this attitude would not become "normal"!

Chapter Fifteen

AND THE NOT-SO-NORMAL

Easter weekend 1971 … and the extra cabin space of the Cessna 206 was put to good use. I had been asked to take a team of ten young adults from the Campaigners for Christ "Everyman's Centre" in Port Moresby down to the high school at Salamo where they were planning to run a series of special meetings (Easter Convention) especially for the students there. Because we now had the capacity for six passengers on each flight I was able to include Rose and our two boys so that we could spend this weekend at Fergusson Island. But in those days there was no airstrip at Salamo, so we had to fly to Esa Ala, on Normanby Island, 240 nautical miles from Port Moresby – a flight time of two hours, and then make a three or four hour boat ride across to Fergusson Is.

The first plane load with six team members left Port Moresby at 6 am. After safely delivering these fellows to Esa Ala they had to wait at the unattended airstrip for something like six hours or more while I returned to Moresby, with a couple of stops on the way, to get the rest of the team, plus Rose, David, and our infant son Stuart. It was nearly three in the afternoon before we even started loading our things into the boat for the second stage of our journey.

Fortunately the sea was quite calm and we found this section of the trip very interesting as we putted slowly past these islands — beautiful with their white sand and coconut trees along the beaches. Sometimes we were close enough that we could see children waving as we went past. We made a brief stop at Dobu Island (pronounced "door-boo") where two team members left the boat as they were to take separate meetings there. Dobu is a dormant volcano, and as we watched the sun setting behind the mountain it was really beautiful. By the time we reached the Salamo wharf it was nearly 7 pm, light rain was falling, and everyone was feeling rather sleepy.

The last part of our journey was a one-mile ride through a coconut plantation with the trees meeting overhead. In the dim light from the headlights of the tractor we could see many of the local folk holding banana or taro leaves over their heads to shelter from the rain as they walked along the track. Outlined through the arch of palms ahead of us we could see an illuminated cross on the front of the Church. Although we were being bounced along in an open trailer Rose described the experience as being like an adventure in a dream. When we finally reached the settlement we were greeted by Doug McKenzie, headmaster of Wesley High School, and his wife Leonie (fellow Kiwis!). Rose and I, and our two boys, stayed with Doug and Leonie while the Everyman's team members went on to the Bishop's house – at least for tea. They were probably billeted with different families, and for some of them this was their home territory.

On the Saturday Rose and I were invited to go with some other visitors on a tour of the historic spots in the area, particularly the one-time mission station on Dobu Island. It was here, a place that had once been an important cultural centre for the local population, that Methodist missionaries to the area held their first Christian church service on June 15th 1891. Many of the headstones in the local cemetery bore epitaphs that suggested tragedy: wives who had died in childbirth; children who died in infancy and missionaries who had died of malaria after only a few months in the area. For many of those pioneers, some of them Fijians, their calling and commitment to serving the Lord had obviously involved real sacrifice. But we could see some of the fruits of their efforts in the genuine Christ-like testimony of the young men and women who had come to run these special meetings during this weekend.

We were also taken on a conducted tour of the Vulcanological Observatory at Esa Ala. This station, with its extremely scientific instrumentation, keeps a close watch on the 'dormant' Dobu – just in case! I remember, at one stage of the tour, we had stopped beside a huge concrete block, which would have measured possibly one-and-a-half metres by three metres, when our Papuan guide noticed one of the tourists leaning with her hand on this block. He expressed some concern and said, "Please, don't lean against that. It will be registered as an earth tremor."

The Everyman's team received a very good response to their meetings and many people came to them asking for counseling and guidance, or to make a definite statement about their decision to accept Christ as their personal Saviour. This meant that many of the team did not get to bed until nearly midnight on Sunday. But I had warned them we would need to be at the wharf by 5 am on Monday ready for our 3-hour boat ride to Normanby Island. This was to be the exact reverse of Friday's exercise and it all went smoothly and according to plan but, in spite of the early start, it was another 12 hours (5 o'clock in the afternoon) before I had the aircraft parked back at Port Moresby and was free to call it quits for the day.

* * * * *

December 1971 – our time in Port Moresby had come to an end. We were asked to prepare ourselves for a move into Indonesian territory. MAF had recently based an aircraft and pilot at Kupang, in Indonesian Timor, and we had been asked to go there and relieve the Charlesworth family who would be due for furlough at the end of 1972. So for the latter part of 1971 Rose and I attended classes at the University of Papua New Guinea (two hours in the afternoon, five days per week) where we were trying to develop a working knowledge of *Bahasa Indonesia* (the Indonesian language). We had also been warned that in Kupang we would be without many of the privileges we had taken for granted in PNG, so we should plan to take all the footwear, clothing, and chemist supplies we might expect to need during the next three years. And we had been told we would need to have an accurate inventory of what was packed in every individual drum and box, and an estimate of its monetary value. We weren't even sure about access to electricity in Kupang. So the record-player and reel-to-reel tape-recorder (much of which I had actually manufactured myself as a hobby project) would have to stay behind – I decided to sell the unit, along with many of my (precious to me) LP records.

It was planned that we should leave Port Moresby on December 22nd then, after a brief holiday and five or six weeks of deputation meetings in New Zealand, return to Australia for more language study, after which we would move to Sentani, West Irian, on June 22nd and finally to Kupang in November 1972. But, as someone once said, "Man proposes but God disposes." Apart from the departure from Port Moresby on Dec. 22nd and the holiday in New Zealand, none of these plans eventuated. Instead I spent some time in a hospital in NZ and two doctors in that country contacted MAF with the recommendation that we should not (ever) be sent to work in Indonesia and we should spend at least one year in Australia before returning to what was then known as 'the Territory of Papua and New Guinea'. I will come back to this part of our "adventures" later.

Chapter Sixteen

WE NEED TO TAKE A BREAK

Just because we ended up back at Ballarat for 18 months, or so, did not mean that life became dull and boring.

Shortly after we settled back there I was able to get involved with the assembly and modification of MAF's newest aircraft – a Cessna 185 that was to bear the registration letters VH-MFW. Then on Wednesday 21st June (1972), I left Ballarat on what was supposed to be a very routine flight, to deliver this aircraft to New Guinea. The flight, normally via Bourke, Charleville, Normanton, Horn Island and Daru, usually took two days, at least as far as Daru on the southern coast of Papua, and sometimes a third day to get from Daru to Wewak on the north coast, or to Mt Hagen in the New Guinea highlands. However, it was not always a straightforward operation, as I was about to learn.

After the usual weather delays (anyone who really knows the place would not be surprised at that) I left Ballarat with two passengers on board and set course for Dubbo, NSW, where I was to collect a third passenger, David Lowrance, son of a MAF-USA pilot who was working in West Irian. This all went according to plan. But later in the day, as we crossed the NSW - QLD State border, the HF radio made a squawking sound like a dying chook and apparently stopped transmitting. I had planned this flight, as I usually did, to be on full position reporting and this meant I was obliged to call Flight Service with a position report every 40 minutes, or thereabouts, so one of their operators would be expecting to receive a report as we crossed the border. Yes, I know things are done differently nowadays, but this was “the good old days” - and if I failed to call in with that position report then Flight Service were obliged to initiate an "uncertainty phase", which is the first step before they start a search to go look for the missing aircraft. We were now too far away from any ground-based station to raise any of them on the VHF radio, so I just had to keep going, and keep trying. After about 30 minutes I finally did manage to raise Charleville on VHF.

We made a brief stop there for fuel, and since I was able to speak to the Charleville station on the HF radio while I was on the ground there, we took off again hoping to get to Longreach 20 minutes before daylight ended. However, once I was airborne again it was impossible to raise anyone on the HF radio. So I told the operator at Charleville that I would continue on to Longreach and set a SARTIME (time nominated by a pilot for the initiation of SAR – search and rescue) of last light. In other words, an 'uncertainty phase' would only be initiated if I had not arrived at Longreach by the time it was dark. I had hoped to find some kind of a radio serviceman in Longreach but this was not to be. Apparently all the aircraft owners there go to Townsville if they need any radio repairs done. So next morning it was off to Townsville where the technician at the AWA workshop (on Townsville airport) managed to get the set working again. After discussing the options with my passengers, we decided to head for Cairns, overnight there, then clear Customs and try for a Cairns to Daru flight first thing Friday morning.

We enjoyed a very pleasant evening in Cairns and I made a mental note that it would be lovely to come back to this place for a holiday, even though the locals told us, "This is the first fine weather we have had for at least two weeks." That night I watched anxiously as the stars disappeared behind layers of cloud. But Friday dawned fine and clear, so after the usual formalities with HM Customs, we set off for Daru at 8 am. But once again I was having problems with the HF radio. I could not raise any Australian station but I did manage to raise Port Moresby, once. This one, chance contact persuaded me to believe it was just atmospheric conditions and so I kept heading north. I was able to contact other aircraft on the VHF radio and they passed my position reports on to the appropriate Flight Service units. I was hoping it would be possible to fly across Torres Strait at such a height that I could maintain contact with Thursday Island on VHF and cancel SARWATCH with the operator there when I got to a position over the top of Daru. But as soon as I had passed my position report at Horn Island I was instructed to "Call Moresby now on HF." Of course I could not raise them now – even though I had managed to do so once earlier in the day. The Senior Operations Controller in Moresby then simply "put his foot down". If I was not able to communicate with Moresby Flight Service on HF radio then permission to enter the Moresby Flight Information Region was absolutely refused.

"So what do I do now?" I had no choice but to land at Horn Island. The airport here had two long sealed runways, a small hangar, a shed where aviation fuel was available, a passenger terminal with a telephone and one cold water tap (yes, there were toilets) and three houses occupied by airport maintenance staff. The nearest town was Thursday Island. How could we get there? Well, there was a boat operated by a local transport firm, if we were prepared to pay the cost of chartering that – but then the wharf at Horn Island is more than six kilometres from the airstrip. And what about radio repairs? Yes, well, "Wot about it indeed, Sir?"

It looked like we were in for a weekend with nothing to do and nowhere to go. But ... good fortune! I discovered there was a light aircraft just about to leave for Port Moresby and the pilot was planning to return on Sunday afternoon. Now I knew there were a couple of good aircraft-radio repair shops in Port Moresby, and the pilot was agreeable to take the radio for me, and if it was repaired, bring it back on Sunday. (Remember, this was all happening on Friday.) So, that was the radio problem accounted for. Now, what about somewhere to sleep? Again, fortunately, the boat that had just brought the pilot and passengers for the Moresby flight over from Thursday Island was about to return there. So it looked as though our transport problem might be solved.

But where would we stay on Thursday Island? We were told that there were several Hotels and a Guest House, if we could find them. We finally chose "The Grand Hotel" (It has since been burnt to the ground — but not while we were there). The town of Thursday Island (as it was then) was one of those that had to be seen to be believed. Most of the buildings appeared to date from the very early 1900's or the Depression years of the 1930's, and from all appearances, had never had a hammer, saw, or paint-brush near them since! It could be scary to think what would happen to a place like that if a real cyclone hit the town.

We lasted one night at *The Grand* and then realised that if we were going to be here for the whole weekend we would never be able to pay the bill, even if we could get out of the place and on to Daru, in Papua New Guinea, on Monday. We eventually managed to contact the Anglican Archdeacon's wife, Mrs Fox, who, with the help of Bishop Hawkey, very graciously arranged beds for us. Suddenly our view of Thursday Island changed dramatically. Instead of being a huddle of ancient and dilapidated hovels it became another tropical island. We noticed the weather was warm and fine, the sea was a beautiful blue (but full of sharks, we were warned); we noticed the hibiscus and frangipani trees, and began to enjoy our enforced stay at this little spot.

And then to have the privilege of listening to the Church service on Sunday morning, where the Torres Strait Island people sang in beautiful harmony with nothing more than a drum for accompaniment — wow! It was some of the most beautiful singing I have ever heard. Before the service someone had tried to get them to sing with piano accompaniment, but that attempt was "dead" by comparison to the "unaccompanied" singing with just a drum to keep the right rhythm.'

On Sunday afternoon we journeyed across to Horn Island again and I hoped our friendly pilot would have a serviceable radio for me. But, after waiting for him to go through the regular procedure with Health Inspector, Customs Officer, etc., he came and handed me a note from Laurie Darrington, the MAF pilot in Port Moresby at the time. The radio was still not repaired. A technician had spent some time on it but had still not got the thing back in working order. So now we were really "sunk". Here I was with an aeroplane on Horn Island, refused permission to go any further on our journey to New Guinea without an HF radio — but that was now about two hundred miles away in Port Moresby, and no chance of another flight from there for several days. Now thoroughly disheartened I had to start thinking about making arrangements to get back to Thursday Island. Then someone suggested I make a phone call to Port Moresby. I had never thought of that. Those fancy telephone micro-wave links were still very new and I hadn't even considered such an idea. Yes. The system was now serviceable, and "in no time at all" arrangements were made for Ted Crawford to fly from Kawito to Horn Island sometime on Monday. I would then be able to fly in company with him as far as Daru — that arrangement was acceptable to the Flight Service officials in Port Moresby – and the radio for MFW (the aircraft I was flying) would be sent to Daru on a regular airline flight, so I could collect it there and all would be well. And so it was done. We finally arrived in Mount Hagen on Tuesday 27th. It had taken us a week instead of the usual two or three days.

Readers who are familiar with normal radio communication procedures will know that the registration letters "MFW" mean that the aircraft I was trying to deliver to New Guinea, therefore, had the radio call sign "Mike Foxtrot Whiskey". Within our own company we usually referred to our own aircraft by just using the last letter of the callsign. Hence in all the radio communication between the various MAF bases where there was discussion about the problems I had been having, the pilots and engineers simply referred to the aircraft as "Whiskey". They were so familiar with the International Phonetic Alphabet that they never recognised any problem with this at all. But apparently a rumour did begin to spread that Roger Young had been grounded at Horn Island because he was "Having trouble getting whiskey into New Guinea." Well, yes, it was true – sort of! But I do hope the story, whenever it was told, was done so with the appropriate touch of humour.

The return flight in Cessna 185 VH-BVJ was not without incident either. This time I had two passengers, one of whom was Rose's sister Dawne who was coming to Australia to begin her nursing career. For some reason the Customs officer at Horn Island decided to "go through everything with a fine-tooth comb". We were delayed for two or three hours at least, until suddenly he seemed to notice it was nearly four o'clock, stamped and signed the last of our papers, closed his brief case and was gone, just like that. We hurriedly threw all our things back into the suitcases, stuffed the cases back into the aircraft, scrambled into our seats and were airborne as fast as possible, heading for Coen about two hours' flying to the south. But by the time we should have arrived there I realised I must be slightly east of track and the setting sun was now hidden behind cloud, so light was fading fast. Fortunately I spotted the airport amongst the scrub and sand hills, and we were on the ground before the light had completely faded. As I disembarked from the aircraft I was greeted by a man I recognised — the ever-helpful George Anderson. George was the airport groundsman back in the days when I had been flying an aircraft out of Buka. You may remember he was the man who had returned to work late one afternoon when he realised that I was still not home and it was starting to rain. On that occasion he had sat there in his little office passing weather reports to the Flight Service operator in Rabaul just because he figured I would need to know what the weather was doing. Once again he had taken a personal interest in the progress of my flight.

"You made it, just in time." He said. "I've been listening in on the Flight Service frequency and was just about to go and get the flares out [for a night landing] when I heard the sound of your engine. So I knew you'd make it okay." When I asked about a taxi to take us into town, 14 kilometres away, he shook his head and said, "No need to worry about that. You can sleep in the little flat we have here. It's supposed to be for DCA staff when they visit, but I can let you use it for one night." This was still the same George Anderson – always thoughtful and willing to go way beyond the call of duty. The world would be a better place if we had more men like that.

When my two passengers crawled into their beds they seemed to go to sleep very quickly, but I sat at the table for another couple of hours working on my flight plan for the next two days. Obviously, because of our unexpected delays at Horn Island, we could not make it to Ballarat by Friday night but, in spite of that, the next two days of flying – Longreach, Bourke (overnight), and then to Ballarat, were without incident.

You may remember that we had left Port Moresby in December – which is the official "start-of-wet-season" month. Shortly after we had left there was a very heavy rainstorm, and the shed where our boxes and drums had been stored – well, ... when someone thought to check our boxes it was discovered that they had been sitting in "several inches of water." So they, very thoughtfully, lifted the boxes and stacked them on top of the drums. Of course the drums were perfectly watertight (that's why most missionaries pack their goods into drums whenever they move to a new location). But all those boxes stayed there in Port Moresby, in the steamy tropical heat, for several months before it was definitely decided that we would not be going to Indonesia. They were then all shipped to Ballarat. When we opened those boxes – phew!! It was just stinking black mould. Bed and bathroom linen, tablecloths, books ... everything virtually fell apart in our hands. All of the contents were consigned to the November 5th Guy Fawkes Night community bonfire we had at the airport that year.

But there were blessings as well, wonderful blessings, such as the encouragement of receiving a letter from a previously unknown friend who was moved by God to get up at 1 o'clock in the morning to pray for us and to write to us. And the teenage boy whose Sunday School teacher had given each member of her class ten cents. Like the men who had been given the talents in the parable Jesus told, she had suggested that they see what they could do — "build on it, use it to earn more money so you have something to give to others". By the time he decided to give it to us it had grown to several dollars. He did not know that just that very morning we had realised we did not have enough money to buy the petrol we needed to drive home to Ballarat. What a very precious and timely gift! And another day Rose went to buy warm pyjamas for the two boys but found she only had enough money for one pair. When we returned home we found a gift waiting for us — there was more than enough money to buy the second pair of PJ's.

Amongst the blessings we received at the hand of God was a prolific garden. I doubt that we have ever had such good crops either before or since. It seemed that everything we planted flourished, even to the two fruit trees in the backyard. We were living in House 5 on Ballarat Airport and there was one plum tree and one peach tree in the backyard, but neighbours warned us that these trees never bore any fruit. Undaunted we still pruned them during the winter months and during spring-time Rose went around pollinating the blossom flowers with a small paint-brush. We had such an abundant crop of peaches that it almost broke the branches off the tree.

During our stay in Ballarat, which spanned two winters, we were given or loaned all the warm clothing we needed, even to the luxury of an electric blanket, which in the cold damp of a Ballarat winter (especially in those draughty and poorly-insulated Airport houses), was almost an essential – especially after several years in the Tropics. But, in spite of the cold and wet winter weather, I was appreciating the regular meal times made possible because of the regular and consistent hours of work as a maintenance engineer, instead of the very irregular hours and often very long and sometimes stressful days (sometimes without any opportunity to stop for a meal or a drink) that had been a normal feature of everyday life as a pilot in Papua New Guinea.

Nevertheless, when in July 1973 we were asked if we would be prepared to take on a short-term assignment of six to nine months flying on Bougainville, we both agreed that we would be happy to go. The work on Bougainville had now developed to the extent that it involved two (soon to become three) Cessna 185 aircraft and scheduled (RPT) flights with a twin-engine 10-seat Britten-Norman *Islander* aircraft. But the final outcome of this decision to return to the tropics was to bring changes that we could have never imagined.

Once again our journey between Australia and New Guinea would be in a little MAF Cessna. For our family the idea of travelling in a big jet airliner was the exception rather than the rule. But this time, just for variety, I diverted from the normal route of Bourke, Charleville, Normanton, and instead chose to travel via Broken Hill and Birdsville to Normanton, sharing the flying with our newest candidate pilot Leo Hume. Alex Jardine, who was still the manager of MAF-AIR Services in Ballarat, was also travelling with us. I will let Rose describe the flight as she wrote in a letter to her parents:

> "We left Ballarat at 7:20 am [on Wednesday 13th August] and our first stop was at Broken Hill for fuel, and then it was on to Birdsville. Broken Hill to Birdsville was very interesting: one of our landmarks was supposed to be the airstrip at Tibooburra, but when we got to the place where we expected to find it there were three airfields, all with two runways in the form of an X. Altogether there must have been one runway for every resident in the area. Leo finally did identify one building with the name painted in large letters on the roof, so we were then satisfied that we had found the correct airfield. Then out in the desert we saw several nicely laid-out airstrips but not a sign of life anywhere in any direction as far as the eye could see.
>
> "The ground (sand, soil, earth – call it what you like) was a fantastic sight, colour wise. From the air it looked like a beach where the tide has gone miles out – all ridges, which varied from bright orange, with the hollows definitely maroon, to pinkish-red ridges with purple hollows, and odd patches of greys, blues, mauves – NO green or brown, or any of the colours we usually expect, and no trees at all. We could have been on another planet it was so completely different from anything I had ever seen before. Then we followed the mighty Cooper Creek and after that more desert through to Birdsville – all of ten houses there; lots of birds, flies, and dust . . . and tracks leading away from the place in all directions. It looked desolate and lonely. Birdsville, as you probably know, was so named by early explorers because of the prolific bird life they found there.
>
> "We were half an hour on the ground there and then took off for Cloncurry. But when we had almost reached Cloncurry the pilots decided that we were making good time and still had enough fuel to go on to Normanton, at the bottom of Cape York Peninsular.

"We had taken off before the sun had risen this morning and we saw it set before we landed at Normanton. [My log book shows that Leo logged eight hours' flying, I logged two hours - a total of ten hours in the air, with two stops along the way.] Our two boys were surprisingly good all the way."

[In later years we often gave our children a map so that they could follow the progress of the flight - and check on Dad's navigation, perhaps (?)]

"The Motel at Normanton was full so we were obliged to go to the Hotel – a rare old place ... up three flights of stairs to the first floor. Our room had double doors from the passage into it and double doors opening out onto the veranda – no windows, no mosquito wire, no mozzie nets. It was far too hot and stuffy to leave the doors shut, so we had to leave them open and the boys were soon covered in bites (which all turned into big red itchy lumps and lasted for a couple of days at least).

"We went to the Café next door for tea – another 'Outback Special'! Two of us ordered cold meat and salad, the other two ordered ham and eggs, while the two boys had sandwiches. After waiting about twenty minutes, and drinking a couple of cold drinks each and admiring the Aboriginal children customers, a chap came out from somewhere beyond the counter and said to the man behind the counter, "What will I do with these meals?" The reply was, "Serve them, of course!" And so we finally got our meals.

"We left the hotel at 6.30 next morning and were airborne at 7.10. The sun was just up then. Our first stop was at the one-time Presbyterian mission station of Aurukun, 50 kilometres south of Weipa. Our friend Frank White had recommended that we call in. Frank was an aircraft engineer who was working in the hangar at Ballarat at the time, and he had once worked at Aurukun. Also Alex Jardine, as elder of a Presbyterian church, which had provided some support for the work here, was also interested to see the place. We refuelled there, also had a cup of tea and a quick tour around the "station". All in all this had taken just over one hour, and it was then on to Horn Island where we cleared Customs at midday and then to Daru.

"We had been enjoying perfect weather until we reached Horn Island, but it got worse as we flew across Torres Strait, until we were dodging around rain showers and low cloud. However, we eventually found Daru and did our inwards Customs processing there, we also refuelled, and then took-off into the murk. We dodged around cloud build-ups and finally managed to get on top of the cloud and set a compass course for Mount Hagen."

What Rose did not know, although I would have explained this to Leo, was that there are two almost permanent build-ups of cumulonimbus cloud in this part of the country. One is over Kikori, and the other is over Mount Murray, which is just to the east of the APCM mission station and airstrip at Samberigi. Once past the Samberigi-Erave area it is often possible to get down below the cloud and fly in to Mount Hagen, either through the Ialibu basin or to track east of Mount Ialibu and follow the Kaugel River, and then via Kauapena and the Kuta Ridge in to Mt Hagen.

"When Roger got to the point where he thought we should be almost over Samberigi he called on the Mission Radio frequency to ask for a weather report as it was now just after 4 o'clock, the start of an APCM radio *sched.* The folk at Samberigi reported that they could hear an aeroplane overhead, so we figured it was almost certainly us. It took them five minutes to run outside and take a look at the weather to the north, but by that time we could see Samberigi on one side of the aircraft and Erave out the other side. We finally arrived in Hagen just before 5 pm.

"We had tea with Gloria Penberthy and her mother (who was visiting for six to eight weeks) and stayed the night with Rob and Sandra Willis Jones, who had just arrived in Hagen one week before. We had a lovely sleep. We needed it!!

"When we arrived at the hangar at 8 am next morning we found that the aircraft we were to take to Kieta was still not ready, so we did not get away until 11:30. This did not give us enough daylight for the six-and one-half hour flight over to Kieta, so we knew we would almost certainly be spending the night in Rabaul. Then, when we stopped for fuel at Talasea a Government LandRover pulled up and out stepped Ian Warner. Ian had been a fellow student in Bible College when we were there in 1964, so it was a pleasant surprise to see him – wow, the people you meet when you think you are so far from home you couldn't possibly find a soul you would know.

When we finally arrived at Kieta at midday on Saturday it may have been the start of yet another adventure for us, but it was also the conclusion of a most interesting journey. We had flown over and contemplated the incredible barrenness of some of the Australian desert; we had flown along mountain valleys in the highlands of New Guinea; we had dodged around rain showers over a dull grey-green tropical sea; we had seen one of those huge oil-tanker ships leaving a dead-straight wake behind it in the sea between New Ireland and Bougainville. And now here we were at Kieta, and since the advent of the Bougainville Copper mine at Panguna, were about to begin the process of discovering a completely different social environment from that we had known when we lived at Hutjena (Buka) only five years previously.

In her letter Rose expressed amazement at the fact that she could now pick up a telephone and dial Australia direct. This was such a huge change from the situation we had known back in 1968 when such a thing was unheard of and 'telephone' calls around Bougainville had used HF radio links, so virtually anyone on the island could be listening to everything you said.

Chapter Seventeen

CULTURE SHOCK

Almost everybody who has ever travelled overseas or who has lived and worked with people whose cultural and social norms are different from their own must be aware of the term "culture shock". But in no way do I wish to give any impression that people are in the wrong just because their ideas are different from ours. On the contrary, in many cases we discovered that the Melanesian people of Papua New Guinea held to value systems which were better than those of the industrialised and materialistic society where we had spent our childhood.

Rose and I celebrated our first wedding anniversary with a holiday as guests of John and Ann Hitchen at Christian Leaders Training College (CLTC), near Banz in the highlands of New Guinea. In those days the Highlands Highway, from Lae on the coast through to the many growing towns in the highland valleys, was still a bit of a novelty. From what we had been told this "highway" had only been opened in 1964. This was now 1967 and, although the highway was a road, of sorts, it was still only a gravel surface and subject to frequent closure due to land-slips.

Anyway, Rose and I decided we would like to do a shopping trip to the town at Mount Hagen, so we hired a vehicle from CLTC. Two elderly ladies who were also visiting the college asked if they could come with us, for the scenic ride. Those who know this highway in its present form may be interested to know that the road we used was along the northern edge of the Wahgi Valley – the road on the southern side of the valley (site of the present highway) was either non-existent or usable only for all-wheel-drive tractors. About half-way in to town we came across a utility stopped on the side of the road, so I stopped to see if there might be anything I could do to help. The driver of the stranded vehicle was a New Guinean man, but before I even had a chance to speak to him another vehicle stopped. Driver leaps out and demands, "Wassa matter?" To which the New Guinean replies, "*Ensin e dai, masta.* (The engine stopped, sir)". "Oh. You run outta petrol?" With that, the "helper" turns on the ignition key, watches the fuel gauge and then angrily says, "Look at that, you fool. You're out of petrol!" Tapping his finger on the glass of the fuel gauge he adds, "What does this mean? See that … what does that 'E' there mean?" The stranded driver, anxious to defend his sense of dignity, replies, "It means '*benzine Enuf*' (enough*) masta.*" The "helper" (who may possibly have been his employer) turns on him (rather unkindly, I thought) and continues, "Okay, smart-alec!!" And then pointing to the "F" at the other end of the dial, growls, "So what does this mean?" "It means '*benzine Finish*', *masta.*" The helper throws up his hands in an expression of despair and stomps back to his own vehicle. Then, as a parting gesture, shouts at the poor stranded driver, "I'll send someone out with a can of petrol for you!" and drives off.

Why is it that people of my race so often behave in such an arrogant manner? Why couldn't he just throw his arm over the shoulder of the stranded driver and, with good natured humour, say something like, "So sorry, my friend. Good try – ***very*** good try! But you guessed wrong." And then explain that the "E" is for Empty and the "F" means Full.

A few days later we were invited to fly (as passengers) over to Goroka as Laurie Darrington, who at the time was the MAF pilot in Hagen, was going down to collect a new vehicle and he thought we might enjoy the opportunity to have a close look at the country alongside the highway. And so it was that a few days later we were in the passenger terminal building at Goroka airport. Nothing unusual about that, but suddenly Rose grabbed my arm, "Roger. Look … look at that!" There, walking across the tarmac, having just disembarked from an aircraft, came two men … dark suits, crisp white shirts, both wearing a tie. We probably would not have even noticed them if we were in Melbourne. But here … surrounded by dozens of people wearing genuine traditional tribal attire (very little) – bare-breasted women casually breast-feeding their infant children as they had done for countless generations … those two businessmen looked like a couple of penguins who had just arrived on a flight from Antarctica. They looked so out of place, and perhaps we hadn't realised, until then, the extent to which we were happy to accept the scene within the terminal building as perfectly normal, and hence perfectly acceptable.

The craziness of my own culture, in this regard, was reinforced to me many years later when we were living back in Australia. We were attending a Baptist church, and as a friend of ours was to be baptized that morning, I had been asked to go to the Manse, next door to the church, and ensure that all was in order with the room where our friend expected to get dressed again after the baptism. When I entered the house I discovered, to my surprise, a young mother who seemed to be in a bit of a panic. She had also just come from the church building and was desperate to find a room with a lockable door where she might sit and breast-feed her baby. To me, this was a form of "culture shock." I had just recently returned from a country where most of the women would unconcernedly nurse (to use the American term) their babies in church, in the market place, and even while riding as passengers in aircraft. What was wrong with the people of "my" culture?

Back in the 1960's there were many parts of the country where people still lived in what had been a traditional lifestyle for countless generations. And of course this affected the clothing they wore – or didn't wear. This was most noticeable in areas of the West Sepik and in particular some outstations around the Telefomin area such as Miyanmin. On one occasion one of our MAF engineers had arranged to take his wife and family in to Telefomin but on the flight in from Wewak the plane had to make a stop at Miyanmin.

As they were on final approach to land the wife suddenly began to wonder how her two young daughters, who were also on board the aircraft, would react after they had landed. She knew that at this location they would see women whose clothing consisted of little more than a brief grass skirt, and men whose only attire was a small penis gourd, held neatly in place with a length of thin vine tied around their hips. But she need not have worried at all. After the aircraft was safely in the parking bay she heard one of her daughters squeal with laughter, "Hey. Look at that man with the funny hat!"

It had been the practice of many Patrol Officers to nominate one village elder as the community leader, and his position of office was thereafter indicated by the wearing of a special hat provided by the Australian Administration.

Not the same airstrip, but I have included this photo just to show the type of hat which caught the children's attention

It is beautiful the way children can so often accept cultural differences without any nonsense. But many adults seem to react very differently.

I had taken the dentist, from Wewak, in to spend the day at Telefomin. On the way home we had to make a call in to Miyanmin. Now I need to digress briefly and explain that although nowadays it is normal for torch batteries to be encased in a thin layer of plastic (to provide electrical insulation), back in the 1950's it was normal for Eveready batteries to be protected with heavy cardboard. The standard "D size" torch battery-cell was provided with a solid tube of hard cardboard about 2 or 3 mm in thickness.

Obviously someone who had visited this area had at some point in time used equipment powered by one or more of these torch batteries. Once the battery had been discarded one of the local gentry had obviously discovered it, and realised that the cardboard tube would make a very neat modern-looking replacement for his penis-gourd. As soon as my Dentist passenger realised what the man was wearing he laughed out loud and ran back to the aeroplane to grab his camera. Unfortunately his potential photographic subject, having realised that his new "high-tech" clothing may have been the subject of the visitor's humour, turned and walked towards the jungle. The dentist in his haste to get a photograph dropped a piece from his camera and we spent the next half-hour scratching through the grass looking, unsuccessfully, for it.

Over the next few years we saw many changes in what was considered acceptable behaviour and clothing styles, especially with those who moved to live or work in the major towns. The young man whom we "inherited" as our house-help person when we moved to Port Moresby told us that he spent all of his spare time at the movie theatre, so he could learn more about Australia. With some evidence of pride in his achievement he said, "*Mi save olgeta long Gene Autry*." (I know all about Gene Autry). We hastened to tell him that Gene Autry did not live in Australia, and the places and activities he saw in those movies were not what he would see if he ever visited Australia. I am not sure that he was convinced. And it wasn't long before we were hearing stories of armed hold-ups and highway robbery modelled on the scenes from those "benign" and "harmless" cowboy western movies.

In regard to the clothing styles, I began to wonder if there may be some hint of denial of their own cultural background when, at the Goroka Show in 1979, we noticed some of the performers whose supposedly traditional attire included things like leather work boots, sunglasses, "grass" skirts made of plastic and other touches which definitely looked as though they had been imported from another culture.

A highly respected anthropologist told us that he also had noted these changes and when he asked some of the women from his area why they didn't just dress the same as they would if they were back in their home village, he was told, "We have no problem in our home village, but the way the young men look at us when we come to these big gatherings makes us feel very uncomfortable. Never again will we wear true traditional clothing when we come to places like this." In some parts of the country, in their traditional culture, a man who stared lecherously at any woman could find himself facing a death penalty. So, in many cases the sense of culture shock being experienced by the Papua New Guinean people was possibly worse than anything we might have thought was worth complaining about.

Not long after we had moved to Anguganak I was given the opportunity of speaking at church services in the surrounding villages. So on one Sunday afternoon we accompanied Austin Roach on the forty-five minute hike to the village of Wulukum, the first stage of which involved a walk through thigh-deep water to cross the Opan River, which runs alongside the airstrip. By the time we arrived at the village we were all pouring perspiration. Melanesian hospitality made us feel very welcome and we were given a green coconut – the cool liquid that it contained was very refreshing.

These people had no concept of clock-time. For them the day started when it was light enough to see and ended when it became dark at sunset, and church simply started when enough people had arrived. Instead of a church bell one of the village elders took hold of a heavy shaft of wood and began rhythmically thumping this against the side of a hollow log. The noise travels well throughout the rainforest and for all of their known history these people had used similar log-drums (known as a *garamut*) for sending messages.

The church building, perhaps big enough for 40 people, was, like our house at Anguganak, made of bush materials that had never been through a sawmill or known the touch of a smoothing plane. The "pews" were split logs supported at each end on a short stump. Men sat on the right and women on the left – the idea of husband and wife sitting together accompanied by their children had not yet become acceptable to these people.

As soon as she was seated Rose found that she had a companion – one of the senior women from the village sat herself down on the log beside her, in fact pressed right up against her. This wonderful lady then spent the entire service swatting at mosquitoes and making sure that any fleas or other such "bities" that crawled onto Rose's feet were dealt with and despatched before they could possibly bite her. The unwritten message was, "We appreciate you and for that reason we will look after you and will do all we can to make certain you suffer no undue discomfort when you come to visit with us." It was only after we had finished the Communion Service that we discovered the woman beside Rose had leprosy.

When we were living on Bougainville in 1968 I was asked to do a flight one Sunday to take Bishop Brian Sides down to Rotokas. The people there were planning a special thanksgiving church service to recognise the work done by Skip Furchow in translating the Bible into their own language. Normally we tried to avoid accepting flight bookings on a Sunday, but this was a special occasion.

We arrived at the Rotokas airstrip midmorning and then, after a fairly long church service, had a fairly long walk down to the village where the local people were preparing a huge feast. By the time we arrived at the village I was beginning to feel very thirsty and was impolite enough to ask Skip if I could possibly have a drink of something – anything to quench the thirst. I was politely told that the people nearly had everything ready and if I could just wait a little bit longer then everything would be done decently and in order. I looked at the rows of blackened meat, roasted on open fires and now being laid out along the ground on banana-palm leaves. Apart from the native vegetables, which had mostly been cooked in a *mumu*, we saw the charred evidence of pig, possum, and flying fox on the meat menu. My stomach heaved in protest and I repeated my request for something to drink, please. A green coconut was produced and I drank from that. Thank you very much!

Soon everything was ready. Excited talking and shouts went out and those who had not been involved in the preparations now gathered to share the feast. A prayer of thanks was offered, after which it was "Everybody, help yourself." I'm sorry. But I tend to be a bit picky about my food sometimes and from what I had seen of the preparations I did not want to admit that I felt hungry at all. But then, before I had any time to decide whether I just might try some of this bush-tucker, the local Pastor came over to me, took me by the arm and said, very quietly, "We have prepared something special for you folk over in this house here." And he led us all into a well-designed and well-built village dwelling. There he had laid out a linen tablecloth, plates and cups made of delicate china, jugs of cool refreshing *mouli* juice, and the most delicious tender roast chicken I have ever tasted!

Words failed me! How does one adequately express thanks in a situation like that? I felt not just humbled, but shamed by my own snobbishness. My mind went back to a skit from one of my favourite radio comedy shows. After Stan Freberg had interviewed a rather unpleasant character, Peggy Taylor had commented, "Gee, Stan. He didn't even open the door when he left!" And Stan had replied, "That's okay Peggy. Men like that don't need to. They are so low they just slide out underneath!"

My experiences of mild culture shock extended to dealing with missionaries who came from different cultural backgrounds and who were troubled by things that I considered perfectly normal, or those for whom English was only a third or fourth language. It took a lot of self-control to remember that I needed to use *Tok Pisin* when talking with some of these folk as they had such a limited understanding of English. And I possibly offended many of my German friends when I spoke to them on the radio by using their first names. This is a normal level of familiarity in my own culture, but I later learned that most of the German (Lutheran) missionaries referred to each other by the use of surnames only, especially when talking on the radio.

Another experience of culture shock added considerably to Rose's trauma over the birth of our first child. In those days many of the natives believed that the woman contributed little to the birth of a child – she was merely the incubator in which the foetus developed. It was the responsibility of the man to provide sufficient "material" to ensure that a proper child would be produced. But in the event that a child was born with any sort of deformity then it was probably the woman's fault because she didn't know how to "do it" properly. So when Rose appeared in the main street of Wewak with a child who had a minor deformity of the top lip she had reason to feel very uncomfortable very quickly. Although she could not understand one word of what the young men were saying, she knew from the leering looks and crude laughter that they were making some very unkind remarks about her. Emotionally it was an extremely painful experience for her.

Chapter Eighteen

"WHATEVER YOU ASK ..."

"[*Jesus said*] ... *And I will do whatever you ask in my name ...*"
John 14:13 (NIV)

It all started out so innocently. We were enjoying a day-off and sitting on the beach near Kieta, on the island of Bougainville, when one of my friends asked me, "Roger. If money was not a factor what would you really like to be doing?"

Well, knowing that, at that point in time, Australian MAF had no radio technicians and we seemed to be forever having problems with our radio equipment, I replied by saying, "What I would really like to do would be to take leave of absence for two years so that I could then go somewhere and study and get the necessary experience to be able to fix some of our radio problems." Having said that, I put the idea aside, knowing that what I had suggested was somewhere beyond the impossible. The year was 1973.

We had left Port Moresby, as planned, in December 1971, and had begun to prepare for our expected move to Kupang in Timor. That move never eventuated – for several reasons.

Firstly, in order to obtain visas to work in Indonesia we needed chest X-rays for all four of us – Rose, myself, and our two boys, David and Stuart. However the radiologist in Auckland, who took the X-rays, told us there was a shadow on David's chest X-ray. A course of antibiotics and repeated X-ray photographs several weeks later showed that the shadow was still there. And the radiologist assured us that if the Indonesian authorities needed chest X-rays before they would issue a work-permit for us to enter their country then we could be quite certain we would not get a visa on the strength of that shadow on David's film.

In addition to the problem of David's chest X-rays I had suffered from recurring tonsillitis for many months during the latter part of our time in Port Moresby. So a doctor-surgeon friend of mine, John Mandeno, who had been our family doctor since my childhood and whom I had also known in the role of Sunday School teacher and Scout Master, admitted me to hospital and removed my tonsils. Based on his own experience working as a mission doctor in Indonesia he strongly advised, on the basis of my health, that we should not go ahead with our plans to move to Kupang, and he even wrote a letter to MAF expressing his concern in this regard. So, after a few weeks holiday in New Zealand, we moved back to Ballarat (Australia) where I worked as an engineer in the MAF-AIR Services hangar for something like 18 months. We then moved to Kieta, on Bougainville, where I was flying with Bougainville Air Services, a subsidiary company of MAF, which is how we happened to be on a beach in Bougainville when my friend asked that strange question, and is about where this adventure started.

Incidentally, the mystery of that shadow on David's chest X-ray has never been resolved. While we were in Ballarat later that year Rose had taken David to a doctor and asked if he would arrange for another chest X-ray, purely to see whether or not the shadow was still there. The doctor virtually confiscated the X-ray prints and did not cooperate in arranging for any further X-ray to be taken. When we tried again, a couple of years later, to investigate this mysterious shadow we were told curtly that the original prints had been destroyed. We were, understandably, annoyed. Admittedly it was by now just pure curiosity to know whether or not that mystery shadow was still evident – since, in effect, it had been a factor in a major decision which we had had to make. But, regardless of what happened to those prints, that decision just may have saved my life.

We had moved to Bougainville as a temporary appointment, just for a few months so that two other pilots could consecutively take some holidays (furlough). By mid January 1974 our time on Bougainville was complete. We were then asked to consider moving to Mt Hagen, where there was need for an engineer to help setup a new maintenance workshop, since MAF were in the process of moving their PNG headquarters from Wewak, on the north coast, to Mt Hagen. This was a sensible move since Mount Hagen was a far more central location and the work in PNG was expanding rapidly.

We agreed to this move on the condition that we could make a brief visit to Melbourne, as our son David was due for a check-up at the Royal Children's Hospital. This was a necessary follow-up to do with the surgery he had when he was about 12 months old. And we also needed to collect a few more of our belongings, since we had moved to Kieta with just the very minimum for survival. So arrangements were duly made for this brief trip back to Australia. But as it happened the next few weeks turned out to be a real obstacle course. In some ways it seemed to resemble those Confidence Courses they put you through at Teen Missions Boot Camp, or even at a Military Training course.

Making appointments for David at the Children's Hospital in Melbourne was no problem, and we were given dates in May (1974). But then there was discussion, at MAF management level, about our travel arrangements. There was one aged Cessna 185 aircraft which was nearly due for a visit to Ballarat where it would be given a good overhaul – in fact it was the same aircraft I had flown to Ballarat back in 1966, just the week before our wedding. But it was not really due to go to Ballarat for another few weeks. So there was much discussion as to whether I should fly this aircraft down, or whether we should just make a booking and travel by Airlines.

In the midst of this confusion we heard that Laurie Darrington's mother had died, suddenly, and he, understandably, headed off to New Zealand leaving the Port Moresby base without a pilot. The only pilot who was properly qualified to "fill-in", and to operate the Port Moresby program in Laurie's absence was me. No other pilot, at that point in time, was familiar with the areas east of Port Moresby. So, on April 24th we, as a family, moved to Port Moresby, with about one day's notice. We did not have to take much in the way of personal belongings with us for this was only a temporary move and we were to be accommodated in the MAPANG guest house in Boroko, a suburb of Port Moresby.

For family reasons Laurie had to delay his return from New Zealand, so I had to remain at Port Moresby for longer than originally expected. Rather than try to change David's appointments at the Children's Hospital in Melbourne, we purchased Airline tickets for Rose, David, and Stuart. We had now also been told I would definitely not be taking the Cessna 185 VH-MFB down to Ballarat. And so, because Rose, with the two boys, would be entitled to a greater airline luggage allowance than I would have on my own, we decided that I should be left with just the bare minimum of luggage and Rose and the two boys would take almost all of our gear with them.

I well remember the day: It was Sunday, and at midday I was at the airport terminal where I had waved farewell to Rose and the two boys. I then drove back to the MAPANG missionary guest home and almost as I walked in the door the telephone rang. It was a call for me – to advise that a decision had finally been made. I would fly VH-MFB down to Ballarat, "leaving on Wednesday" that is, three days time!

"Oh, great!" I said. "I have only just got back from saying goodbye to Rose and the boys, and they have taken all of my Australian aeronautical charts in their luggage! I thought this flight was definitely off."

"Ah-h-h, well … we'll find some more charts for you – somewhere."

And there was another problem – the week in which I now had to get myself to Mount Hagen was the beginning of school holidays and there were no spare seats on the regular airline flights. No worries, I thought. I will contact my good friend Max Garlick – if anyone can get me a seat on a flight to Mount Hagen he can. And so I left that "little problem" with my friend Max.

Oh what a day! Tuesday 1st May 1974. My flight commitments for the day involved six landings with more than four-and-a-half hours time in the air. And I had to be back in Port Moresby very soon after midday so I could, hopefully, get a seat on a flight to Mount Hagen, ready to leave there at first light on Wednesday. As you can imagine, on that Tuesday morning I was airborne as soon as it was officially daylight, about 6 am.

My furthest away point form Port Moresby was KaloKalo, but when I landed there I learned that they had a full load to go back to Salamo. Why was that a problem? Well KaloKalo is a one-way airstrip, and there was a fairly strong southeasterly wind blowing, so I could only get airborne off the KaloKalo airstrip with a half load in the aircraft. Well, with hindsight, I agree that I may have made a wrong decision, but I was really feeling under pressure about the time. I told the missionary that I could only take half of the load he had ready for Salamo and I did not have enough time to do a second KaloKalo to Salamo flight. As it turned out, we probably spent so much time messing about and re-organising the load that it would have been less time-consuming to have done that second flight. As it was, I left that airstrip feeling very "stressed" and also left a rather unhappy customer! Sorry fellas! But that's the way it is sometimes. Nobody is infallible!

When I finally got back to Port Moresby I quickly parked the aircraft in its hangar and ran down to the main terminal building. A quick check of the entire building soon revealed that there was no sign of the "amazing Max Garlick".

To add to my growing consternation I heard an announcement over the PA system advising passengers that seat allocation on the flight to Mt Hagen would be "closing shortly". I was almost in a panic. "Why didn't you organise this yourself?" I chided myself for having been so foolish as to leave such an important task to someone else who was, as I well knew, a very busy man. And then that fateful announcement, which I did not want to hear: "Seat allocations on Flight 'xyz' to Mt Hagen are now closed."

"Oh. You fool Roger! Why..." But then, in his inimitable manner, Max suddenly came into view, heading straight for the Airline counter. I ran across to him. "They have already closed seat allocation for the flight." I gasped. He looked at me, like a magician teasing his audience, and with a flick of his head that said, "follow me" continued his march to the Airline counter. Well, one thing I do have to admit – that man had a lot of friends in a lot of useful places. I was issued with a boarding pass, my luggage was checked-in and I was directed to a boarding gate. Wonderful! Why did I ever get in such a panic? The plane from Brisbane was late, and so seats, which had been allocated for some passengers booked through from that flight were available.

But, once on board the airplane for Mt Hagen and securely strapped into my seat, we were greeted with a cheerful announcement over the cabin PA system: “Good afternoon. This is your captain speaking. It will be a few minutes before we depart. The plane from Brisbane has just landed and we will be waiting for a passenger from that flight.” I looked around the aircraft cabin. There was not an empty seat anywhere. I slid down and tried to hide behind the seat in front of me.

After the expected delay, now one of the flight attendants is walking down the aisle. Behind her is a young teenage schoolboy. She is obviously looking for an empty seat. Now feeling very guilty I slunk even lower into my seat. But before she even got to my row she stopped and spoke to a young mother. “I know you booked a seat for your child,” she said, “But he is young enough to be allowed to sit on your lap. If you would be good enough to cooperate it would allow this boy to get home to his parents. I will arrange a refund of the money you paid for the extra ticket.” Great! At least the boy now had a seat. But I still felt sort of guilty.

The flight to Mt Hagen was a direct run of something less than one-and-a-half hours in the Fokker Friendship and was without further incident.

When I walked into the passenger terminal in Mt Hagen one of our pilots, Graham Goss, was there to meet me. “Your plane is already fuelled and loaded,” he said, “I have checked the weather reports for you. Kawito is fine with blue sky, and Graham and Jenny Brice are happy for you to spend the night there with them. It will save you any risk of fog delaying your departure out of here tomorrow morning. So, if you want to get away from here right away, here is a copy of the flight plan I have already prepared for you. ”

Well. Thank you Graham! I gladly accepted the offer of an immediate departure. Fog could be a problem in Mt Hagen and sometimes the morning fog would not clear until about 9am. So, having left Port Moresby early that morning, and having flown just a little more than six hours for the day (not counting the time in the Fokker F27), I spent the night of May 1st at Kawito. And I had been provided with a set of Aeronautical charts covering the eastern half of Australia. I didn't ask where they came from. I was just very grateful that somebody had found them, somewhere.

Next morning, after a routine departure from Kawito, I cleared Customs at Daru and flew on across Torres Strait to Horn Island. In my experience in the past, Customs procedures at Horn Island had usually been fairly straightforward. There was a routine check of documentation but all the other formalities were completed in Melbourne after the aircraft finally arrived in Ballarat. But for some reason on this occasion the officer at Horn Island insisted that I must proceed to Cairns and complete the formalities with the Customs officer there. This to me was quite a frustration. Usually on these flights it is possible to make the entire journey from the south coast of PNG and right through to Ballarat in just two days. But this diversion into Cairns would not only cost me valuable time (and possibly make it a three-day flight) it could also increase my chances of running into problems with the weather. Because Cairns is on the coast it was possible that I may have problems with cloud build-up along the Great Dividing Range when I tried to head back inland to pick-up the more direct route to Ballarat.

Nevertheless, I submitted a new flight plan and eventually landed at Cairns. As it turned out, the Customs officer there was busy when I arrived. He was involved with clearing an international airline flight and would come and attend to matters with me as soon as he had finished that task. It was nearly two hours before I saw him. He took one look at the aircraft I was flying and said something like, "Don't you blokes normally get all your paperwork done in Melbourne?" I agreed that was the normal procedure. "Then why did you bother to call on me?" he asked. I explained that it was purely because the officer in Horn Island had insisted that I do so. But, no – my documentation was no business of his. By now I was running short of daylight and was not anxious to spend the night in Cairns. It would be impossible to reach Ballarat the next day if that happened. So I quickly did some navigation sums, submitted yet another flight plan and departed Cairns, feeling very fed-up with the turn of events. I landed at Ingham just before last light.

At Ingham I got talking to the pilot of a crop-spraying aircraft. He offered me a ride into town, dropped me off at a Motel and assured me he would pick me up at about 5.30 next morning, as he also was hoping to get airborne at first-light. I wondered – will he remember? Can I trust his memory?

Next morning at 5.30 the sun had still not appeared over the eastern horizon but I was out there standing by the side of the road, waiting. "Will that guy turn-up, or should I call a taxi?" Why had I doubted his word? About 100 yards down the road was a telephone box. I looked at my watch. It was now getting light enough to be wishing I was already in my aircraft with the engine running. I debated in my own mind, "Should I continue to wait, or should I go and 'phone for a taxi?" "But," I told myself, "As sure as I leave here and walk to that phone box that Ag pilot will turn up."

"No. He must have forgotten me. It's way past first light. I'd better go and phone for a taxi." So, somewhat reluctantly leaving my suitcase unattended on the side of the road, I ran toward the telephone box. But before I had covered half the distance the "toot" of a car horn drew my attention. Sure enough, there in the driveway of the Motel was the utility from the aerial spraying company. I turned and ran back.

The poor fellow was full of apologies. "I clean forgot about you," he confessed, "but then when I saw your plane at the strip I remembered. So I came back to get you." Well, that was a very generous act. This guy had now made himself late in departing for his day of work, just so he could keep his word to a total stranger. His thoughtfulness was very much appreciated.

Fortunately the weather was fine and I had no trouble crossing the range as I headed inland, first right across to Longreach and then south to Charleville and Bourke. But it was a long day. My log book shows an entry for 10 hours and 20 mins flying.

Nevertheless, in spite of the late start, I made it right through to Ballarat before it got dark. Alex Jardine was there to meet me and after the usual greetings and technical questions about the aircraft I had just delivered, he looked at his watch and said, "There is a train leaving for Melbourne in about 15 minutes. If you hurry and get your things I will drive you in to town and you should be able to catch that train. When you get to Melbourne take a suburban train to Dandenong. Rose has phoned to say that she will be waiting for you on the platform at Dandenong Station." And so I made it, and Rose and the boys were there to meet me.

Early the following week I contacted the MAF office in Box Hill. "Do you know of any doctors in the Melbourne area who are knowledgeable about tropical things?" I asked. I had a strange looking infection on my foot, and suspected that it may be some weird tropical fungus. I was given the name of a Dr Inches and duly made an appointment to see him. The infection on the foot turned out to be a non-issue – merely a variation of something like tinia. No problem. But I did have another question, which in my ignorance was not a great cause of concern to me. It involved a spot on my back just near my right kidney. A mole, which had been there for years, had recently begun to persistently leave spots of blood on my clothing. The doctor took one look at the spot and asked if I could possibly wait until he had dealt with his other patients. He said the spot needed to be removed and sent away for analysis (biopsy). I agreed to his advice and the minor surgical procedure was carried out later that afternoon. A further appointment was then arranged for the following Wednesday, by which time the results of those tests should be available. These arrangements were all fine by me as we were planning to leave for our return to PNG the day after the planned follow-up appointment.

It was raining as we loaded the car for the drive to Ballarat that Wednesday morning and the rain continued to get heavier as, with windscreen wipers on full speed, we slowly and carefully picked our way through the streets of Melbourne and on to the Western Highway. For some reason the doctor's receptionist had telephoned us at Caldermeade, where we had been staying with Rose's parents, to advise that my appointment time had been changed from 10 am to 3:30 pm. So we simply altered our plans and decided to drive through to Ballarat and leave some of our luggage there and also to check that the aeroplane I was to fly back to Papua New Guinea was in fact ready to go. This meant a trip of something like 200 kilometres, or more, to Ballarat, west of Melbourne, and then 150 kilometres back to Forest Hill, a suburb on the eastern outskirts of Melbourne … and the rain was torrential! Even as we drove through the city on our outbound trip some of the streets were already flowing with water. We found out later that this had been the wettest day ever recorded in Melbourne's history – and we had no trouble believing that!

Nevertheless we made it back to the doctor's surgery for my appointment at 3:30 pm.

In spite of the doctor's immediate reaction when he had first seen that spot on my back, and in spite of the altered appointment time, I arrived for the appointment still quite convinced that we would be leaving the next day for PNG as planned. But, when we arrived at the consulting rooms the receptionist indicated that Rose should be with me when I went in to talk with the doctor. It was not Dr Inches as expected. He was away, and it was a young locum who greeted us as we entered the room. After the usual formal greeting his first remark went something like, "I hope you haven't already paid for your return tickets to New Guinea?"

"Not a problem," I glibly replied. "I fly myself – well it's a company aircraft really."

"Well that's good, because you won't be going." As my mind was struggling to come to grips with this piece of news I realised the doctor was still talking and he was now explaining to me that the "strange spot", as I had called it, had proved to be malignant melanoma. I had never heard the term before. But I soon learned that because of the malignancy, it would be necessary to remove a significant amount of surrounding flesh to ensure that all of the dangerous tissue had been removed. This would involve surgery, skin-grafts, and a couple of weeks in hospital.

"Do you know any surgeons in Melbourne?" he asked.

"Nope. I wouldn't know one from Adam, except that I suspect Adam didn't have a navel." I replied, still treating the situation a little too flippantly.

He looked thoughtful for a few seconds, then picked up his phone and dialled a number. After speaking quietly to someone on the other end of the line – and I honestly could not hear what he was saying – he lowered the handpiece, looked at me and asked, "Do you know a man named Bill Ramsey?"

"Yes I do. He used to do reconstructive surgery at a leprosarium in the New Guinea highlands."

"Then speak to him." And the doctor passed the telephone handset over to me.

I do not remember all of the conversation that followed, but I do remember Mr Ramsey saying something like, "Roger, this may not be quite like the usual emergency but you will be in ward 2-West in Box Hill hospital at 7 o'clock this evening." He then went on to explain the procedure I should follow in order to make that commitment.

We drove back out to Caldermeade (near Lang Lang, east of Melbourne) through floodwaters over the highway two or three inches deep in places. By 7 pm that evening I was in a bed in the appropriate ward with a "Nil Orally" sign over the head of the bed indicating that I was scheduled for surgery the next day.

I do not remember much of the next two or three days. I certainly do not remember how or what I ate, or even if I ate anything. The one thing I do remember is that for three days I lay facedown – on my stomach. The skin-graft patch on my back was very delicate and I had been warned that I must not even allow clothing to touch the area. A light framework had been provided to keep the bed sheet and blankets from touching my body. So I lay, facedown and virtually naked – wearing just a hospital gown, which normally would have fastened down the back but had to remain unfastened, for at least three days. Fortunately the ward was heated, for this was mid May – the last month of autumn – and Melbourne can be very cold even at that time of the year.

One of Rose's aunts had given me a book to read entitled *The Things They Do To You,* a most hilarious story about a farmer who had been admitted to hospital. The story had me with tears in my eyes, from sheer laughter! It was excellent therapy and certainly helped to take my mind off my own problems. But in spite of that, I was not without some level of discomfort.

It was at least the second day after the operation that I had to ask a nurse if she would please remove the blanket and frame from my bed so I could get up and visit the toilet. I was told, "Remove your blanket, yes. But let you walk to the toilet? No way!! I will get you a bottle." It was no use. Somehow the operation seemed to have affected my nervous system or muscle control in a certain area of my anatomy and, with my standing leaning against the side of the bed, the necessary muscles simply would not relax enough to allow even one drop to flow from my bladder. It was no use. I positioned myself back on the bed and waited for the nurse to come and replace the frame and the blanket.

By midnight the discomfort had reached a level where I simply had to try again. I pressed the call button and a petite nurse with a lovely smile arrived at my bedside. I explained that I needed help to get out of bed and why. She obliged by folding the blankets back and removing the frame – an arrangement, which I referred to as "my kennel." But it was still no use. No amount of conscious control could undo the clenched condition of those muscles. When the nurse returned a short time later to make sure I was comfortably back in bed I explained my problem. She looked thoughtful for a minute and then suggested, "Okay. I'll get you a commode. Perhaps if you can sit down it will help things to relax." Her idea worked and I was very grateful! But I was still not allowed to walk to the toilet.

Probably because I often slept during the day (being confined to bed as I was) I didn't always sleep soundly at night. The next night, sometime after midnight, the same nurse with the lovely smile was doing her rounds, checking that all was well with the patients in her care, when she noticed that I was obviously awake. Quietly she walked over to my bed and whispered, "Is it true that you are a pilot with Missionary Aviation Fellowship?"

"Why, yes. That is so." I said. "And why do you ask?"

"Do you happen to know Alby Waters?"

"Yes. Indeed I do. So how did you come to know him?"

"Well, I used to have a boyfriend in Ballarat. Often when I went to visit him we would go to Bible studies, and Alby was one of the study leaders." So we chatted briefly and then she said, "Next time you see Alby, please pass on my greetings to him."

"Certainly I will do that. But who do I say sends her greetings?"

"Bibi. Tell him that Bibi sends her greetings."

I peered at the nametag she was wearing, trying to make out the rest of her name, but in the dim night light of the ward it was impossible to read. "Okay." I said. "I'll tell him you said 'hello'." Other nurses referred to her as "Nurse Fraser", but I soon learned that she was Dutch and the correct spelling of her surname was

Vrazier. Because of our common acquaintance with persons who were totally removed from the hospital scene, I felt I could look to her as a friend in something more than just the patient-nurse relationship, which had caused us to meet in the first place.

I was discharged from hospital on Saturday 25th May, but before I was permitted to leave there was one little task that still needed to be done. Skin to perform the graft on my back had been taken from the rear part of my right thigh. As a result of the skin removal my thigh had been wrapped in bandages and what I had always assumed was a wooden splint. On the morning of my planned discharge I asked my doctor why the splint had been included. "Oh that's not a splint," He said. "That will be dried blood." When the doctor left I started to remove the bandages but found that the "splint" was bonded firmly to the skin of my right thigh and I could not pull it away from my leg at all. So I turned to the nurse, who had come to check me out of the ward, and asked, "Can I leave this dressing in place and remove it when I get home? I could soak it in a warm bath and see if it will come away then."

"Most certainly not!" I was told, in a stern voice. "You will not leave these premises with any medical dressings at all, apart from that one on your skin graft." So I went to take a shower (I was now allowed to walk that far), but even though I stayed under the shower for 20 minutes or more, that "splint" simply would not let go of my leg. Forlornly I returned to my bed. "It won't come off" I said to the nurse. She gave me a look of contempt and said, "What sort of a wimp are you? Get on the bed and I will take it off for you!"

I lay, face down again, on the bed. The nurse grabbed hold of the hardened and blood-soaked "splint" and tugged, hard. It stayed where it had been, stubbornly refusing to yield to her grasp.

"Oh. Yes, it is stuck, isn't it!" she said, finally acknowledging that I really did have a problem. "The dressing has actually become part of the new skin as it formed on your leg." Then she added, "Wait a moment. I have an idea." She disappeared briefly and returned with a bottle of freezing-cold saline and poured some over my leg, intending that the icy-cold liquid should act as a form of anaesthetic. The tears that came involuntarily to my eyes now were certainly not from reading funny stories about farmers in hospital! I grabbed a corner of my pillow, stuffed it into my mouth and bit down … hard! The "splint" eventually came away, but the nurse then had to install another dressing to protect the now very tender skin on the back of my right thigh.

I dressed and limped out to the hospital entrance. Rose drove the car right to the door to save me the extra walk.

The skin-graft on my back still had to be washed and dressed three times every day for the next three weeks. Mr. Ramsay, the surgeon, had already given Rose specific instructions on how to perform this delicate task. A large circular dressing was placed around the skin-graft area so that I could sit in a chair (and eventually the pilot's seat of an aeroplane) without damaging the newly grafted area of skin.

After two or three follow-up visits to my cheerful and friendly surgical expert I was given a clearance to return to work, so we finally left Ballarat on June 11th, flying in the newly overhauled Cessna U206, P2-MFY. The "P2" registration indicating that this was now a Papua New Guinea registered aircraft. And Aviation Medical authorities now required that I undergo a pilot's medical examination every six months, instead of the usual once-a-year check-up.

Chapter Nineteen

BUT HE ANSWERS IN UNEXPECTED WAYS

We now "fast forward" six months, to Sunday, 3rd November 1974:

As I was getting dressed after my morning shower Rose asked, "Was that lump in your leg there yesterday?" I had not noticed it before but it stood out very obviously now, a small lump, about the size of a pea, right at the top of my right leg. "Looks like a swollen lymph node," I said, thinking out loud. But I could see no scratches or injuries that might have caused infection, and hence a swollen lymph node, in that leg.

"I wonder ... ?" I had noticed that during all of the medical checks I had undergone since the melanoma spot was removed from my back, doctors had always been careful to check for possible swollen lymph nodes around my neck, under the armpits, and in the groin.

"I wonder how urgently I should get that checked?" I said, still thinking out loud.

"Fairly soon, I would say," said Rose.

"But I'm rostered to fly tomorrow. How long before I can get a day off flying so I can get to see Doctor Beavis?"

"Well, since you're the Flight Programmer it should be up to you to organise that!"

"So do I reorganise all of tomorrow's flying program just so I can get to see a doctor? Is it that urgent?"

"How would I know? I'm not a doctor."

I was still wrestling with this unanswerable question when the telephone rang. I answered it and heard, "Good morning. This is the Hagen Control Tower. We have just received a message about a medical evacuation needing to be done out of Lapalama. Are you able to help with that?"

"Sure can," I said, knowing I now had an answer to the question that had been troubling me for the last half-hour. If I flew out to Lapalama to bring that patient in to the hospital it would mean I had flown seven days in a row and could not roster myself to fly on Monday. I would therefore be free to go and see Doctor Beavis. I did not accept the timing of this chain of events as mere coincidence.

In spite of the Medical Evacuation status of that 45 minute flight to and from Lapalama it was very routine, but I did not know at the time that it would be many years before I would again pilot an aeroplane in Papua New Guinea. During the years that followed, the Lord was arranging some remarkable events towards satisfying what I had expressed as "the desire of my heart" while sitting on that beach in Kieta, something like twelve months previously.

On Monday morning the 4th November I was one in a long line of patients waiting to see Dr. Beavis. When he saw the swollen lymph node he said, "I will have to refer you to Mr Sharma, the surgeon." So I waited until Mr Sharma was available. When he saw the swollen node he said, "I will have to take that out and send it away for biopsy." That meant a visit to his operating theatre, so it was arranged for Tuesday morning. The scar where the node had been removed was a little bit painful – enough to keep me from flying but not, I considered, enough to keep me from doing office work. So, on Wednesday I reported for work as normal, expecting to still carry on with Flight Programming and other office work. But instead I was confronted by David Grace, the Chief Pilot, who ordered me to, "Go home and rest."

Mr. Sharma had made a point of emphasising to me the seriousness of my situation if the lump he had removed proved to be malignant, and he suspected that it most probably would be. "We do not have the facilities in this country to provide the post-operative care that you will need. I strongly advise you to return to Melbourne and put yourself in the care of the same surgeon who performed your skin-graft."

On Thursday of this same week Rose also made a visit to the hospital. She was now nine months pregnant with our third child, and her gynaecologist told her, "Your baby is now fully developed. If you have not given birth by Thursday of next week then come into the hospital and we will 'bring it on'."

Rose and I discussed whether or not we should start packing for a possible imminent departure from New Guinea. But at the same time I had a very strong feeling that even if the lump was proven to be malignant, God not only could, but also would, heal me of this cancer, which had now possibly entered my lymph system. I even wondered whether I should agree to this proposed trip to Australia for further investigative surgery. But as I prayed for wisdom on this question the thought that came very strongly to my mind was related to aircraft maintenance. "If someone had told me I had possible contamination of the oil system in my aircraft engine then I would be foolish indeed to continue flying that aircraft without having the oil filters checked. Now a knowledgeable medical expert has recommended I have some filters in my blood system checked. It would be foolish to ignore that advice." But we still hesitated to start packing.

Then John Johnston, manager of MAF in Papua New Guinea at the time, paid us a visit. His request was clear and to the point. He said, "Mrs Young, we do not want you doing anything that will prevent you from leaving here with your husband, if that proves to be necessary, in a few days time. Please do not do anything foolish, like trying to start packing up all of your household goods. Just take it easy, and sit tight. If you end up having to leave here in a rush then we will arrange all of the packing after you have left."

When the report came back from Pathology it stated that the lump removed from my lymph system had proved to be metastatic malignant melanoma. The condition was every bit as serious as Mr Sharma had feared.

So on Wednesday 13th November, the day before Rose was supposed to be admitted to Mount Hagen hospital for an induced birth, John arrived at the door of our house with tickets for our flight to Melbourne, documents that would be needed for our son David to enrol in a new school, and a certificate, signed by a doctor, to say that Rose was fit to travel on an airline flight "without risk of parturition", and the news that "Your flight departs at 10 am tomorrow." This was an incredible bit of organising on John's part, and we were very grateful to him for his efforts in this regard.

Rose, with her pregnancy now very obvious, did get some strange looks from cabin crew as we boarded the aircraft, but we made it to Melbourne quite safely. It was another four weeks before our daughter was born. By that time I had recovered from the surgical procedure required for the "complete excision of the inguinal lymph nodes" in my right leg, and far from "not living to see your daughter born" (as some had feared) I actually drove Rose to the Box Hill hospital on the night Esther was born.

What with the birth of a new baby, Christmas holidays, and a chance to catch-up with friends and relatives, it was actually February before we began thinking seriously about any plans of returning to my flying job in Papua New Guinea. But my Australian Commercial Pilots Licence was due for renewal so I decided to deal with that while I was still in Australia. A few circuits with Ken Cooper, the MAF Flying Instructor, proved that in spite of the recent "injury" to my right leg, I could still handle a Cessna 185 in a stiff cross-wind. Then on Thursday 6th March, 1975, I took my licence in to the Civil Aviation Office in Melbourne. The young man behind the counter took my licence but returned a few minutes later and said, “I can't renew this.”

“What do you mean, can't renew it. What's the matter with my licence?”

“It’s not your licence that is the problem, but you are not physically fit.”

“What do you mean, ‘not physically fit’? I walked up the stairs to this office. I didn't even take the lift!”

“Well, there is a letter in your file stating that because of your physical condition your flying licence has been suspended.”

“That's news to me. I have seen no such letter.”

“Then I will show it to you.” He left the counter briefly and returned with a copy of the letter, addressed to me and signed by the Superintendent of Aviation Medicine. The letter had been written several weeks earlier, but had been sent to my Mt Hagen address, which explained why I had never seen it. But there was no question about its message – due to my recent medical history my flying licence had been suspended. This news came as a shock to me although, with hindsight, I agree it should not have come as any surprise. There was a possibility of review in two years time. But I did notice a clause near the end of the letter that indicated I could appeal against this decision.

"I want to talk to the person who wrote this letter. Where is her office?"

"You can't just go and talk to her. You will need an appointment."

"Then will you please arrange one for me. And where is her office anyway?"

When I eventually did get to talk with Dr Potter I agreed with her that, under the circumstances, it was reasonable to call for a temporary suspension of my flying licence. But I then went on to explain that if my flying licence was left unused for 24 months I would then have to redo all of the written exams, as well as a flight test, just the same as if I were applying for an initial issue of the licence. And I certainly did not want to have to go through all of that procedure again. (I understand that the regulations relating to this matter have since been changed). She listened sympathetically and was very understanding of my problem. But as she explained, "We cannot change, or even deliberately overlook, any regulation just to suit one person. There is a specific standard that applies for professional pilots, and with your present medical history you simply do not meet those standards." She was fairly guarded and careful in some of her comments, and possibly did not wish to frighten me by admitting the official prognosis for a person with my medical history. I have only learned since then that, according to statistics and medical knowledge of the time, there was only a five-percent chance I would still be alive in two years' time. However, she eventually agreed to just downgrade my licence, possibly even to a student licence, on the condition that I would continue to undergo six-monthly medical checks with a properly approved doctor. This was perfectly acceptable to me, although it would mean that I now faced an unknown future. I would certainly not be returning to flying in New Guinea, but at least I could retain a flying licence of some sort. Her parting words to me were something like, "Mr Young, I don't think you should ever consider returning to the tropics."

Sometime after that interview I happened to be talking again with the same man who had asked me that thought-provoking question when we were sitting on the beach in Kieta, some 15 months previously. "So what are you going to do now?" he asked.

"I honestly don't know" I said. "We certainly won't be going back to New Guinea. I am reluctant to go back to working in the hangar at Ballarat because, since the recent operation affected the lymph system in my right leg, it gets very swollen if I spend too much time standing. And standing all day, especially on a concrete floor in the hangar — well, I could end up with a leg that looks like I have elephantiasis."

"Are you aware of the fact that you could do retraining? Since you have had to leave your previous job for health reasons you would be eligible for retraining. Do you remember what you once said about wanting to take two years off work to study electronics?"

"Yeah. Now why didn't I think of that? So where do I go to ask about that idea?"

"Probably the CES office in Ballarat."

And so it was that in July 1975 I again became a full-time student, on a 2-year course in Electronic Communications at the Royal Melbourne Institute of Technology.

*****

Delight yourself in the Lord and he will give you the desires of your heart. Psalm 37:4. (NIV)

*****

As a postscript to this chapter I would like to add that it was not until several years later I began hearing comments from friends, fellow workers, and hospital staff that brought home to me just how serious many people had considered my condition to be when I entered Box Hill Hospital for this second lot of surgery. I have already described in the opening pages of this book how my friend Bibi (Nurse Vrazier) reacted when she saw me back in hospital. But she had maintained a very professional standard of confidence and never really let on (to me) that according to one prognosis, which seemed to be popular at the time, Roger Young had "secondary cancer in the lymph system and may have only another two weeks to live." Not only was I fit enough to drive Rose to hospital on the night our daughter Esther was born, but can you even begin to understand the thrill it was for me, more than 23 years later, to deliver that same daughter to church and walk down the aisle with her on the day of her wedding.

Feb., 28th 1998. Esther and husband Simon

Photo by Gordon Harvey

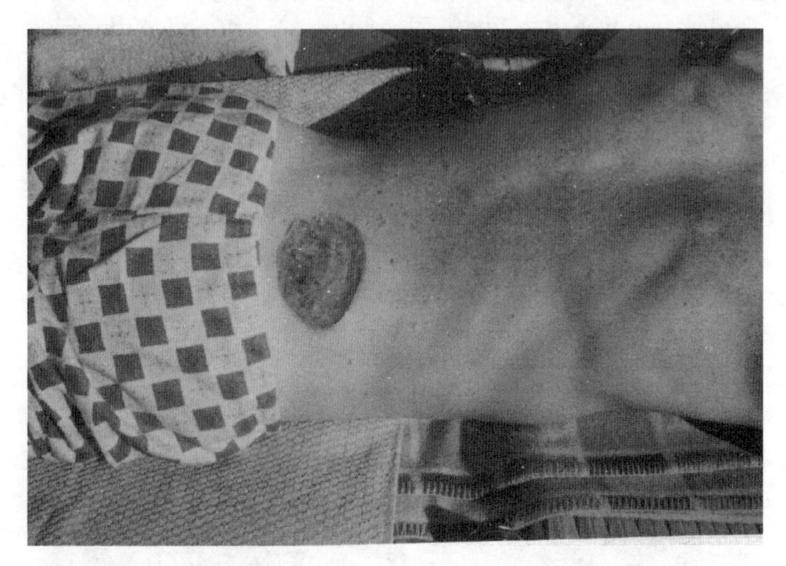

May 1974. I put this in because my daughter wanted you to know that, although the "black mole" may have been only the size of a thumb-nail, the actual skin-graft was much bigger.

Chapter Twenty

MORE OF GOD'S PROVISION

For the most part I enjoyed my studies at RMIT. Some of the stuff was not entirely new to me as I had dabbled in electronics as a hobby since I was a teenager. But the whole scene of electronics was in a state of change. Some of the material I had to learn was biased towards the newer technology, but at the same time much of the theory, even in digital electronics, was still based on older technology where thermionic valves had been used. Does anyone now remember those ancient radio sets and gramophone amplifiers that contained many little glass "bottles" each with an electrical filament inside that glowed a dull cherry-red when the thing was working? Remember, this was only 1975 – personal computers and microprocessors were still virtually unheard of, and for the first six months of my course we were required to use a slide-rule for all complicated mathematical calculations. It was only after persistent demands from the student body that we were permitted to use pocket calculators (the "scientific" variety) in the classroom or during exams.

And I was beginning to find that the subject of electronics – even just the bit that applies to radio communications – was like a vast and immeasurable ocean. During my second year at RMIT one of my lecturers asked me how I was coping with the studies – and he wanted an honest answer! I told him I was feeling a bit like a boy who had dived into a river thinking he could possibly swim across, but had suddenly found himself in the middle of a vast ocean and now didn't even know where the shore was anymore. It was more awesome than just feeling "out of my depth." Nevertheless, just in case you think I was wasting my time at this Technical College, perhaps I should mention that I gained top marks in most of the study modules, and also collected at least one of the prizes that were awarded to students at the end of each of the four semesters. And there was a lot more on my mind than just being a full-time student again.

Because our future was now rather uncertain, Rose and I had been advised to buy ourselves a house. The person who gave us this advice also mentioned that a boom in the price of houses was anticipated in the near future and for this reason we would be well advised to get ourselves established while they were still affordable. But for us, a house of our own was virtually unaffordable anyway. I was trying to live on a student allowance. Rose was trying to sell Amway products just so we could pay the grocery bills. But God was good to us.

I went and spoke to the manager of the Commonwealth Bank about a possible housing loan, as I had banked with them since I first arrived in New Guinea in 1965 – there was no other banking organisation available in Wewak. But I was told, in effect, "Don't waste my time, and I won't waste yours." Rose and I then made arrangements to speak to someone else about low-interest Government-guaranteed loans that were supposed to be available for people on low incomes. When I asked, "What would happen if we ever do manage to get on our feet, financially, and are able to pay off this loan in less than twenty years?" I was told, very curtly, "Then you don't need our money!" At the end of that interview we were told, "You should receive a letter from us within the next fortnight." Thirty years later that letter has still not arrived. Feeling very discouraged by this time Rose and I made arrangements for an interview with the manager of the ANZ Bank, since I had started an account with them when I first arrived in Ballarat in 1963 and, a fact that I had almost overlooked, had a small sum of money invested in a long-term deposit with them. This had been a monetary gift sent to me by my father while I was a student in Bible College back in 1964. The response from the bank manager was a cautious, "I will have to have a look at it and will let you know."

At that point we pretty well gave up on any idea of ever owning a home of our own. And anyway, we thought the Bank would probably not consider a student allowance sufficient to be repaying a housing loan. But we were mistaken.

When MAF-AIR Services had established their workshop in one of the hangars on the Ballarat airport, the local Shire Council had also granted them access to 10 or 12 of the houses and 6 of the two-bedroom flats, which had once been accommodation for RAAF officers when the Air Force had a base in Ballarat. As soon as I had sufficiently recovered from the cancer surgery and Rose was feeling well enough to travel after the birth of our daughter, we moved to Ballarat and were living in one of those houses on the Ballarat airport. One Sunday evening, when I was not at home, Rose answered a knock at the front door of our house to find John Brett, the Chief Engineer, at the door. John lived in one of the two MAF-AIR staff houses that had a telephone and he had an urgent message: there was someone on the telephone who wanted to speak to either Roger or Rose Young. When Rose ran down to Brett's house to answer the phone she heard the voice-at-the-other-end say, "It's Hugh Earnshaw here, from the ANZ Bank. I was just wondering when your husband is going to come in and talk about that housing loan?" Rose's reply was, "We didn't think it was worth it." "Oh yes," he said, "It will definitely be worth your while." So we did go ahead with the interview and were approved for our housing loan. Apparently the money, which I had cautiously placed in a long-term deposit more than ten years previously had earned me sufficient "credit points" that I was now entitled to take out a housing loan.

After discussing the nitty-gritty details of income and expenses, and how we managed to survive on an income that most people would have considered to be well below the poverty level, the bank manager looked earnestly at Rose and said, "Mrs Young, I wish that my wife could have a long talk with you." But it was said in a tone of voice that implied a compliment to Rose on her thrifty housekeeping practices, rather than a genuine request to educate his wife on the subject. And an additional benefit of immense help to us at this time was that one of Rose's uncles offered us an interest-free loan (to be repaid in the next year or two). We were now able to start to dream about owning a place of our own, but this was only possible because other people had been so thoughtful, generous, and helpful in very practical ways.

Rose and I spent many hours looking at houses for sale but eventually decided that the best and cheapest answer was to buy a block of land near the airport and have a house built for us. It would be a small 3-bedroom design, but comfortable and very cosy even during the miserably cold, wet, and windy Ballarat winters. In order to keep costs to a minimum we decided to do all the painting, paths, driveway and fencing ourselves, and we worked hard to establish a good garden. Certainly there was a lot more to occupy my mind than just studying electronics and associated topics.

As for my pilot's licence – within a few weeks I received a letter from the Superintendent of Aviation Medicine to advise me that rather than suspending the licence, the decision had been made to simply downgrade it to Private Pilot level. This meant I was still allowed to pilot an aeroplane, but not on a professional basis. And I was (still) required to undergo 6-monthly checks with an approved Aviation Medical Examiner. Two years later (April 1977) I received another letter from Dr. Potter to inform me that as a result of my latest medical check-up, I had now been assessed as fit enough to have my Commercial Pilot Licence revalidated. This time, when I visited the office in Melbourne, the man behind the counter happily completed the necessary procedure and handed back my flying licence, all approved and valid at commercial pilot level for the next 12 months.

What would you have done if the next decision had been your responsibility? Yes, my flying licence had been revalidated at commercial pilot level but I was not really convinced that I was ready to return to the stress and pressure of work as a pilot in PNG. So, at least for the meantime, I returned to work in the hangar with MAF-AIR Services in Ballarat. At first tentatively, as I wanted to see what effect this might now have on the oedema problem in my right leg, as it was now two-and-a-half years since the operation, and also hopeful that what I had learned over the last two years would at least be some help in resolving most of the radio problems we had been experiencing with our aircraft. MAF were also happy to make use of the experience I had already gained as a pilot in New Guinea when they asked me to "sit in" (as in the role of a check pilot) with some of their new candidate pilots – such as a flight to PNG with Max Chapman, and a flight to North Australia with Paul

Summerfield. So my knowledge and experience were certainly not being wasted.

Then towards the end of 1978 a couple of significant things did happen: My parents came across from New Zealand and while they were staying with us in Ballarat my father, a public accountant by profession, got to know a man in the same profession who lived in Ballarat. This man was also a very keen amateur radio enthusiast. I don't know what transpired between them before I was brought into the discussion, but by the time I was invited to do so they had already come to the agreement that if I could obtain an Amateur Radio Operators Certificate of Proficiency within the next 12 months, there was a perfectly serviceable amateur radio transmitter and receiver that would be "mine for the asking." As two of my brothers back in New Zealand (Graeme, the oldest, and Russell, the youngest) already had "ham" licences, this was definitely an incentive for me to start learning Morse Code and pass the necessary exams so I also could have a similar licence and would then be able to arrange regular chat times with family back in NZ. The other significant thing was a request from MAF that I consider returning to PNG as a commercial pilot, as the need there was quite desperate. However, as a "trial run" to see how (or if) I could cope with a return to the pressures of a flying program as well as the heat of the tropics, it was arranged that we would spend two months with MAF in North Australia.

So on December 8th 1978 we, as a family, set off again in a MAF Cessna 206 for another little adventure – this time in Arnhem Land, and we would be living at Elcho Island. However, while we were there we received some rather sad news. My brother Graeme had been involved in a car accident. When investigations were made (apparently he had not even seen the parked car he had crashed into) it was discovered that he was, in effect, half-blind. A brain tumour had grown to such an extent that he had virtually lost all vision on his left side. And the tumour was inoperable. We cut our time in Elcho Island short (left there on Friday 12th Jan) and made plans for Rose and me to make a hasty visit across the Tasman. By the time we got to visit Graeme he was confined to bed, but reasonably cheerful and resigned to the fact that he did not have many days left of life on earth. We then rushed back to Ballarat, frantically packed up everything in our house, packed into drums all the items we planned to take back to PNG, and arranged with a Real Estate Agent to lease our three-year-old house to tenants.

Two months and one day after our rushed departure from Elcho Island we again all bundled ourselves into a MAF Cessna – this time a newly refurbished and re-engined Turbo 206, P2-MFG – for yet another adventure.

Chapter Twenty One

MOVE AGAIN, FRIEND

Our destination this time was Goroka, in the Eastern Highlands of PNG, and we were accompanied, as far as Mt Hagen, by our friend Neil Johnston who, incidentally, had also done some flying with Bougainville Air Services in the 1970's. And the reference to a "re-engined" aircraft is not insignificant. This was one of the first to be modified with the new 310HP TSIO-520M engine. The difference in performance compared to the sluggish response we had put-up with from aircraft fitted with the old 285HP engine was just about unbelievable. P2-MFG almost leapt into the air and climbed eagerly to cruising altitude, and I found myself wishing that a machine with a performance like this had been available back in those days when I was operating out of Port Moresby. If we'd had a machine like this those awkward and embarrassing times when passengers had been asked to leave one suitcase behind – not because it wouldn't fit into the aircraft, but because we lacked the performance to get airborne off their short and/or soft little airstrip – would not have happened.

After arrival at Goroka we were given the weekend to get comfortably settled, then my check-out flights began in earnest as most of the airstrips in the Eastern Highlands were new to me and the entire area of the Huon Peninsula, including all of its airstrips – some of which needed very careful handling – were all a totally new experience for me.

On Monday 26th March 1979, with Alan Stray as check and training pilot, we headed south from Goroka, then east and into Lae and finally visited most of the airstrips between Finschhafen and Madang. It was late Wednesday afternoon before we saw Goroka again. During this time the town had been hit by an earthquake – 6.5 on the Richter scale – but I had been quite unaware of that as we were airborne at the time. There had also been a telegram from New Zealand (dated Saturday 24th) which appeared in our mailbox, with Monday's mail delivery – after Alan and I had left, advising us that my brother, Graeme, had died that same Saturday. The Post Office had not bothered to phone the message through and the funeral was well and truly over before I had even heard about it.

In spite of this we enjoyed our time in Goroka. The Asaro valley, at just over 5,000 feet above sea level, has a most pleasant climate – like eternal springtime. The company had managed to rent a very nice house – one of the staff houses at the Melanesian Institute for Pastoral and Socio Economic Service – certainly the nicest we had ever lived in. Our daughter, Esther, started preschool and absolutely loved it. Stuart set about establishing a garden, and our older son, David, joined the swimming club as there was a swimming pool available for public use. And we enjoyed meeting many of our old friends again.

There are a couple of memories here that I think are worth a mention: One rather thrilling experience was to see the expression (of thanksgiving for answered prayer?) that flashed across Dr. Beavis's face when he saw me in his waiting room one morning in Mount Hagen. I was due for another of those routine pilot's medical checks. Before he even started to fill out the paperwork he just looked at me and said, very quietly but obviously very sincerely, "It's good to see you back here again!" The other was one morning when I was doing the radio *sched*, a missionary friend recognised my voice and broke in with, "Hey, is that you Roger? Welcome back! And how are you anyway?"

"One hundred percent! And it's good to be back again."

"Hundred percent?" He echoed. "I didn't think there was that much of you left."

"Ah, yeah, well … there's enough that I'm still standing up." And we both laughed.

But it wasn't long before I began to suspect I had lost more than just a pound of flesh on my last visit to the hospital operating theatre. Or maybe it was that I had gained something I didn't really need, or want. Even while I had been a student at RMIT I had visited our doctor in Ballarat several times in order to try and identify the cause of my greater than normal fatigue. I presented myself for blood tests and was told the results were "strongly suggestive of glandular fever." "But," they added, "you are too old (aged 35-36 yrs) to have glandular fever." Peter Evans, the apprentice who had been boarding with us at the time, had awoken one night with a raging fever. When we took him into the hospital they diagnosed glandular fever, and the blood tests confirmed it. He was given six weeks off work. I didn't even get so much as one day. But the doctor in Goroka decided he would not take any chances. I was sent off to Brisbane for extensive tests – they did a brain scan, (and yep, they confirmed that I had one of those!) and a liver scan. But I soon began to realise that as a result of the "holiday" in Brisbane I was feeling much better. So I returned to work.

While in Goroka I sat, and passed, the exam for my Amateur Radio Operator's Certificate of Proficiency. I also sat and passed a Department of Civil Aviation exam that gave me a licence to work on aircraft HF radio transceivers.

At the beginning of 1980 we were asked to move yet again. (As some people quip, MAF means "Move Again, Friend".) This time we would be moving to Mt. Hagen so I could take on the role of Acting Chief Pilot while Noel Hawke was away on furlough. There was also an added advantage in this move as our son David was due to start high school. Being in Mount Hagen meant that he would be able to attend the Bamboo Heights International High School where, although students still did correspondence lessons, they were all in a classroom situation with supervising teachers, who could answer questions or present classroom type lessons when there were enough students doing a particular subject to justify it. And, as it turned out, one other big advantage was that we were now within easy driving distance of the Christian Radio Missionary Fellowship station at Rugli – on the road between Mt. Hagen and Baiyer River. It wasn't long before my friend David Brewster, from CRMF, came and spent an afternoon with us and helped me get my amateur radio station operational.

I had never intended that this hobby should take up too much of my time but I remember the first evening I switched the set on just to have a listen (without David's supervision) and see what other amateurs were talking about. It wasn't long before I heard another PNG "ham" chatting with an operator in the USA. Before they concluded their brief "QSO" (meaning *conversation* when you're "speaking" in Morse code) I heard the American say, "If I can just get one more P29 station then I'll be right for the Bird of Paradise Award." I gingerly picked up my microphone and, as soon as there was a break in their conversation, I broke in. Addressing the American station I said, "This is papa two nine romeo yankee. I may be able to help you with that award." (P29RY was my amateur call sign.) I was not even sure if he would be able to hear my transmission, or what would happen, but I received an enthusiastic response. "Hey there. Papa twenty-nine Romeo Yankee you're rompin' in loud and clear. Can you give me a signal report and send me a card to confirm the contact?" Wow! This was awesome. Here I was sitting in a house somewhere in the mountains of New Guinea talking to some guy in the USA and we could hear each other more clearly than most of the PNG mission stations that I spoke to on the radio most days of the week.

The next evening I turned on my amateur radio again. This time I started with a general call (known in "ham" jargon as a "CQ call") which is sort of like calling out, "Anybody out there who will speak to me?" I was not prepared for the response: Immediately three or four stations replied, all speaking on top of each other. I had to try and identify one call sign out of that jumble. I eventually did manage to make out an intelligible call sign and gave a signal strength report. Most of these operators were very keen to confirm our contact with the exchange of post cards, because they needed this evidence to apply for various amateur operator awards. And since Papua New Guinea had at that time only about 20 or so licensed "hams", any contact with a P29 station was considered a rare treat. Before I had managed to sort out the next station that was waiting there were even more stations calling me. The next two hours were absolute chaos. I remember reading a note on one of the cards I received as a result of that evening. The American operator had written, "*Thanks so much for the contact Roger. My wife woke me at 3 am when she heard you on the air. I called for at least an hour before you finally heard me*!" Another evening I talked for more than an hour with a man who owned an oil-palm plantation in Hawaii. He had been a professional weather forecaster before he purchased the farm. We had a very interesting chat.

It wasn't long before this became a real family-oriented hobby. Rose and the three children sat behind me with an open Atlas, and as soon as the person I was speaking to gave me a location, or an address, there would be a race to see who would be first to locate the place on a map. We all enjoyed the geography lessons. But not all of my contacts were with people on the other side of the world, although it was perhaps a good idea to remember that, quite literally, anyone in the world could be listening. Rose often likes to remind me of one evening when I had been chatting with an American Lutheran missionary who lived "just over the hill" at Wapenamanda. As a reinforcement of my invitation for him to call in and pay us a visit next time he was in Hagen, I had explained how to find our house: "Right behind Heagney's store – that's the blue one on the left just as you turn onto the road that takes you out of the airport. Just look for the two big bamboo poles with the antenna wire strung between." At the end of our QSO a very definitely North American voice chipped in, "Yeah, copied all of that …" He had a regular time each week (a *sched*) when he would call in and talk with his missionary friend in Papua New Guinea (the one I had just been talking to) and we had actually been encroaching on his *sched* time. And of course I soon arranged a regular *sched* with my brother Russell, in New Zealand.

When I think back over those days in Mt. Hagen I sometimes wonder how I survived. Not only was I supposed to be Acting Chief Pilot, but I was also given the task of Area Manager, responsible for MAF bases at Hagen, Mendi, Wapenamanda and Tari (a job that I absolutely hated, incidentally). By this time MAF had actually employed two other pilots who were also radio technicians, but one of them had recently returned to Australia for health reasons and the other had been based at Wewak. Since most of the maintenance work was now being done at Hagen there were days when I had things to do in the radio workshop, which was part of the MAF Headquarters hangar in Hagen. On top of all that, of course, I was expected to do my fair share of regular day-to-day flying.

All of our aircraft departures were made from the Airport Terminal building, which we shared with Air Niugini, and the Area Manager's office was in the Terminal building. But the Chief Pilot's office was part of the administrative complex, attached to the maintenance hangar. As far as I was concerned most of the time this worked to my benefit because it meant that it was almost impossible for anyone to keep track of where I might be at any given time of the day. So I didn't get hassled with incoming phone calls. The office staff did an excellent job in answering most calls that might otherwise have been passed on to me, but occasionally one of our traffic officers would come looking for me with a message asking me to return somebody's phone call.

This was also the time in history when many of us were still struggling with what we referred to as "metric madness". When I had started flying in New Guinea all airstrip lengths were quoted in feet; all mountain heights on our navigational charts were given in feet; and all weights were quoted in pounds. Now everything had to be metricated – the heights of all mountain peaks marked on our charts were now quoted in metres (although the aircraft altimeters still registered in feet); all airstrip lengths were now given in metres; all aircraft loads now had to be calculated in kilograms; and all fuel was measured in litres, instead of gallons. This was creating confusion for a lot of people. I remember one evening I was listening as a couple of real old-timers were chatting on the "ham" radio. They sounded like WWII veterans and it was interesting just to be able to listen. Then they got on to this problem of metric madness. One of them said, "It's just so crazy. I went down to the hardware store the other day – I needed a new garden hose. When I got there I told the sales assistant I needed 50 feet of garden hose. 'Oh, you can't have that,' he says. 'You'll need to give me the length in metres.' So we spent some time doing a few sums and decided what I needed was 15 metres of garden hose. Then he turns to me and asks, 'So what size will it be? Three-quarter-inch, or half-inch diameter?' So have we gone metric or not!?"

But the danger of this confusion became very real when one of our pilots was at Laiagam one day and was asked, "How much load (weight) can you take out of here?" Now I need to explain that although the strip at Laiagam was about 850 metres in length it was 7,000 feet above sea level and it had a 1.5% down slope to the south. For this reason it was the normal practice to make all take-offs towards the south. Although this meant that the pilot was facing rising ground after take-off, it was normally possible for the aircraft to out-climb the hill. And the pilot, on this occasion, was flying a normally aspirated Cessna 206 (ie: NOT turbocharged). I do not know what figure the pilot had given the missionary at Laiagam, but from my own experience, it would normally be in the order of 350 to 420 pounds weight (depending on how much fuel he still had on board the aircraft). But the missionary thought he meant kilograms, and gave him a load that was "that many" kilograms. Yes, the aircraft got airborne, but could not out-climb the rising ground. Fortunately the pilot was not killed, although he was trapped in the wreckage for 45 minutes before anyone could get there to rescue him. The aircraft was a total write-off.

Partly as a result of this accident I decided that one of my tasks, as Acting Chief Pilot, must be to produce a complete revision of what we referred to as our "Mini Manual". This was a little handbook which listed most of the airstrips used by MAF. It gave details of length, altitude, surface slope (if any), and the normal *load penalty* (the weight that the aircraft had to be below maximum permissible all-up weight) that had to be applied for a safe take-off. But I decided this revision should include ***all*** airstrips on the Mainland of PNG – not only Government aerodromes and MAF mission strips, but also Catholic Mission strips, those that had been built by SIL/WBT, Seventh Day Adventist, New Tribes Mission … you name it, if it was a recognised, usable airstrip then it was included. In addition to quoting all data in the now required metric figures I also included cautionary notes where appropriate, and a list of the normal take-off and landing penalties that could be expected for normal conditions (ie: average day-time temperature with no wind). The listed penalties included data for Cessna 185, normally aspirated (300HP) Cessna 206, turbo-charged (310HP) Cessna 206 and, where appropriate, the twin-engine Beech Baron as we now had one of these in our fleet.

When I presented my notes to our typist she complained that the layout would not fit on a normal size sheet of paper. So I took the notes home, typed them all up on my own portable typewriter, took these pages back to the office and said, "Now I have shown how it can be done, please do it all on your electric typewriter so that we have a good black copy to use as a master." This was before the days of modern desk-top publishing and good quality laser printers. So the problem was to get good, readable copies in a convenient sized booklet. After discussing the matter with our Admin' Officer, Ron Kingsley, we chose to take the pages to a commercial printshop in Hagen and ask them to do the job. I was very happy with the finished product.

However, my efforts got a very mixed reaction. Almost all of the MAF pilots were very enthusiastic and appreciative. MAF management complained bitterly because I had spent money, and since I was only *acting* in the role of Chief Pilot, I had no business in taking on a new project such as the one I had just finished. And the Civil Aviation flight-testing officers (when they saw the publication) condemned it because I had actually listed take-off and landing penalties. In their opinion the pilot was expected to wait until he was actually on the ground at a particular airstrip and then, having assessed the *actual* temperature and wind conditions, he was obliged to take the aircraft performance charts and calculate the exact penalty that would have to be applied for those specific conditions. They mumbled about things like legal liability and such, but did not seem to really comprehend that even a Flight Programmer, sitting in his office and trying to work out how best to deal with all the flight requests he has for a day, needs some idea of what might be the expected penalties for take-off or landing at the airstrips he has included in any plan he hands to a pilot.

One of the other responsibilities dropped onto the Chief Pilot's desk was that of research into alternative aircraft types. Because of the many different demands for flying in a mountainous tropical country, and especially mission flying, it is very difficult (virtually impossible) to find the ideal aircraft to do the job. Whatever choice is made will always be a compromise. The United Church had presented MAF with a request that they extend their service out into the many islands scattered throughout the sea off the eastern end of the mainland – places like Kiriwina (Trobriand Islands) and out towards Misima, and possibly even from this area across the sea to Rabaul, on the island of New Britain. Because of the over-water flying involved this required a twin-engine aeroplane, and MAF had actually purchased a 6-seat Beech D-55 "Baron" aircraft for this purpose. Not the ideal aeroplane but, as I have said, it is virtually impossible to find the "perfect" machine for the job. I had also been asked to do an assessment on a Robertson STOL version of the Cessna 210 because a number of pilots, myself included, believed that for some of the longer flights we needed something faster than the trusty old Cessna 206. There were a number of reasons why I eventually gave the idea a "thumbs down", and was not popular for doing that. But now I was being asked to assess the need for a cabin-class twin-engine aircraft, such as the 10-seat Cessna 402. We had looked at performance charts for the aircraft and had already decided that a Robertson STOL modified Cessna 402C could handle many of our airstrips. But the question that really needed to be answered was whether or not the expense of such a machine was justified. Was there really sufficient demand for a machine of this capacity? Our friends at SIL/WBT (JAARS) had been using one for some time, and many of our pilots were insisting that there was a genuine need for MAF to be doing the same. I wrote a letter and what I considered to be an appropriate questionnaire, and sent this to most of the mission and church-based organisations that appeared on our list of customers. From an analysis of the responses I received I was still not entirely convinced of the need for such a machine, but as Noel arrived back from leave about this time, I left all the data for him to make the assessment. I have mentioned these facts mainly in an attempt to explain how these aircraft came to be part of the MAF-PNG fleet, although they were both sold some years later.

Laiagam: (pg 209) 7000 ft above sea level, length 850 metres. View looking south. Because of the 1.5% slope to the south (away from the camera) take-offs were normally made towards the south, but this meant that the pilot was facing rising ground. This was one of the main reasons for the load restriction on take-offs from this airstrip.

Porgera: View looking down the airstrip – 7200 ft (2195 metres) above sea level, length 518 metres with a surface slope of 10%. You cannot see the 12,000 ft peaks of Dini and other mountains because I had my back to them when I took this photo.

Chapter Twenty Two

IT COULD HAVE ENDED HERE

There have been times when people have told me, in all seriousness, that they believe Satan tried to get rid of me, especially while we were living in Papua New Guinea. I am never quite sure what to make of those claims, but I have to admit that such ideas could probably be easily justified. And I would not be truly honest if I tried to insist that I had never been scared at any time while flying in that country.

On Friday, November 14th 1980, I was rostered to do the regular Wapenamanda – Porgera – Paiela mail and freezer-goods flight. Now it is probably only fair to admit that I had never been particularly happy about operating into Paiela. This is no criticism of the people who made that airstrip – it was a bit of an engineering masterpiece really. Located 6,150 feet above sea level they had shaved the top off a mountain peak and managed to create a perfectly level strip, but it was only 487 metres in length and the ground dropped away steeply at both ends of the runway. Landing here was a bit like landing on an aircraft carrier, except that this "aircraft carrier" was more than 6,000 feet above sea level and there were no arrester wires to stop you sliding over the end if you messed up the landing. This meant that for most of our aircraft there were severe load penalties, both for take-off and for landing. But, fortunately we had one aircraft that was specially modified with Robertson STOL (Short Take Off and Landing) equipment and this allowed us to land at Paiela with the aircraft at gross weight (with a full load). And this aircraft was also fitted with the 310HP turbocharged engine, so it was definitely the most logical machine to use for any operations into Paiela.

I had not slept well on the Thursday night, partly due to a nagging premonition that something awful would go wrong on Friday. And the flying originally scheduled for that day meant I could still be working in the area after 4pm, by which time it is normal for the weather to have turned quite nasty. Consequently I prayed specifically for God's protection over all of Friday's flying.

The load out of Wapenamanda was a mixture of goods, some for Porgera and some for Paiela, but I also had two passengers to collect at Porgera and take to Paiela. It was planned that I should then collect a second load of goods from Porgera, take these across to Paiela, and the men would return to Porgera on the back-leg of the second flight.

On my first landing at Paiela there was only a very gentle breeze blowing, and if I may say so myself, the landing was quite a good one. We stopped comfortably, well within the available airstrip length, and the passenger in the front right-hand seat actually commented favourably on my performance and asked why it was that the airstrip had a reputation for being uncomfortably short. I do not recall what I said in reply or whether I ever really answered his question.

My second load into Paiela consisted of a 200 litre drum of kerosene and some trade-store goods, but this time the approach for my landing was not what I would call "good". The wind strength had increased and was now creating some choppy turbulence, so I had to maintain a slightly higher airspeed on the approach. I made a mental note that this extra speed would require heavier breaking than on the previous landing. But, in spite of the extra speed the aircraft touched down cleanly at my aiming point and I immediately selected "flaps up" (a normal and accepted technique for STOL performance in this model of aircraft), stood hard on the brakes and pulled back on the control wheel to increase the weight on the main wheels. Almost immediately the right-side brake pedal went "flat" (went to the full extent of its travel with no resistance) indicating that there would be no braking effect on the right-side main wheel. Of course, in order to keep the aircraft tracking straight down the line of the runway, I had to release all pressure on the left brake. This meant I had no effective braking at all. I quickly pumped both pedals again and confirmed that there was absolutely no braking effect at all on the right-hand side.

Now, in order to put my dilemma into an understandable context, I need to explain that at the point of touchdown, about 50 metres in from the airstrip threshold, we would have been travelling at something like 100 kilometres per hour (60 knots). I would have had no more than 430 metres of runway left, and at that speed, would have rolled off the far end in less than 16 seconds. Try to imagine how you would react in a situation where you are driving a car at 100 kilometres per hour when you suddenly realise that the bridge 430 metres ahead of you has been washed away, or you may prefer to imagine that a mob of kangaroos has suddenly appeared out of the bush and jumped onto the highway. You stamp your foot on the brake-pedal and it goes flat to the floor. You have no brakes!! What would you do? Could you possibly stop in time? And remember – for every second that you think about it you have travelled a further 27 metres closer to the scene of your potential accident.

Well, of course, in my case there was *no* time to think about the problem, so I decided the safest move would be to abort the landing and make a "go-around". I slammed the throttle to full-open and selected take-off (20°) position on the wing-flaps. This was definitely one of those experiences that we describe as "heart in mouth".

About two-thirds of the way down the airstrip I realised with some horror that the engine was not producing full power and my imagination started "doing gymnastics". I had a fleeting mental image of rolling off the end of the airstrip and tumbling down the hill and into the jungle. Even though the drum of kerosene behind me was firmly secured with a cargo net and belts made of strong webbing I still had a horrible picture of the cabin structure crumpling on impact and yours truly becoming the meat-in-the-sandwich, crushed between a full drum of kerosene and the solidness of the aircraft instrument panel. The words, "So this is how it happens" flashed through my mind — perhaps only for a fraction of a second, but it was not a pleasant thought.

I had possibly travelled at least one-third of the way down the airstrip before I decided to abort the landing, but I really have no way of accurately measuring the distance at that point in time. And, although the turbo-charged engine is capable of producing full sea level power at this altitude, it is not always instantly available. When the engine has been at little more than idle power for several seconds, such as during an approach to land, the exhaust-driven turbine slows down and does not have sufficient power to drive the compressor on the air-intake side of the system. So when I had slammed the throttle from fully closed to fully open the turbo-charger had to build-up speed again. This meant there would be a few seconds delay before full power was available from the engine. Well, having told you all of that, and obviously I am still alive to tell the story, I can now tell you that as I flashed past the last set of markers on the airstrip I noticed the airspeed indicator was showing 65 knots and the engine was now giving enough power that the machine was flying – just. But the drama was not over yet.

The next question was, "What do I do now?" As soon as I had the aircraft safely established in a steady climb I loosened my seat harness so I could move across and peer out the right-hand side window. From what I could see of the starboard main wheel, the brake assembly had disappeared completely. I assumed it had snapped off and must be lying somewhere on the airstrip behind me. So what do I do now? Do I go all the way back to Hagen, or should I just return to Porgera? I tried making a call on the company HF radio channel. But I knew that this was normally a waste of time. In those days we had a teletype (or telex) machine in the administrative office at the hangar and when that machine was switched on it created such a tremendous amount of interference on the radio that our traffic officers usually turned the radio off. In desperation I tried calling the CRMF station at Rugli, knowing that they could make a telephone call to our hangar and thus alert them to give me a call on our company radio channel. No joy with that either. Dr. Calvert was using that channel for his daily medical *sched,* and even if he had heard me, he gave no indication of having done so. I was completely on my own. No one was available to discuss the various options. It was completely up to me to make a decision. Ouch!

The Porgera airstrip in those days was 7,200 feet above sea level but it had a 10% slope. I knew I could stop there easily, even without brakes. So that was my decision. Return to Porgera, land

and investigate the problem and then contact the Chief Engineer.

But as soon as my wheels touched the ground at Porgera my eyes registered a flash on the right-hand side of the airplane as something appeared to fly forward and into the arc of the propeller. "What on earth was that?" I wondered. But I was fully occupied with the task of landing the aircraft and taxying to the parking bay at the top of the airstrip knowing I had little or no effective braking. Once the engine was stopped I jumped out. My first thought was to check the propeller for damage – had that stone, or whatever it was, damaged any of the blades? Uh-oh ... what a horrible sight! I certainly would not be flying this aeroplane back to Hagen today. Yes, there were still three blades on the propeller, but one blade was sitting at a crazy angle. When I took hold of it I began to wonder how it had not simply departed company from the hub! Even as I stood there, looking in horror at the busted propeller, one of the local men came over to me, holding something in his hand. "I found this at the end of the airstrip, just where you touched down." In his hand he held the remains of the brake assembly from the right-hand wheel.

I could only guess at the chain of events that must have caused it to be thrown forward and through the propeller, rather than just breaking away and staying where it fell when the aircraft had touched down. Be that as it may, I was now well and truly "grounded"!! And there were passengers at Paiela who would be wondering why I wasn't coming to bring them back to Porgera.

I just stood there dumbfounded as I looked at the damage and considered what might have happened if that brake assembly had suddenly decided to tangle itself in the right-hand wheel and been thrown forward into the propeller before I had become airborne out of Paiela! At full engine power the blade would have been immediately torn away from the hub, the unbalanced propeller would have then ripped the engine out of the airframe. There are absolutely NO forced landing areas in the jungle-clad mountain slopes around Paiela. It just didn't bear too much thinking about! I crawled back into the aircraft, switched on the radio and listened to traffic on the Flight Service channel. Soon I was able to identify one of our company aircraft – Rob Willis-Jones was operating in the Tari area, not too far from Porgera.

I gave him a call, "Rob, can I see you on company frequency, please?" When he switched over I gave a brief run-down on my "little adventure" for the day but added, "Any chance you could come over this way and get me out of here?"

After arriving at Porgera, and making the right sort of comments about my decision to leave the aircraft where it was, Rob very graciously made the 12-minutes-each-way flight over to Paiela and brought the two Department of Works fellows back to Porgera. I was then able to explain to them why I had not stopped after my second attempted landing earlier in the day.

The following week two engineers, Bert Kater and Alex Jewett, flew into Porgera and repaired the damaged aeroplane. My logbook has an entry indicating that I flew that same aircraft back to Hagen on Friday 21st November. My logbook also has an entry indicating that four days later we moved again – back to Goroka. My new responsibilities, apart from normal day-to-day flying, now included Area Manager for the MAF bases at Goroka, Madang, and Lae, Senior Check and Training Pilot for the same area, Flight Programmer and, since MAF still had a maintenance workshop in Goroka, I was also the Base Engineer. But it didn't last long. I soon caught myself making some potentially serious and dangerous mistakes. I needed to face the fact – I was not just weary, I was exhausted and I obviously did not have anything like the stamina I used to enjoy before that second cancer operation. If I continued to work in this condition I could be making more mistakes, and there could be accidents where people would get killed. It was time to pack-up and go back home.

We explained this decision in a letter that Rose wrote to some of our friends:

"In our last letter we mentioned moving back to Goroka after living in Mt Hagen for one year. As we write this letter we have just fastened the lids on the boxes and drums after packing yet again!

"Most of you know that we came back to Papua New Guinea in 1979 just to help out for that year. We then stayed on for six months into 1980 to relieve while Noel Hawke (Chief Pilot) was on furlough, and then we agreed to extend at least until the end of 1980.

"About July last year Roger began to feel that we should leave PNG at the end of 1980, but as the months went by we heard of more and more staff who were leaving and so, despite the feeling that it was time to go, we agreed to move back to Goroka where, in addition to his normal flying commitments Roger would also be the Area Manager and Base Engineer, and make it a normal 3-year term before returning to Australia (or New Zealand).

"However, we have not had any real peace-of-heart since moving back to Goroka (or rather, staying on in this country) especially as compared to our feelings when we arrived here in 1979 – when we had that real joy of knowing we were in the right place. Also, since October the whole family has been in considerably less than one hundred percent health.

"So, after that long explanation – but we wanted you to understand – we have been packing again, and plan to leave PNG and MAF on March 24th.

"As yet we are not certain where we will be settling down or working, but we are planning to have a holiday until we feel fit again. Present plans are to fly to Cairns on 25th March, then travel southwards visiting friends along the way, to reach Rose's family in Bairnsdale [Victoria] by Easter and continue our holiday there before finalizing job decisions.

"We want you to know that this decision has not been made lightly. We tried to "put it off" for several months before accepting what we believe to be the Lord's guidance for us. In many ways a decision to leave full-time missionary work is more difficult than the decision to become involved in the first place.

"Two verses of Scripture have been an encouragement to us during these past weeks:

"*I will instruct you, says the Lord, and guide you along the best pathway for your life; I will advise and watch your progress.*"

(Psalm 32:8. Paraphrased).

"*Behold I send an angel before you, to guard you on your way and bring you to the place which I have prepared. Give heed to him and hearken to his voice.*"

(Exodus 23:20-21. RSV)"

Our Air Niugini flight out of Goroka on 24th March was a morning departure and the weather was still fine as we flew down the Markham Valley towards Nadzab. In fact, even the Finisterre Ranges were clear of cloud so it was an emotional experience for me, and I was having a bit of a dialogue with God:

"Thank you for the wonderful experiences I have been allowed to enjoy during the years I have been flying in this country. They have been good years."

"I am pleased that you enjoyed your time in this country. But this is now the third time I have caused you to leave. I do not want you to come back again."

So it was mixed emotions: Sad to be saying goodbye to a part of the world I had grown to love, in a way. But the way I was feeling at that point in time I didn't really care if I never saw another aeroplane again, and certainly I had no great desire to have to work on one as a maintenance engineer, nor ever again to be acting in the role of a pilot and flying one.

Photo taken late 1981: David (13), Roger, Esther (6), Rose, Stuart (11)

Chapter Twenty Three

YOU CAN'T GO HOME AGAIN

When I think back over the years we spent working in Papua New Guinea I don't think we ever seriously looked at the question, "Where will we go if or when we have to leave this work?" And perhaps if we had been asked, we may have mumbled something like, "I guess we'll just go back home." But I need to tell you, you cannot really do that. You can't go back home. "Home" does not exist anymore – the people have changed, and the place has changed. It sounds so obvious when I read what I have just written. But for some strange reason, facing the reality of that fact still comes as a shock to many missionaries who have had to return home – particularly when the return has been due to ill health. Some very senior and sane ex-missionaries have told us it can take more than ten years to get over the "culture shock" of returning to their home country.

It is not just the nonsense of dealing with huge Supermarkets and peak-hour traffic. It cuts much deeper than that!

No one had ever explained to us the simple basics of human emotions. Although many of us may try to deny it, we all depend to some extent on the emotional support of a group of friends. This is one of the reasons why some mission societies insist that before any of their candidates head out on an overseas assignment they must first have a group of supportive friends who will not only contribute financially to the support of the missionary but also pray for them and offer emotional support in the form of written letters or emails.

Although we had made many moves – our son David changed schools at least 13 times in his 12 years of schooling – I had not realised how much we depended on the friendship of the staff we worked with and the people we served. When we made the decision to leave Papua New Guinea we left much of this support behind. And of our prayer supporters who lived in

Australia and New Zealand we even had one who wrote and said, "Since you are leaving the Lord's work I won't be writing to you anymore." We have had other missionaries tell us they also received letters like that when they retired or returned home for health or family reasons. And in any case, in our situation, what place did we now call "home" anyway?

MAF had already told us there was no vacancy for me in their workshop at Ballarat, so we would not be returning to the little house we had built there back in 1976. I wrote to the General Aviation Division of Mount Cook Airlines in New Zealand, as they were using a fleet of Cessna 185 aircraft to fly folk in and out of the ski-fields in the Southern Alps. But they could only offer to add my name to the list of hopefuls and [possibly] let me know if or when they ever did have a vacancy for a Cessna Pilot. I wrote to the firm I used to work with in New Plymouth – they had since moved to Ardmore and gone through several name changes – but there had been a down-turn in General Aviation in New Zealand and they were not even employing new staff to replace those who left or retired.

So we did not really know where we were going to call "home" for the next few years, or what I would be doing to earn an income. We just trusted that God would show us the answer to these questions all in his good time.

The few days' holiday we had in Cairns, thanks to the generosity of church folk we had never even met before, who loaned us a car and a caravan (and the van had been moved to a very nice Caravan Park, just for our benefit), was probably the best holiday we have ever had – before or since. But by the time we got to Bega, in NSW, where we spent a day or so with one of Rose's sisters, I was feeling nauseous and most unwell. Next day we travelled to Bairnsdale, where Rose's parents were now living. The first thing I did was to arrange two appointments – one with a doctor and one with a naturopath. As it turned out, the naturopath was available the next day but I had to wait an extra day to see the doctor.

When I walked into the naturopath's consulting room, almost before I sat down, he said, "You've got a problem with the liver, but I can give you tablets that will help to get it working properly again." Later in the consultation he warned me not to eat anything greasy and not to eat oranges or drink commercially produced orange juice. When I asked, "Why not eat oranges?" he admitted that he did not really know the reason but believed it had something to do with the soft white pulpy part of the orange skin.

The doctor's approach was quite different. Although, when I visited his consulting room, I was already beginning to show the yellowing skin and eyeballs and the chest-rash typical of hepatitis, he took the cautious approach of requesting a blood test to check liver-function, and eventually sent me to the hospital in Sale for a liver scan. When I asked whether or not I needed to be careful with my diet he shrugged his shoulders and said, "No. Just eat anything you feel like eating." Rose claims that I turned almost green with jaundice.

A few days later, when I really felt I would enjoy a drink of orange juice, I decided to find out if the naturopath's warning about orange juice was really justified. It was!!

When the report from Sale came back indicating that there was no evidence of cancerous growth in the liver, the doctor suggested, "Well, perhaps you just had a dose of hepatitis." (Blood tests taken about 20 years later have confirmed that at some time in the past I have been a victim of "Hepatitis A".)

But a bloke can't spend the rest of his life on sickness benefits. So in July I started looking for work. To cut a long story short, I was offered a job with the General Aviation Division of Amalgamated Wireless Australasia (AWA) if I would be prepared to move to Parafield, in South Australia. Well I had no real problems with that, and gladly grabbed the opportunity. But I hadn't really thought enough about how the children would react. Our oldest son, David, was now in his second year at high school. He had already made one dramatic change; from the NSW curriculum correspondence lessons he had been doing while we were in Goroka (with a class of only eight or ten people) to a high school in Bairnsdale, Victoria, with more than 1,000 students. And now here we were in August and he was facing yet another change, this time to a South Australian curriculum at a high school with more than 1,200 students. And, as we discovered later when David enrolled at Playford High

School in South Australia, their curriculum is six months out of step with the Eastern States. He was also suffering from Chronic Fatigue Syndrome at the time. It is to his credit that he accepted these moves without bitter complaint.

On the work scene I felt I had been thrown in at the deep end. But then perhaps I had asked for it, as I was so keen to consolidate the theory I had learned at RMIT with some solid hands-on practical work. But I was not prepared for an attitude that seemed to prevail here. At every place I had worked in the past, other staff members, particularly those who were more knowledgeable and experienced than I, had been very happy to share their knowledge and offer helpful instruction as and where appropriate. But here it was not so. Instead, with one notable exception, I found an attitude where knowledge and experience were jealously guarded. If I wanted to learn, then I would have to read the manufacturers manuals for myself and learn what I could. So I did a lot of photocopying and wrote pages of notes, and perhaps it was a good thing I did. I rather suspect that there is a human tendency to always take the easy way out, if one is available.

For months we struggled with emotions we did not really understand. We were renting a house in the suburb of Elizabeth East, an area with a high rate of unemployment and all the associated social problems. It is only now, years later, it has been explained that we would have been going through a grieving process – grieving the loss of regular contact with Christian friends in an environment where we had felt significant, accepted, and very much at home. When we had first gone to New Guinea it was with a sense of excitement and anticipation, and we expected things to be different. But no-one had ever warned us about the emotional shock of re-settling amongst what we thought would be “our own people” and then finding that the social environment was nothing like the home we had left so many years ago.

But there was more to it than that. The church we attended in Elizabeth was like a desperately needy mission field on its own. But we were both so exhausted we could not really make any contribution. Many days I would come home from work and collapse into bed before tea. Only after a couple of hours sleep was I able to get up and eat my evening meal. My brain felt like it was trying to run on flat batteries. But about once in every six weeks or so it was suddenly as though I emerged out of a fog and was able to think clearly and had energy to do things with some enthusiasm. These episodes lasted only about one day – just long enough to reassure me that it used to be like that all the time. So I was encouraged to keep going, hoping and trusting that one day my health would be back to normal again.

I stuck to the job in Parafield for 12 months, then one evening I received a phone call from Jim Charlesworth, who had now taken over the role as manager of MAF-AIR Services in Ballarat. Basically the message was … if I wanted a job back in Ballarat then they now had a vacancy. But I would not be doing any radio work. My job, if I wanted to take it, would be overhauling alternators and starter motors, and boring stuff like that. Yes, it would be electrical work, but I would not be making any use of my radio licences.

Well, there were other factors that convinced me that God was behind this, and so I accepted the offer … not too willingly, I should add. I had enjoyed the weather in South Australia and I was certainly not looking forward to going back to those miserable wet winters in Ballarat. And this time both boys did complain, justifiably, about having to make yet another move, to a different State and different curriculum. And we didn't have a house to go back to in Ballarat. We had put our house on the market as soon as I had made the decision to take the job in South Australia and we had just signed the contract to sell the place a couple of weeks before I got the phone call from Jim Charlesworth. And …we had just looked at a house for sale in Elizabeth Fields, which fitted the description of our dream home almost exactly. Leaving South Australia was not easy and it took me years before I reconciled myself to the move.

The experience of studying all those radio installation and service manuals during my time in Parafield now paid off. During the next 15 months I sat and passed at least eight exams on aircraft radio systems, and the experience I had gained with AWA meant that I was now permitted to apply for the respective licences. And during the next 12 months at MAF-AIR Services I spent possibly a total of only two days in the Electrical Overhaul shop. All the rest of the time I worked in the hangar on tasks, which for the most part were related to the radio licences I had just earned.

I have to admit that after this move life did seem to become a little more predictable and "routine". But I use those terms in a relative sense, because over the next twenty years or so Rose and I did make many visits to the MAF fields in Arnhemland (Gove) and Alice Springs. Some of these visits were only two or three weeks but some lasted for months. All of these tours-of-duty involved at least some time spent trouble-shooting and re-working or repairing aircraft radio and auto-pilot systems. The level of involvement in avionics was far greater than I had ever dreamed when I made that wishful-thinking response to a question back in 1973. But by the grace of God I had been provided with training and experience far beyond what I had ever asked or hoped for. And throughout this time we continued to discover that one can never really know what a day may bring forth. Perhaps this is best illustrated by again quoting from one of the letters we wrote:

6 June 1997
"We have had so many interesting things happen in the last few months that we are not sure what to skip over, and what to mention. We would have mentioned David and Tracey's wedding when we wrote last November, but probably not mentioned that during our brief visit "home" in Ballarat last August they had shared with us a very sad report to the effect that they may never be able to have children of their own. We grieved with them at this disappointment. But the Bible does say something about the Lord giving people the desires of their heart, so we asked Him if He would be gracious enough to grant another miracle. Can you imagine our delight when David and Tracey came to our place for tea, on the occasion of celebrating Esther's 22nd birthday early in December, and told us that Tracey is expecting in July!!! When Tracey went to the doctor that morning for confirmation, the doctor had beamed and said, "You have made my day!" Sort of made our day too! Things like that make being expectant grandparents doubly special.

On 25th December (Christmas day) our son Stuart phoned us from Brisbane airport just before he, with four other leaders and a team of 22 teenagers, left for Zambia with Teen Mission. Then on Saturday 25th January he again phoned us reverse-charges from Brisbane. This time, to give a run-down on their trip – talked for over an hour, and we weren't complaining!!

Our own next adventure was another drive from Ballarat to Alice Springs (2,300 kilometres each way). This time our visit to the Northern Territory was not so much on MAF work, but mainly to relieve the locally based Avionics technician who was in need of a good holiday. Nevertheless at least half of the work I had to do was on Aboriginal Air Services (MAF) airplanes.

However, our drive up to Alice this time was not quite "routine". We took the precaution of having our car (Mazda 323) serviced the week before we left. Then on Sunday 19th we drove 45 minutes north to attend church in Maryborough, because our son David was preaching there. We had already decided that we would continue on towards Mildura, or somewhere, to give us a good start for our trip north, but after only about two hours on the road we noticed the engine was running very hot – even allowing for ambient temps of over 40°C – so had to slow down to a maximum speed of 80-85 kilometres per hour. Then we tried to take a short cut, and ended up on a road, which did not seem to be marked on the map.

We decided to stop at the next Motel, and finally limped into Renmark (over the border in South Australia) a little before dark. Next morning we found a busy, but very obliging, mechanic at NatRad radiator specialists. Temperature for the day was forecast to be 42°C (108°F), but by 10am it was already hotter than that! However the mechanic did a fantastic job and our car was ready just after midday. We had a good run to Port Augusta, and then on to Coober Pedy on Tuesday.

We reckon Coober Pedy (opal mining town) is an interesting place. We booked into an underground Motel, visited the Old Timers Mine (very interesting – really needed more than the 50 minutes we had allowed ourselves before closing time), and met a couple who invited us to dine at the Italio-Australia club, where they run the Restaurant.

Tom, our host, had mentioned that they had not seen rain in Coober Pedy for four years, so when I noticed spots of water on the window I called Tom to, “Come and see the rain.” Well I tell you, in no time at all everyone in the bar-room next door ran outside to dance in the rain. Talk about “singing in the rain,” like a bunch of kids they were. Then we were treated like guests of honour. “You brought the rain. Please come and visit us again some time.” But before they even had our meal cooked, Tom came over to us and said, “I don't wish to cause you alarm, but Ballarat is on fire, along with a lot of Victoria.” So we kept an eye on the TV news, but all the coverage they were giving was simply the Dandenongs, just out of Melbourne. When we got back to our Motel room we rang David, back in Ballarat, and were able to confirm that the fire was mainly at Creswick, at least ten kilometres from our house. We found out later that friends of ours, who were not home at the time of the fires, reported that the fires came to within less then one kilometre of their property.

After leaving Coober Pedy it was cloudy or raining most of the time – so much for the "unbearable Central Australian heat" in January. Actually when we reached Erldunda, 200 kilometres south of Alice Springs, we discovered that the highway was closed with floodwaters between there and Alice Springs. So we spent that night at Erldunda, where the locals were complaining about “cold weather in the middle of summer”, and completed the final 200 kilometres to Alice Springs on the Thursday morning. However, we were not really surprised at all this rain. 1996 had been one of the driest years on record, and statistics indicate that a very dry year in the Centre will often be followed by a very wet one – so we were half expecting to encounter some form of mild flooding. It seems strange: all our friends in Victoria, who were commiserating about us having to spend time in Central Australia at the hottest time of the year, were themselves sweltering in scorching heat, while we were "complaining" that the solar-powered hot water in the Alice Springs house was only just warm.

During our three weeks in Alice Springs the Todd River flowed almost every day. (It is normally just a dry sandy river bed), and in fact one man, who had been floating down this river on an air-mattress was killed when he was tipped off and hit his head on a rock. For our return journey we wanted to make the trip in easy stages, so we planned to drive the first three or four hours on the Sunday afternoon. On Sunday morning I phoned the Police to check the condition of the highway south, and was told that the Finke river was in flood, and the road was closed with water more than one metre above the level of the Finke bridge. "Try again on Monday," the man said. However, when we checked again at 1 pm (on Sunday) we were told that the road had been opened about 20 minutes previously. So we quickly threw our last few things into the car and headed south. In the first hour of driving we encountered at least fifty places where there was evidence of flood water having been over the road, and the Finke river itself, normally a dry sandy river bed (like the Todd River) was a roaring torrent, just touching the bottom of the bridge. Sandy gravel all over the road surface on the bridge approaches, and logs jammed in the bridge railings, were evidence that the flood waters had been much higher.

We had also noticed that there were big rain clouds in the Finke river catchment area, and were told later that the flood waters came up again some time after we had passed, and the road was closed for another two or three days. But the continuous rain for three weeks had transformed the desert. What had been a red wilderness on our northbound trip in January was now an almost unbelievable vast expanse of green grass. Whereas we had seen no cattle at all on our way north, now we saw many herds grazing within a couple of kilometres of the highway, and literally lost count of the numbers. Rose saw this as a parable, and likened it to spiritually thirsty people, just waiting for some refreshment from the Lord, and the Church would then experience abundant new growth, like this desert. The ground, which had appeared so barren and sterile, was actually full of seed and potential. It only needed the right conditions for it all to spring into life. Remember, Jesus talked about "living water." The first lake we saw, normally a pan of glistening white salt, was like an inland sea of blue water stretching almost to the horizon. I was tempted to stop the car and take a swim, but it was a couple of kilometres to the water, and the ground at the side of the road was soft and muddy. I was scared of getting our car bogged, so did not take this rare opportunity for a swim in the desert.

We were in Victoria three weeks before heading north again, this time back to Gove (Nhulunbuy), right on the north coast of Northern Territory. During this time I tried unsuccessfully to get some relief for a problem with my right shoulder, which was becoming "frozen" – very restricted movement, and quite painful at times.

Three days before we were due to leave for our flight to Gove, a cyclone appeared off the coast near Cairns, and people were asking if we would still be able to travel. We had to change planes at Cairns, and I have read enough horror stories of airliners damaged by flying through violent storms, so I was a little concerned myself. However, when we got to Cairns the weather was beautiful – the cyclone had moved way out to sea. A few days after we arrived in Gove the cyclone moved back again and wreaked havoc on the Queensland coast. Perhaps not quite as dramatic as Moses at the Red Sea, but the Lord seemed to have moved floods and cyclones to let us pass."

This time on our visit to Gove we did not stay in the town of Nhulunbuy (a mining town of 4,000 people) but were given use of a house in the nearby Aboriginal community of Yirrkala. There was a funeral in progress when we arrived, and the wailing and clap-sticks continued every night for the entire two months that we were there.

We had been in Gove for just two weeks when one afternoon, just after lunch, our friendly neighbour, who is also a qualified doctor, phoned me at work to tell me that Rose had just been taken to hospital, suffering from a sore leg, and perhaps I ought to go in and visit her. At the time I was in the middle of a task which had to be finished that day so the aircraft would be airworthy for the next day. Having no real idea of the drama that was about to unfold, I asked Daina, "Do you really think I need to go?" She quietly said, "Yes, I think so." So I managed to excuse myself from work, with an assurance that, "I will work back tonight to get that job finished", borrowed a car and headed for town.

I will let Rose tell the story from here on:

"On Tuesday 25th March, along with several other MAF ladies, I had attended an informal meeting at Shady Beach. But when I stood up to go home I felt really unwell and could hardly walk. When dropped off at the house where we were staying I lay down for a while, then noticed that my left leg was a pasty blue colour, and swollen.

I managed to hobble over to Daina Wall next door (she is a doctor) who immediately arranged for Alrena Martis to take me in to the Gove hospital. By the time Roger arrived at the hospital, arrangements were already under way to fly me, as a medical emergency, across to Darwin (700 kilometres away — Nhulunbuy is a very isolated mining town). So Roger left again within a few minutes to drive back to Yirrkala and pack an overnight bag for me. At this stage I was thinking that I was only going to Darwin for tests, and might be home by the weekend. Thus, I was flown to Darwin, flat on my back, with a drip in my arm, and a nurse sitting beside me. Roger later told me that as the nurse was about to close the door of the "Super King-Air" aerial ambulance, she turned and asked him, "Have you said your goodbye's?" As he watched our plane taxi to the runway he wondered at the significance of the way she worded that question. But he had a task to finish, so he returned to work. Other engineers quietly expressed words of encouragement, and at least one specifically mentioned that they would all be praying for us. A couple of hours later he tried to phone me at the hospital, and when he asked if he could speak to Mrs Rose Young, was told, "No. But ring back in 20 minutes. She will be in the ward by then, and you will be able to speak to her." Only then did he really relax, knowing I had obviously arrived safely.

Because the following weekend was Easter, and most specialty services in the hospital were shut down, it was ten days and many tests later before the diagnosis was confirmed – that I had a 15cm (6 inch) blood clot (Deep Vein Thrombosis) between my groin and my navel. Although Roger was able to spend one week of this time in Darwin with me, it was quite a worrying and uncomfortable time. On Friday 4th April, when I had been in hospital ten days, I was feeling discouraged, but when I opened my Bible I "just happened" to read these words:

"*Pity me, O Lord, for I am weak. Heal me, for my body is sick, and I am upset and disturbed. ... Come, O Lord, and make me well. In your kindness, save me. For if I die I cannot give you glory by praising you before my friends. I am worn out with pain; every night my pillow is wet with tears.*" (Psa 6:2-6 TLB).

I found this a tremendous encouragement. It was so appropriate, and comforting to know someone else had been there before (in the emotional sense).

After two weeks in Darwin hospital I was discharged and returned to Gove – being loaded and unloaded onto aeroplanes via a wheelchair on a forklift. I felt this was a little undignified, and embarrassing, and didn't know whether to laugh or cry.

Looking back, after learning much more about it all, I realise my life was at significant risk at least three times. However, I did not know the danger at the time and it was an experience where God's peace in my heart and mind, and the comfort of His presence, was with me in a very special way.

After returning to Gove (Yirrkala) I was told to have total rest, except for regular visits to a doctor to check that my blood thinning medication was remaining stabilised, and within safe limits. So I had to lie on a bed and watch my MAF friends and neighbours do the house cleaning, the washing, bringing in pre-prepared meals, etc. They were all such a blessing to me in my time of need, and I pray that God will bless them, for they were such a comfort and support when I could not have coped alone. I do thank God for such Christian love in action.

After a few weeks at "home", on Friday 2nd May I rang the doctor to check results of my latest blood test and was told that things were way out of limits. "Don't cut yourself, whatever you do!" I was warned. This report made me feel very depressed. Now, although I do not normally recommend random selection of Bible verses, I did open my Bible at random and this is the verse I read:

"*Yes, now I see it all -- it was good for me to undergo this bitterness, for you have lovingly delivered me from death ... for dead men cannot praise you. They cannot be filled with hope and joy. The living, only the living can praise you as I do today. Think of it! The Lord healed me! Every day of my life from now on I will sing my songs of praise.*" (Isa 38: 17-20 TLB).

And then a couple of pages further on, I read, "*But now the Lord who created you ... says, 'Don't be afraid for I have ransomed you; I have called you by name; you are mine. When you go through deep waters and great trouble, I will be with you. When you go through rivers of difficulty, you will not drown! When you walk through the fire of oppression, you will not be burned up ... others died that you might live ... for you are precious to me ... and I love you. Don't be afraid, for I am with you'.*"

(Isa 43: 1-5 TLB).

After six weeks of rest (for me – although Roger was working, even Saturdays and public holidays) we left Gove as planned. We flew to Brisbane (four hours) where we were able to visit our son Stuart at Bible College of Queensland. I was so glad we had this break, for I was very tired by the time we got there, and am sure that the extra four hours of travel to Melbourne and Ballarat would have been too much. We continued our trip home to Ballarat after three days in Brisbane, and again that trip was all I could take for one day. It has been good to catch up with David and Tracey's news and to see Esther again – and we should add that a nice young man named Simon seems to visit several times a week.

However, since arriving back in Ballarat I have gradually been doing more, and slowly getting back on my feet. I have had another CT scan, which apparently shows "no abnormality". So we assume the blood clot has been dissolved, and we praise God again for this answer to the prayers of so many people. We are so thankful to those who have prayed – some of you not knowing why you were prompted to do so. The Lord has blessed us through all these adventures, and we thank Him for that, and give Him the praise and honour.

And so there we have it. Yes, I could have written much more, but this has been my answer – or rather ***our*** answer – to that question Bibi asked when I was confined to a hospital bed and "not expected to live long enough to see our daughter born." No, it's probably not as dramatic as "The Air Adventures of Biggles". But Squadron Leader Bigglesworth was a fictitious character. What I have told you is the story of a somewhat mediocre but very real individual – a very ***human*** being; one who can still wake up in the middle of the night almost overcome by feelings of guilt about silly little things such as those times when I had told passengers they would need to leave one suitcase behind, because we were overweight. I know some pilots who would have just loaded the extra suitcase onto the aircraft and said nothing. But I also know of some awful accidents where the significant item of evidence in the report was that the aircraft was overweight on its fatal take-off attempt. Or my mind will be replaying that incident at Paiela and I find myself wondering if perhaps I could have stopped in time even with only one wheel-brake working. Or I remember times when my attitudes or actions may have been completely misunderstood and I had probably been judged as unsympathetic or arrogant. Certainly I was far from perfect.

So have I wasted my life? Should I have stayed in New Zealand doing a job that I enjoyed and where I thought I was well paid? No. I do not believe for one minute I would have ever been truly happy if I had done that. I may have grieved the heart of God many times where I have failed to do the things I should have done. But I still believe the greatest satisfaction in life starts with an intimate personal relationship with God and then continues as I seek to learn His plan and His purpose for me, and endeavour to pursue that pathway through life.

Life is not some kind of a vain competition. What I have recorded in this book is not my attempt to earn God's favour in some way, but rather it is the story of my very inadequate response to His love. If God has provided for my needs, and perhaps blessed others by the things I have done, then that is because He chose to do it that way. There is no other explanation.

A MAF Wife

Folk are often asking me
"What did you do in PNG?"
"Are you a teacher?
Or a nurse?
Or are you ***just*** a mother?"

When someone asks me a question like that
And they bring it out - right off pat
I don't know what to say!
I'm not a teacher. I'm not a nurse
I ***am*** a wife and mother.

The Lord has called me to so much more,
More than I ever dreamed of before
I came to PNG.
But how can I tell them and still be brief
Of the caring and sharing, the joy and grief?
That's an M-A-F wife and mother.

Our husbands are flying in all kinds of weather
Sometimes they're bringing families together
Or bringing mail from far away
To brighten a lonely missionary's day.
We wives stay home and pray.

It's my turn to take the children to school
8 am departure is the rule.
Buy veggies at market for the afternoon plane
Then hurry back to the airstrip again
To meet a plane at half past ten
With a new family on board.

I've made their beds and prepared their tea
Collected their luggage, now let me see …
Home for a cuppa, then let them rest
They're looking tired so that will be best
Before we show them around.

Many Adventures Followed

The cloud is thick on the hills out there
"Please Lord keep him in your care."
The phone, "A plane is delayed till half past two
Can four passengers come to lunch with you?"
"Of course they can, send them over"
Um ... Cool drink, salad, bread and butter.

Time to show the new folk around
So they begin to know the "lie of the ground"
Their first impressions of this beautiful land
Where God has called them to take a stand
By sharing in our work.

My lunch guests' plane is delayed till tomorrow
The guest house is full, but if I borrow pillows
And move Esther out, they can sleep in her room
tonight.
With the new folk as well that's eleven to tea
What's something I can prepare quickly?

Roger isn't back yet, where can he be?
Oh ... "diverted for a medical emergency."
It's nearly dark, the ambulance is here
Then through a valley that is still in the clear
The little plane at last is near.

Another victim of a tribal war
Gently they lift him out the door
"Lord we commit him to You
And thank you for bringing Roger home too."
Now home … and we have guests tonight.

What did I do in PNG?
I find it hard to tell, briefly …
Made beds by the dozen
Extra meals by the score
Shopped for outstations
And still much more …
"Lord. I did it for You."

Rose Young 28/10/1981

Glimpses of Glory

(Written by Rose while she was a patient in Darwin hospital)

Heaven is a beautiful place
   Filled with glory and grace
If I get there before you do
   Remember I'll be waiting for you.
Out of the limitation of time
   Into Eternity' s space sublime
Out of distress and pain and grief
   Into wholeness and perfect relief.
My grip on life seems insecure
   But my hope of Heaven is certain and sure
Don't grieve for me when I am gone
   It means my work on earth is done.

I know the One who saved my soul
   Who paid the price to make me whole
He died that I might be forgiven
   He arose and secured my place in Heaven.
He gave me breath for these few years
   I've lived my life with joy and tears
I've had my share of hopes and fears
   And now, as the door of eternity nears,
I rejoice in the plans He has for me.
   I'm glad I've been able to walk by the sea
And been able on mountain tops to stand
   And look far out across the land.

He's shown me the beauty of a flower so small
   And of mosses growing on an old stone wall
I've seen the cathedral of trees pointing high
   Seeming to reach right up to the sky.
I praise my God for the gift of sight
   To be awed by creation, by colour, and light
I thank Him when I see my husband's smile
   And when I hold Megan Rose in my arms awhile.
I rejoice at the gift of sound
   The distant baying of a hound
The morning chorus of bird song praise
   In prayer and song my voice I raise.

He gave us our senses — He gave us touch
Without which we would miss so much
The comforting touch of a loved one's hand
Or wriggling our toes in soft warm sand
The wind on your face, the heat of the sun.
I know I've only just begun
But consider too the gift of taste
Without that, eating would be a waste.
The tang of lemon, or honey so sweet
Without taste strawberries would not be a treat.
God is the giver of all things good
I thank Him for the taste He gives our food.

He also gave us the gift of smell
Most noses do this very well
The smell of hot bread from the oven, just baked
The smell of fresh turned earth, just raked
The perfume of roses, violets, flowers
And the wet earth after summer showers.
I thank God too for the gift of memory
For I look back over life, and see
His goodness to me in so many ways
His care and protection through all my days
I know that I should praise Him more
For past and present, and for what's in store.

Don't grieve too much if I should die
Don't weep and sob and mourn and cry
The Lord is glad that I am free
From all those things that limited me.
For me to die is greater gain
I no longer have to live in pain
I'm whole, complete, perfect at last
All the guilt and shame is passed.
I am receiving all that He prepared for me
Out of earth's reach, in eternity --
I'll praise Him while I wait for you
To join me so you can praise Him too.

What is Heaven like? What will I do there?
  I have a mental picture, which I'd like to share
A celestial symphony I'll arrange
  From earth that will be quite a change ...
"Cheep, cheep," says a sparrow as he hops along
  Then all the other sparrows join in the song
Then, singly and in chorus, all the birds begin to sing
  A song of praise and worship to their creator and their king
Along come all the roses, all the flowers ever seen
  The daffodils, the lilacs, the lilies in between,
The colour, the texture, the perfumed smell
  All the flowers ever made are praising Him as well.

Here come the animals, frolicking, bounding
  Each in their prime – it's really astounding
Praising their Maker for all that they are
  The trumpeting and roaring can be heard from afar.
A chuckling happy little brook, a sparkly little wave
  A mighty thundering waterfall, big and strong and brave.
Let all creation praise Him -- hear the sound once more
  A hundred mighty oceans crashing on the shore
The trees of the forest will clap their hands
  Joined by shrubs and bushes from across all lands
Palm trees and grasses all come to share
  In praise of the One who kept them in His care.

In line-dances, pirouetting, here come the fish
  All together praise Him, swish swish swish ...
Mountains and hills, and valleys too
  The rocks cry out, "Lord praise You".
The hidden treasures of every mine
  See them glitter and sparkle and shine
Thunder and lightning flash and roar
  The praises reach through Heaven's door.
Let all creation praise Him, let them praises bring
  The universe is gathered, hear the stars all sing
The beauty of holiness, perpetual light
  The earth and the sun were never so bright.

Again a pause in Paradise, then my symphony goes on
 Let everything that has breath join in this new song
The ransomed, redeemed, His loved, His own
 All united before His throne
Our differences past, forgotten, done
 All together join as one
Singing worthy worthy the lamb that was slain
 The lamb that arose, and liveth again
Worthy to receive honour and power, and praise and blessing
 Glory and victory, and thanks unceasing
Even so, Lord Jesus come
 Take us to your heavenly home.

So when I die, don't sob and cry
 I've gone to a better home on high
I've got my new body — not saggy and marred
 But one prepared by those hands that are scarred.

HALLELUJAH

Rose Young 1997.